Field Guide to Orchids of Britain and Europe

D0257710

Field Guide to

Orchids

of Britain and Europe
The species and subspecies growing wild in Europe, the Near East and North Africa
with drawings by the author

Karl Peter Buttler
Consultant Editor: Paul Davies

The Crowood Press

Contents

Symbols used in the species' descriptions

●   The species or subspecies is confined to the area covered by this volume (endemic in Europe, the Near East and North Africa)

Symbols used with the abbreviations for the countries (the abbreviations are explained on page 274)

†   The species or subspecies has become extinct.

*   The species or subspecies is only a casual and not native.

?   Presence is doubtful and requires confirmation.

The pronunciation of the Latin names is indicated by a line under the vowel or diphthong to be stressed.

Some of the drawings have been taken from originals by other authors. They are recognized by initials near the scale line as follows: E G Camus (C), L Ferlan (F), P Gölz and H R Reinhard (GR), R Keller (Ke), H Kümpel (Kü), E Nelson (Ne), L A Nilsson (Ni), H G Reichenbach (R), W Vöth (V), J J Wood (W), D P Young (Y).

This edition first published in 1991 by
The Crowood Press Ltd
Gipsy Lane, Swindon,
Wiltshire SN2 6DQ

© 1986 Mosaik Verlag GmbH, Neumarkter Strasse 18, 8000 München 80, West Germany
© 1991 Revised English edition, The Crowood Press Ltd

British Library Cataloguing in Publication Data
Buttler, Karl
  Field guide to the orchids of Britain and Europe.
  1. Europe. Orchids
  I. Title II. Orchideen. *English*
  584.15094   ISBN 1 85223 591 8

Original title: *Steinbachs Naturfuhrer: Orchideen* by Karl Peter Buttler

The publishers would like to thank **Mr Gordon Strutt** for translating the original German text, and **Mr Paul Harcourt Davies** for adapting the text for the English language and for bringing the nomenclature right up-to-date.

  The new combinations of scientific names proposed in this volume are published in the *Med-Checklist Notulae* of the periodical *Willdenowia* (Berlin). Since first publication of a German edition of this book, nomenclatural changes have been proposed and accepted in *Die Orchide* and *Bulletins of the A.H.O.* These have been incorporated in the text for this edition.

  In the main text, photograph positions are indicated by 'r' for right; 'l/r' for lower right; 'l' for left; 'u/l' for upper left, and so on.

Front cover photograph: Common Spotted Orchids (Bob Gibbons, Natural Image). **Back cover photographs:** left, Southern Marsh Orchids (Peter Wilson, Natural Image); right, Monkey Orchid (Paul Davies, Natural Image).

Typeset by Action Typesetting Limited, Gloucester
Printed and bound by Times Publishing Group, Singapore

Introduction

The number of orchid species throughout the world is estimated at over 30,000, making this family one of the largest in the plant kingdom. It is also one of the most highly developed of the plant groups and of exceptional interest botanically. The most extensive development of the orchids has taken place in the tropics of both the Old and New Worlds, especially in the rain forests.

By comparison, Europe has approximately 250 species and is on the fringe of orchid distribution. Together with various subspecies, these have been brought together for the first time in a single volume, with descriptions, colour photographs and explanatory drawings. The keys enable the genera, species and subspecies to be identified in a logical manner.

The guide covers the whole of Europe, including the few northern species. Also included are the Middle East, that is Asiatic Turkey (Anatolia) and areas of the eastern Mediterranean known as the Levant, North Africa and the islands of the Canaries, Madeira and the Azores. From the botanical viewpoint, this extended geographical area takes into account internationally recognized floristic communities, independent of political boundaries. The amateur botanist taking a holiday in the Mediterranean area, now has a comprehensive work of reference for all the orchid species that may be found there. The additional information, which gives the countries in which each species occurs, should also be of great help.

A complete account of European orchids with colour photographs, including some of recently described species and subspecies, has only been achieved thanks to many colleagues who have readily made their material available. Each photograph has the date and location – important additional information for the orchid-lover who also wants to see the plant in flower. Only one *Goodyera* and one *Ophrys* species do not have a colour photograph, but they have been adequately described.

Just as butterflies enjoy a unique place amongst insects, so, of the flowering plants, orchids catch the imagination not only of scientists but also of amateurs who often approach their chosen speciality with scientific thoroughness. In spite of this there are still many unsolved problems concerning the European orchids. These are referred to under the different species. Identification is difficult and uncertain in some cases.

Added to this is the tendency amongst many orchid species to produce hybrids which have the characteristics of both parents. In this book, a full account has been given of subspecies, but this has not been possible with hybrids — whose descriptions would require a separate volume.

In naming the plants, the most up-to-date nomenclature has been adopted. Since all questions of classification have not yet been resolved, the scientific names of orchids are still undergoing changes and because of this a comparison of the subject literature from different years suffers. To reduce any possible confusion the different synonyms are given, both in the species descriptions and in the index.

By doing this the value of the guide as a reference book and a key to further subject literature is significantly increased. In spite of the accuracy necessary in the descriptions of the individual species, the interested layman who may not have had a botanical training is also catered for.

Apart from the abbreviations for the countries, the text contains no other abbreviations, such as those generally found in the subject literature, and only such botanical terms as cannot be avoided for the identification of the species. Such terms are explained in the general discussion found at the end of the book. This is divided into the following sections:

1. A key for the identification of each species. This is based on the genera, the key for which is given on pages 8 – 11. Each genus is given a symbol and colour code which is repeated on the colour photographs of the species contained within that genus. With small genera, the species can be identified from the photographs and the accompanying descriptions. For larger genera, separate keys are given. These follow the main part of the book describing the species.

2. Description of orchids with an explanation of the specialized terms.

3. Orchid systematics and taxonomy, problems of classification, colour anomalies and hybrids.

4. The biology of orchids including the fungal symbiosis which is characteristic of this family.

5. Distribution. Floristic elements with a map.

6. Protection of orchids.

7. Indexes and bibliography.

In Europe, orchids are protected by law to a greater or lesser degree depending on the country. Trade in natural orchids is prohibited. This guide supports these laws, so that the indigenous orchid species is preserved as an indispensible part of our flora.

Key to the identification of the 36 orchid genera included in this guide

The generic symbols with their coloured backgrounds can be used to refer directly to the species descriptions.

1 Flower spurred 2
1* Flower not spurred or spur very short and inconspicuous 18

2 Labellum slipper-shaped, more than 2 cm
Cypripedium, p12

2* Labellum not slipper-shaped, often shorter than 2 cm 3
3 Plant lacking green leaves; all leaves scale-like 4
3* Plant with at least one flat green leaf (sometimes narrow and grass-like) . . . 5

4 Plant brownish; labellum with two spreading distal lobes, brown
Neottia, p40

4* Plant greenish; labellum undivided, rounded, white with red spots
Corallorhiza, p230

5 (3) Labellum divided into two unequal parts at right angles to the long axis . . 6
5* Labellum not so divided (but sometimes with lobes or teeth) . . 9
6 Leaves with reticulate veining, short-stalked
Goodyera, p48

6* Leaves with parallel veins, sessile . . . 7
7 Sepals and lateral petals form an enclosed pointed hood; flower bracts membranous, similar in colour to the sepals, as long as the flowers including the uppermost ones
Serapias, pp158 – 167, key p245

7* Lateral sepals spreading. Flowers without hood (although sometimes not opening); bracts herbaceous, green, at least the upper ones much shorter than the flowers 8
8 Ovaries sessile or without a clearly defined stalk, held upright at an angle; forwardly directed part of the labellum (epichile) with longitudinal ridges
Cephalanthera, pp 32 – 37, key p238

8* Ovaries obviously stalked, horizontal or hanging; epichile smooth or with very small swelling area
Epipactis, pp14 – 31 key p237

9 (5) Labellum patterned, velvety but less so in the conspicuously coloured central area, which contrasts with the different colour of the surrounding hirsute (hairy) area
Ophrys, pp168 – 229, key p246

9* Labellum bare, without pattern 10

10 Labellum clearly divided with 2, 3 or 4 lobes or teeth 11

10* Labellum undivided or at most a mere suggestion of 3 lobes (in which case leaves grass-like) 13

11 Lower part of the stem with two (very rarely 3 or 4) more or less opposite leaves; ovary clearly stalked (stalk longer than the bract) *Listera*, p42

11* Stem with several leaves arranged along its length; ovary sessile 12

12 Labellum about 4 mm, 3-lobed with pointed undivided central lobe *Herminium*, p48

12* Labellum more than 10 mm, 3-lobed with deeply divided 2-pointed central lobe *Aceras*, p106

13 Inflorescence twisted so that the flowers are in 1 or 3 spiral rows. All perianth segments pointing forward forming a tube *Spiranthes*, p44 – 47 (*see also Goodyera*, alternative 6)

13* Inflorescence not twisted, flowers facing in all directions, not tubular 14

14 Flowers sessile; labellum with a suggestion of 3 lobes, the lateral ones mere tooth-like stumps; leaves grass-like *Chamorchis*, p58

14* Flowers clearly stalked; labellum

undivided; leaves broad, lanceolate to ovate 15

15 Plants with several leaves arranged on the stem; flower bracts as long as or longer than the ovaries *Epipactis phyllanthes*, p28

15* Plants with at most 3 leaves near the base of the stem; bracts not longer than the flower stalks 16

16 Labellum grooved and sickle shaped, may be oriented in different directions – upwards, sideways or downwards in relation to the flower stem *Liparis*, p232

16* Labellum not sickle shaped, pointing upwards (the central sepal pointing downwards) 17

17 Labellum and lateral petals about half as long as the sepals; 3 – 5 leaves up to 3 cm long *Hammarbya*, p234

17* All perianth segments of about equal length; the largest of the 1 – 2(3) leaves more than 3 cm *Malaxis*, p232

18 (1) Labellum pointing upwards 19

18* Labellum pointing downwards 20

19 Plant without green leaves; inflorescence lax with 1 – 8 stalked flowers *Epipogium*, p40

19* Plant with grass-like green leaves; inflorescence dense with numerous stalkless flowers *Nigritella*, pp66 – 69

20 (18) Labellum divided into two unequal parts at right angles to the long axis .21

20* Labellum not so divided, but often with lobes and teeth. 22

21 Leaves and bracts green
Cephalanthera,
see alternative 8

21* Leaves and bracts dirty violet
Limodorum, p38

22 (20) Labellum hollowed into a slipper shape; stem with one flower and one basal leaf
Calypso, p230

22* Labellum not slipper shaped, stem with several flowers and usually with several leaves 23

23 Labellum undivided, sometimes an inconspicuous tooth-like lobe on each side near the base 24

23* Labellum clearly lobed 27

24 Labellum tongue-like, long and strap-shaped, or shorter and narrowly triangular 25

24* Labellum broad, rounded 26

25 Plant dirty violet, without flattened leaves; flowers violet.
Limodorum, see alternative 21*

25* Plant green with flattened leaves; flowers white, yellowish or greenish
Plantathera,
pp52 – 59
Key p239

26 (24) Flower bracts membranous, generally coloured; labellum often crenate
Orchis, see alternative 34*

26* Bracts herbaceous, green, at times shading to violet. Labellum pointed or rounded, never crenate
Dactylorhiza, see alternative 41*

27 (23) Sepals growing together forming a dome-shaped hood, toothed at the point . . .28

27* Sepals not fused, but sometimes tending to form a hood 29

28 Labellum with 4 thread-like points at least 3 cm long
Comperia, p104

28* Labellum with 3 short rounded points
Steveniella, p104

29 Central lobe of labellum extended and generally twisted, at least 3 times as long as wide
Himantoglossum,
pp154 – 157
Key p245

29* Middle lobe at most double, as long as the side lobes, not twisted 30

30 Sepals with extended club-shaped points
Traunsteinera, p108

30* Sepals blunt or pointed, not club-shaped 31

31 Labellum has 2 conspicuous vertical plates, with free tip, decurrent at the base
Anacamptis, p150

31* Labellum without longitudinal plates .32

32 Central lobe of labellum divided, sometimes with a single tooth between the two points 33

32* Central labellum lobe not forked 35

33   Both pollinia stalks attached to a common viscidium (diag p152); bracts cover the ovaries; all sepals are curved forwards
Barlia, p152

33* Eacn pollinium has its own viscidium; bracts often shorter than the ovaries, when longer, the lateral sepals are directed sideways or upwards 34

34   Flower small, 5mm long at most; labellum not dotted
Neotinea, p106

34* Flowers obviously larger or, if less than 5 mm, then the labellum is white with reddish-brown dots
Orchis, pp110 – 151
Key p242

35   (32) Labellum tongue-shaped, 3-lobed near the tip, the central lobe much shorter and tooth-like
Coeloglossum, p60

35* Labellum with a rounded or oval outline, often deeply lobed with the central lobe generally covering the lateral ones . . 36

36   Plant with two heart-shaped leaves clasping the stem at different heights
Gennaria, p50

36* Plant with 3 or more basal leaves . . . 37

37   Sepals and lateral petals forming a hood 38

37* Lateral petals spreading, flower without a hood 41

38   The 3 labellum lobes of about equal length and width 39

38* Lateral and central labellum lobes unequal 40

39   Plant with two basal leaves; spur about as long as the ovary
Habenaria, p50

39* Plant with more than 3 leaves spaced along the stem; spur much shorter than the ovary
Leuchorchis, p62

40   (38) Labellum lobes narrow lanceolate, the central one larger than the laterals; plant with basal rosette and a few scale-like stem leaves
Neottianthe, p60

40* Labellum lobes rounded triangles, the central one smaller than the laterals; stem leaves but no rosette
Dactylorhiza iberica, p74

41   (37) Spur thread-like, diameter less than 1 mm; perianth segments small up to 7 mm
Gymnadenia,
pp62 – 65

41* Spur club-shaped, diameter more than 1.5 mm, very rarely thinner; perianth segments larger generally obviously more than 7 mm
Dactylorhiza,
pp70 – 103 Key p239

Lady's Slipper *Cypripedium calceolus* L.

1 cm

Plants with creeping rhizomes; stem to 60 cm, often just 1-flowered; leaves elliptical to ovoid to 17 cm long; calyx 2-parts reddish-brown 3.5 – 5 cm long, the lower part formed from the fused lateral sepals; lateral petals reddish-brown 4 – 6 cm, twisted; labellum 3 – 4 cm, slipper-shaped; column with 2 fertile and 1 sterile stamens, the latter flattened, about 1 cm long covering the shield-shaped stigma.

Habitat: woodland, scrub; up to 2,000 m; prefers semi-shade and lime-rich soil.

Flowers: May – July. **Photos**: Ge, Niedersachsen, 13.6.83 (l); Br, Yorkshire 16.6.79 (r); *see also* p 256. **Distribution**: occurs widely in Europe, especially in the temperate and boreal zones, in the sub-meridional zones only in the mountains; rare in oceanic western Europe. Also in the whole of temperate and boreal Asia and in isolated sites in the Caucasus and central China. **Floristic element**: sub-meridional/montane, temporate, boreal. **Countries**: Eur: SE Gr, Ju, Bu, Rm, RK, S It, SW Hs, W Ga, Be, Br, C He, Au, Hu, Ge, Da, Cz, Po, RB, N Su, No, Fe, RN, E RW, RE, RC. **Variation**: the species has several forms, especially in North America. Deviations from the Euroasiatic type growing there are generally considered to be varieties. **Key** to the *Cypripedium* species:

1 Stem with two leaves in addition to the flower bract; labellum white, generally with purple flecks, margin round, opening turned up . . . . *C. guttatum*
1* Stem with 3 – 5 leaves; labellum yellow or pink to purple, not flecked, opening margin turned inwards 2
2 Labellum yellow; sterile stamen stalked . . . . *C. calceolus*
2* Labellum pink to purple; sterile stamen sessile . . . . *C. macranthos*

Spotted Lady's Slipper *Cypripedium guttatum* Swartz subsp. *guttatum*

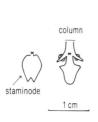

column

staminode

1 cm

Synonyms: *C. orientale* Spreng; *C. variegatum* Georgi. Stem up to 30 cm; leaves to 12 cm; all flower parts less than 3 cm, usually with purple flecks on a white background, rarely unflecked.

Habitat: coniferous and mixed woodland, woodland clearings. **Flowers**: May, June.

Distribution: in Europe only in the Soviet Union. A species with circumpolar distribution in the boreal and temperate zones of Eurasia, western Europe and eastern North America. **Floristic element**: Sarmatic, n-Russian, c- + n-Siberian. **Countries**: Eur: N RN, E RE, RC.

Large-Flowered Lady's Slipper *Cypripedium macranthos* Swartz

Synonyms: *C. m. var. ventricosum* (Swartz) Reichenb. fil.; *C. thunbergii* Blume

1 cm

Similar to *C. calceolus* in appearance differing especially in the flower colour and size of the labellum; labellum 4 – 7 cm, somewhat shorter (*ventricosum*) to somewhat longer than the 4 – 6 cm perianth segments; sterile stamen 1.3 – 1.5 cm sessile.

Habitat: deciduous woodland clearings, rarely in coniferous woods. **Flowers**: June, July.

Distribution: in Europe only in the Soviet Union. Distributed throughout the temperate zones of Eurasia from White Russia eastwards to Manchuria and Japan, also in the submeridional zone in north-east China. **Floristic element**: Sarmatic, c-Siberian. **Countries**: Eur: E RC.

Cypripedium

13

Marsh Helleborine   *Epipactis palustris* (L.) Crantz

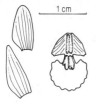

Plant with long creeping rhizome. Stem 15 – 50 (– 80) cm high, with 2 – 4 sheathing basal scale leaves and 4 – 8 stem leaves, the lower ones elongated, lanceolate 7 – 18 cm long and 1.5 – 4 cm wide, the upper ones smaller. Inflorescence lax, 6 – 20 cm long with dense short hairs. Flowers 7 – 20, eventually overhanging with long stalked pubescent ovaries. Sepals ovate – lanceolate, slightly hairy, greenish and reddish-brown merging (rarely without the reddish-brown), the centre one 8 – 11 mm long and 3.5 – 4 mm wide, the laterals somewhat longer and broader; lateral petals 8 – 10 mm long, ovate, whitish or reddish; labellum 9.5 – 13 mm long; hypochile shallow dished, whitish with two orange-yellow longitudinal stripes and on each side a triangular lateral lobe; epichile rounded, white, wavy with 2 toothed, yellow-edged swellings at the base. Cross-pollinated.

Habitat: fens, damp meadows, wet dune hollows; up to 2,000 m; on base-rich (mostly lime-rich) soils which are thoroughly wet throughout the year or periodically. **Flowers:** June – August. **Photos:** An, Vil. Bolu, 22.7.82 (l); Ge, Nordwürttemberg, 23.7.77 (r/u); Br, Hampshire, 21.7.84 (r/l).

Distribution: widely distributed in Europe and the Near East in the temperate and sub-meridional zones, occasionally penetrates into the boreal zone (Scandinavia) and the meridional zone (as far as southern Italy, central Greece, south-east Anatolia). Also in the temperate zone of Asia eastwards as far as central Siberia. **Floristic element:** (c + e-Mediterranean), (oriental), submeridional temperate, (scandinavian).

Countries: Eur: SE Gr, Tu, Al, Ju, Bu, Rm, R, **S** It, Co, **SW** Hs, Lu, **W** Ga, Be, Ho, Br, Hb, **C** He, Au, Hu, Ge, Da, Cz, Po, **RB**, **N** Su, No, Fe, **E** RW, RE, RC; **Asi:** An.

Eastern Marsh Helleborine   *Epipactis veratrifolia* Boiss. & Hohen

Synonyms: *E. consimilis* Hooker fil. (non D. Don), *E. abyssinica* Pax, *E. somaliensis* Rolfe.

Plant with a short creeping rhizome. Stem 15 – 100 (– 150) cm high with 3 – 4 sheathing basal scale leaves and 3 – 9 stem leaves.

Lower leaves narrow to ovate – lanceolate, pointed, 8 – 25 cm long and 1.6 – 6 cm wide. Inflorescence fairly lax, up to 60 cm long with short hairs; lower bracts much longer than the flowers. Flowers 4 – 25, nodding, with long-stalked pubescent ovaries. Perianth segments greenish with reddish-brown edges; sepals 10 – 21 mm long, hairy below, the central one narrowly elliptical, 4 – 7 mm wide, the laterals ovate – lanceolate, 7 – 100 mm wide; the lateral petals ovate with hairs on the nerve behind, 8 – 18 mm long and 4 – 8 mm wide; labellum a little shorter than the sepals; hypochile 7 – 12 mm long boat-shaped, 2 tooth-shaped lateral lobes at the base, the interior dark purple, warty, and with 2 pale reddish-brown tubercles; epichile 9 – 11 mm long with 2 triangular lateral lobes at the base and a longish, pointed central lobe, whitish to reddish with a brownish-yellow band across and a white tip. Cross-pollinated.

Habitat: springs, river banks, wet meadows, water-percolated slopes; 200 – 2,100 m; on wet, base-rich soils, mostly over limestone. **Flowers:** May – August. **Photos:** An, Vil. Maras, 15.6.73 (l); 28.6.75 (r).

Distribution: the Near East from south-east and eastern Turkey (westwards as far as the vicinity of Anamur) along the Levant as far as the Sinai peninsula, on Cyprus, fewer locations also in north-east Turkey. Also eastwards through Iraq, Persia, Afghanistan and Pakistan as far as Nepal with isolated sites in East Africa (Somalia). **Floristic element:** e-mediterranean oriental (e-submediterranian). **Countries: Asi:** Sn, IJ, LS, Cy, An.

Violet Helleborine *Epipactis purpurata* J. E. Sm.

Synonyms: *E. violacea* (Dur. – Duq.) Boreau, *E. sessilifolia* Peterm., *E. helleborine* subsp. *varians* (Crantz) Soó.

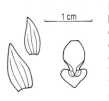

1 cm

Plant with long-branched, descending rhizome, often with several closely packed flowering stalks (up to 10), grey-green merging into violet. Stem 20–70 cm high, with 2–3 sheathing scale leaves and 4–10 leaves spirally arranged up the stem. Largest leaves narrow-ovate to narrow-lanceolate 5–10 cm long and (1–) 1.5–3 cm wide. The inflorescence has a pale green and violet stalk, thickly covered with short hairs, dense with many slightly scented flowers on stalked pubescent ovaries. Perianth segments (whitish) green, sometimes merging into pale violet with a silken sheen; sepals 8–12 mm long and 4–5 mm wide, ovate, hairy beneath; lateral petals somewhat narrower; labellum 8–10 mm long, whitish to pale pink, the hemi-spherical hypochile grey to violet-pink within; epichile heart-shaped, about as broad as long, with (2) 3 smooth outgrowths turning backwards at the tip. Cross-pollinated.
Habitat: shady, mixed woodland, also coniferous plantations; up to about 1,000 m; on deep, fairly damp soils. Flowers: July–September. Photos: Ge, Südwürttemberg, 20.8.74; *see also* p 259.
Distribution: concentrated in the temperate zone of western and central Europe and radiating towards the south and south-east; rare in the Atlantic region; eastwards as far as Lithuania, Poland and the Moldau Republic, southwards to northern Italy, northern Yugoslavia and southern Rumania. ●
Floristic element: w + c-submediterranean pannonic danubian (pontic) s + c-atlantic subatlantic central european. Countries: Eur: SE Ju, ?Bu, Rm, S It, W, Ga, Be, Br, C He, Au, Hu, Ge, Da, Cz, Po, RB, E RW.

Dense-Flowered Helleborine *Epipactis condensata* D.P. Young

Synonym: *E. helleborine* subsp. *condensata* (D. P. Young) Sundermann
Plant with strong descending rhizome, often with several closely packed flowering shoots. Stem 30–75 cm high, with 2–3 scale leaves and 4–8 pale green leaves, sometimes shading to violet on the lower surface. Largest leaves elongated ovate 3.5–9.5 cm long and 2.2–4.5 cm wide, folded, lower leaves rounded short. Inflorescence dense, many-flowered, densely covered in short hairs; bracts strong, longer than the flowers. Ovary stalked, pubescent. Sepals green, 10–11 mm long and 6–7 mm wide, ovate, undersides with short hairs; lateral petals greenish-white often with a pink tinge 9–10 mm long and 5–6 mm wide; labellum 9–10 mm long; hypochile hemi-spherical, inner surface dark violet, outer greenish-white; epichile wide triangular, about 4 mm long and 6 mm wide, whitish with 2 pink to red furrowed protuberances. Cross-pollinated; self-pollination may also occur after the rostellum gland has dried out.

Habitat: open pine woods of the montane zone, 600–2,000 m; on base-rich soils, tending towards somewhat rocky ground. Flowers: June–August, 2–3 weeks earlier than *E. helleborine*. Photos: An, Vil. Denizli, 22.6.75 (l); An, Vil. Burdur, 1.7.76 (r).
Distribution: a species of Asia Minor, rather rare in the mountains of northern Anatolian coast, more plentiful in western and southern Anatolia, eastwards as far as Vilayet Adana, from here southwards to Lebanon, also on Cyprus and Samos(?). Found too in the Caucasus (Georgia). Floristic element: e-mediterranean e-submediterranean. Countries: Asi: LS, Cy, An, ? AE.

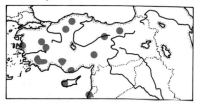

Epipactis

Broad-Leaved Helleborine *Epipactis helleborine* (L.) Crantz

Synonym: *E. latifolia* (L.) All.
Problems: the species has many forms. In the absence of any comprehensive work, this division into 3 subspecies can be seen as a provisional solution.
Key to the subspecies:

1 Leaves with wavy edges, wide ovate to circular, the largest 6 – 10 cm long – 2
.... *E. h. subsp. tremolsii*
1* Leaf edge not wavy; leaves often narrow (ovate to lanceolate) and longer (to 17 cm), if very wide and rounded then generally shorter than 6 cm – 2
2 Stem (normally developed) 40 – 100 cm high; inflorescence rather lax; lower bracts mostly longer than the flowers – 1
.... *E. h. subsp. helleborine*
2* Stem 15 – 35 cm high; inflorescence dense; lower bracts not extending beyond the flowers – 3 ... *E. h. subsp. neerlandica*

1. *E. h. subsp. helleborine*
Synonym: *E. h. subsp. viridis* Soó.

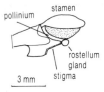

Stem with 2 – 4 scale leaves and 4 – 12 normal leaves. Largest leaves ovate – lanceolate, 7 – 17 cm long and 3 – 10 cm wide, held horizontally, rarely rounded (3 cm) and slanting upwards. Flowers open wide, greenish, mostly tinted with red or violet, rarely without red ('viridis'); hypochile inner surface olive to purplish-brown. Sepals ovate, 8 – 12 (– 15) mm long and 4 – 8 mm wide; lateral petals and labellum 7 – 11 mm long; epichile wide, triangular with 2 basal bosses. Cross-pollinated.
Habitat: woodland, scrub, growing in (semi) shade; up to 2,000m; on damp, nutrient-rich, deep soils. **Flowers:** June – August. **Photos:** He, Kt. Solothurn, 25.7.79 (u/l); Ge, Hessen, 12.8.62 (u/r). **Distribution:** In Europe widespread from the meridional to the temperate zones, reaches into the boreal zone in Scandinavia. In the western Mediterranean area its distribution is still not clear since the records may refer to the subspecies *tremolsii*
in some cases (Hs, Lu, Ag, Ma). It also occurs in the temperate zone eastwards as far as central Siberia and Dahurai, in the meridional zone from Caucasia to Pakistan and Turkestan.
Floristic element: meridional/montane submeridional temperate scandinavian.
Countries: Eur: SE Cr, Gr, Tu, Al, Ju, Bu, Rm, RK, **S** Si, It, Sa, Co, **SW** Bl, Hs, Lu, **W** Ga, Be, Ho, Br, Hb, **C** He, Au, Hu, Ge, Da, Cz, Po, RB, **N** Su, No, Fe, RN, **E** RW, RE, RC; **Asi:** IJ, LS, Cy, An, AE; ? Afr.

2. *E. h. subsp. tremolsii* (Pau) E. Klein
Synonym: *E. tremolsii* Pau
Stem 40 – 60 cm high, shading to purple. Leaves held upright at an angle. Flowers similar to the subsp. *helleborine*.
Habitat: open pine and oak woods, woodland edges, poor grassland; up to 1,500 m on dry, lime-rich soils. **Flowers:** April – July, several weeks earlier than *E. helleborine*. **Photos:** Lu, Prov. Algarve, 14.4.79 (l/l) Hs, Prov. Tarragona, 26.5.82 (l/r). **Distribution:** western Mediterranean area; from the Dept. Pyrénées-Orientales southwards as far as southern Portugal, the south-western foot of the Alps (Dept. Var. Drôme) and also in North Africa. ●
Floristic element: w-mediterranean w-sub-mediterranean **Countries: Eur: SW** Hs, Lu, **W** Ga; ?**Afr:** Ag, Ma.

3. *E. h. subsp. neerlandica* (Vermeulen) Buttler
Leaves ovate to rounded, standing upright at an angle, 4 – 7 (– 8) cm long. Flowers generally open only slightly, bell-shaped, **Habitat:** coastal dunes, especially the grey dunes. **Flowers:** August. **Photos:** Ho, Prov. Noord-Holland, 10.8.79 (p20). **Distribution:** along the coasts of the North Sea and the Baltic; Belgium, Holland, Jutland and Pommern; probably on the English Channel coast and on the islands of north Friesland, possibly in Wales (Glamorgan).
● **Floristic element:** m-atlantic n-subatlantic n-centraleuropean. **Countries: Eur: W** ?Ga, Be Ho, ?Br, **C** Ge, Da.
Related form: A similar plant is found growing on the dunes of north Jutland, but differs in being self-pollinated (autogamous). The pollinia and rostellum gland are reduced and functionless. **Photo:** Da, 29.7.80 (p21).

E. h. subsp. helleborine

Epipactis

E. h. subsp. tremolsii

Small-Leaved Helleborine *Epipactis microphylla* (Ehrh.) Swartz

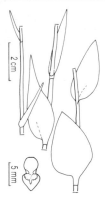

Plant with a short rhizome. Stem 15–50 cm high, with 2–3 scale leaves at the base and 3–12 foliage leaves, the latter up to 1.5× as long as the internodes, often all of them sheathing the stem. The largest leaves are narrow-lanceolate to wide-ovate, mostly shorter than 4 cm, 0.5–2.2 cm wide. Inflorescence lax, 4–20 cm long, with 4–27 flowers thickly covered with short hairs. Flowers nodding, scented, with stalked pubescent ovaries. Sepals ovate, 2–3 mm wide; lateral petals similar in shape and length; labellum 5–7 mm long; hypochile whitish, pale pink inside, greenish outside; epichile greenish to reddish-white, with wrinkled warty outgrowths at the base (2 roundish lateral bosses and a longer central strip). Rostellum gland rarely functional during the flowering period, thus generally self-pollinating.

Habitat: shady broad-leaved woodland and copses, rarely in coniferous woods; up to 1,700 m; on damp, nutrient-rich and mostly lime-containing soils. **Flowers**: May – August.
Photos: Ge, Südbaden, 1.7.65.
Distribution: throughout Europe and the Near East in the meridional, submeridional and the southern half of the temperate zones, absent from the continental regions of eastern Europe. Also in Caucasia and northern Persia.
Floristic element: mediterranean (oriental) submediterranean pannonic s-atlantic s+(n) subatlantic s-centraleuropean. **Countries**: **Eur: SE** Cr, Gr, Al, Ju, Bu, Rm, RK, **S** Si, It, Sa, Co, **SW** Bl, Hs, **W** Ga, Be, **C** He, Au, Hu, Ge, Cz, Po, **Asi**: An, AE.

Epipactis

Dark-Red Helleborine   *Epipactis atrorubens* (Berbh.) Besser

Synonyms: *E. a. subsp. borbasii* (Soó) Soó, *E. rubiginosa* (Crantz) W.D.J. Koch, *E. atropurpurea* autorum (non Rafin.)

Plant with short rhizome. Stem (10 –) 25 – 80 cm high with 2 – 3 scale leaves and 5 – 11 foliage leaves often arranged in two rows, the internode below the inflorescence often clearly elongated. Leaves narrow to broad ovate mostly longer than 5 cm (somewhat shorter in 'borbasii'), 1 – 4.5 cm wide, inflorescence of several flowers tending to one side, thickly covered in short hairs, flowers purplish- to brownish-red, nodding, vanilla-scented, sepals ovate, 2.5 – 4 mm wide hairy below; lateral petals similar in shape and length; labellum 5 – 6.5 mm long, hypochile hemispherical, epichile broad triangular to rounded, mostly wider than long, the two lateral rounded bosses and the elongated central slip wrinkled-warty. Cross-pollinated.

Habitat: open woodland and copses, especially with pines, sand dunes, poor grassland; up to 2,200 m; on dry sandy or stony ground mostly rich in lime. **Flowers**: May – August. **Photos**: Ge, Oberbayern, 22.7.65 (l); Br, Cumbria, 20.7.79 (r).

Distribution: throughout Europe from the boreal to the submeridional zones with individuals penetrating into the eastern Mediterranean in the meridional zone. Also eastwards in the Asian temperate zone as far as central Siberia, rare in the Caucasus. **Floristic element**: e-mediterranean sub-mediterranean pannonic atlantic subatlantic centraleuropean sarmatic c-sibirian scandinavian. **Countries**: Eur: SE Gr, Al, Ju, Bu, Rm, S It, SW Hs, ?Lu, W Ga, Be, Ho, Br, Hb, C He, Au, Hu, Ge, Da, Cz, Po, RB, N Su, No, Fe, RN, E RW, RE, RC; Asi: AE. **Variation**: pale pink- and green-flowered plants occur.

Small-Flowered Helleborine   *Epipactis parviflora* (A. & C. Nieschalk) E. Klein

Synonym: *E. atrorubens subsp. parviflora* A. & C. Nieschalk

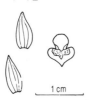

Similar to *E. atrorubens*, but slimmer. Stem 20 – 60 cm high, largest leaves 3 – 6 cm long and 1 – 3.5 cm wide. Stalk and leaves often shading to violet (purplish-red in *E. atrorubens.*). Inflorescence 8 – 25 cm long, rather lax, with 10 – 40 flowers. Sepals lower surface grey-green, sometimes tinged with pale violet, upper surface yellow-green; hypochile brownish-red within, edged green; epichile whitish to pale red or violet. Bosses and central ridge pale to dark violet. Cross-pollinated.

Habitat: open pine (oak) woods in the montane zone; 1,200 – 1,500 m; calcareous (fairly) dry soils. **Flowers**: May, June. **Photos**: Hs, Prov. Tarragona, 12.6.80 (r); Hs, Prov. Jaén, 10.6.80 (l).

Distribution: mountains of eastern Spain. Records for France (Dept. Aude, Pyrénées-Orientales) need confirmation. ● **Floristic element**: w-mediterranean w-submediterranean. **Countries**: Eur: SW Hs, W ?Ga.

Key to the species in the *Epipactis microphylla* group:

1   Flowers small, sepals 5 – 6 mm long, front part of labellum (epichile) 2 – 2.5 mm long .... *E. parviflora*

1*   Flowers larger; sepals (6 –) 6.5 – 10 mm long, epichile 2.5 – 3.5 mm 2

2   Largest leaves (4 –) 5 – 12 cm long; flowers usually purplish-red opening wide (the perianth segments spreading obliquely) .... *E. atrorubens*

2*   Largest leaf 2 – 4 (– 4.5) cm long; flowers greenish, sometimes tinged with pale pink, half opening (the perianth segments bell-shaped inclined forward) .... *E. microphylla*, p20

23

Mueller's Helleborine *Epipactis muelleria* Godfery
(and other autogamous species with hairy inflorescence stalks)

Synonym: *E. helleborine subsp. muelleri* (Godfery) Soó   Type 2, rarely type 1 column.
Habitat: open woodland and woodland edges, poor grassland with shrubs, growing in semishade, rarely in full shade; up to 900 m; on fairly dry base-rich soils. Flowers: June – August. Photos: Ge, Hessen 23.7.65 (u/l); Ge, Südwürttemberg, 2.8.78 (u/r).
Distribution: west and central Europe and the northern part of south Europe: from the northern edge of the central mountains (Be, Ho, Ge) as far as the Pyrenees, central Italy, Istrien, eastwards as far as Slovenia. ● Floristic element: w + c-submediterranean s + m-atlantic s-subatlantic s-centraleuropean pannonic. Countries: Eur: SE   Ju, S   It, W   Ga, Be, Ho, C   He, Au, Hu, Ge, Cz.
Similar species: the following species, each with a restricted distribution (*see also* the 'neerlandica' type on Jutland, p18), along with the widely distributed *E. muelleri* and *E. leptochila*, p28 form a group of similar species which reproduce by self-pollination (autogamy). They are able to do this by means of a special form of column; there are two

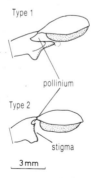

Type 1

pollinium

Type 2

stigma

3 mm

types. Type 1: pollen dish present, rostellum gland non-functional or absent, stigmatic surface at an angle to the long axis of the ovary. Type 2: pollen dish (almost) absent, no rostellum gland, stigmatic surface at right angles to the long axis of the ovary – characteristics
common to both are: flowers nodding, half open, bell-shaped, greenish colour with hardly any red apart from the interior of the hypochile; leaves often arranged in two rows (except *E. pontica. See* the key on p237 for differences.)
Elbe Helleborine *E. albensis* Nováková & Rydlo; column type 1 Habitat: shady river, valley woods. Flowers: August – October.

Photos: Cz, Böhmen, 23.8.79 (lower).
Distribution: Böhmen and Mähren; since the discovery (1967) in the river valleys of the Elbe, Eger, Moldau, Dedina, March and Thaya. ● Floristic element: s-centraleuropean. Country: Eur: C   Cz.
Dune Helleborine *E. dunensis* (T. & R. A. Stephenson) Godfery
Synonym: *E. helleborine subsp. dunensis* (T. & T. A. Stephenson) Soó Column type 1 or type 2.
Habitat: coastal dunes, damp hollows, also in pine plantations. Flowers: June – August. Photos: (p26) Br, Anglesey, 4.8.79 (u/l); Br. Merseyside, 23.7.84 (u/r). Distribution: coasts of northern England (Northumberland, Lancashire, Merseyside) and Wales (Gwynedd), supposed finds on the Continent were mistaken with other species. ● Floristic element: m-atlantic. Country: Eur: W   Br.
Young's Helleborine *E. youngiana* A. J. Richards & A. F. Porter Column type 1
Habitat: broad-leaved woodland. Flowers: July, August.   Photos   (p26)   26.7.84. Distribution: northern England; discovered in 1976, the species has been found in 2 sites in Northumberland. ● Floristic element: m-atlantic. Country: Eur: W   Br.
Pontus Helleborine *E. pontica* Taubenheim
Synonym: *E. helleborine subsp. pontica* (Taubenheim) Sundermann Column type 2.
Habitat: damp beechwoods; 200 – 1,200 m. Flowers: July, August. Photos: (p27); An, Vil. Rize, 3.8.75. Distribution: in northern Anatolia from the Vilayet Balikesir as far as the Turkish eastern frontier. ● Floristic element: e-submediterranean. Country: Asi: An.
Greuter's Helleborine *E. greuteri* H. Baumann & Künkele Column type 1.
Habitat: Fir (Beech) woods; 1,200 – 1,500 m; on calcareous soils.
Flowers: July, August. Photos (p27): Gr, Nomos Trikala, 28.7.82.
Distribution: northern Greece; the species was discovered in 1972 in a few places in the Pindus and Timfristos mountains. ● Floristic element: e-submediterranean. Country: Eur: SE   Gr.

Epipactis

E. youngiana

E. pontica

Epipactis

E. greuteri

27

Narrow-Lipped Helleborine *Epipactis leptochila* (Godfery) Godfery

Synonyms: *e. helleborine subsp. leptochila* (Godfery) Soó, *E. cleistogama* C. Thomas, *E. viridiflava* U. Low

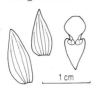

Plant with long descending rhizome. Stem 30 – 70 cm high, with several scale leaves and 3 – 6 limp, often light green foliage leaves, pubescent on the upper surface; largest leaves ovate – elliptical, 5 – 10 cm long and 2.2 – 3.6 cm wide; inflorescence lax with up to 30 flowers; bracts large and conspicuous. Flowers may open wide or remain closed, green, often (especially the labellum) with a reddish tint. Sepals 10 – 15 mm long, sometimes with a long point; lateral petals 8 – 11 mm long; hypochile brownish-red inside; epichile longer than wide, 4 – 5.5 × 3 – 5 mm, pointed, extended; pollinia stalked; rostellum gland absent or non-functional; self-pollinating.
Habitat: shady deciduous woods; to 1,000 m on fairly dry, always calcareous soils. **Flowers**: June – August, 2 – 3 weeks earlier than *E. helleborine*. **Photos**: Ge, Hessen 25.7.65 (l); He, Kt. Solothurn 15.8.80 (u/r); Ge, Bez. Suhl, type population (*neglecta*) 14.7.81 (l/r).

Distribution: patchy in western and central Europe; from northern England to the Pyrenees, into the Adriatic region (Trieste, Krk), eastwards as far as Slovakia. A similar distribution to *E. muelleri*, but concentrated more to the north. ● **Floristic element**: w + c-submediterranean m-atlantic subatlantic s-centraleuropean. **Countries**: Eur: SE Ju, S It, W Ga, Be, ?Ho, Br, C He, Au, Hu, Ge, Da, Cz.

Variation: a less observed aberrant race is known from France, Germany and Austria: *E. l. subsp. neglecta* Kümpel. Leaves dark green, hypochile shallow-dished (not hemispherical); epichile reflexed; pollinia not stalked; flowers about 10 days earlier than the subspecies *leptochila*. **Photo**: l/r.

Pendulous-Flowered Helleborine *Epipactis phyllanthes* G. E. Sm.

Synonyms: *E. helleborine subsp. phyllanthes* (G. E. Sm.) Sundermann, *E. cambrensis* C. Thomas, *E. pendula* C. Thomas, *E. vectensis* (T. & T. A. Stephenson) Brooke & F. Rose

Plant with short rhizome. Stem 10 – 60 cm high, smooth or sparsely hairy; leaves 3 – 7 lanceolate to rounded 3.5 – 7 cm long; flowers hang down on short-stalked (almost) glabrous ovaries, yellowish-green sometimes with a weak violet tinge, may open wide or remain bell-shaped or closed; perianth segments lanceolate 7 – 11 mm long; labellum 6 – 8 mm long, white, very variable in form, may be divided into hypo- and epichile or undivided and tongue-shaped. Self-pollinating.
Habitat: deciduous woods, hedgerows, pine plantations, coastal dunes; on damp to dry base-rich soils. **Flowers**: July – September. **Photos**: Br, Bedfordshire, 24.7.83 (l); Br,
Northumberland 26.7.84 (r). **Distribution**: Atlantic Europe; from Ireland and northern England to northern Spain. ● **Floristic element**: s + m-atlantic. **Countries**: Eur: SW Hs; W Ga, Be, Br, Hb. **Relationship**: *E. confusa* D. P. Young (Syn: *E. helleborine subsp. confusa* [D. P. Young] Sundermann) is generally considered to be a separate species. Distinguishing differences are:

1 Leaf edge slightly sinuate with wisps of ciliate hairs (lens required!); hypochile green interior; after pollination the perianth segments remain fresh for a time .... *E. phyllanthes*

1* Leaf edge straight, evenly covered with ciliate hairs (lens!); hypochile usually reddish interior; after pollination perianth segments quickly wilt .... *E. confusa*

Distribution: Baltic from East Jutland to Götland and Östergötland to Brandenburg. ● **Floristic element**: n-subatlantic n-centraleuropean. **Countries**: Eur: C Ge, Da; N Su. The status of the plants needs verification.

Epipactis

Persian Helleborine   *Epipactis persica* (Soó) Nannf.

Synonym: *E. helleborine subsp. persica* (Soó) Sundermann

Plant with long descending rhizome. Stem 10–60 cm high, upper part slightly hairy, 2–3 basal scale leaves, 2–4 foliage leaves about half way up, these 3–8 cm long and 1.5–4.5 cm wide held hotizontally. Inflorescence lax with large bracts. Flowers open wide, slightly nodding; perianth segments green to reddish; hypochile brownish-red inside; epichile whitish with green tip and reddish base, slightly notched round the edge. Self-pollinating. Rostellum gland present, but not functional.

Habitat: shady woodland, hazel plantations; up to 1,700 m; on base-rich deep soils. **Flowers**: June, July. **Photos**: An, Vil. Artvin, 10.7.82 (r); An, Vil. Ordu 26.6.82 (l).

Distribution: Turkey, especially in northern Anatolia, also in the mountains of Persia, Afghanistan and western Pakistan. **Floristic element**: e-mediterranean oriental e-submediterranean. **Countries**: Eur: SE Tu; Asi: An.

Relationship: similar plants are known from Greece (Nomi Imathia, Larissa, Pela) and Italy (Prov. Naples, Frosinone, Isernia); their affiliation requires verification.

Key for the species of the *Epipactis troodi* group:

1   Front part of the labellum (epichile) has 2 longish, many-furrowed horizontal swellings; points of the lateral petals bent forward .... *E. cretica*
1*   Epichile with 2, rounded, almost smooth swellings at the base; points of the lateral petals turned backwards – 2
2   Sepals 10–12 mm long; stem and leaves (especially on the under-sides) shading to intense violet .... *E. troodi*
2*   Sepals 9–10 mm long; stem and leaves dark green .... *E. persica*

Cretan Helleborine   *Epipactis cretica* Kalopissis & Robatsch

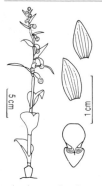

Stem 10–40 cm high with 1–2 rounded sheathing and 2–4 ovate leaves, the latter up to 5 cm long and 3.5 cm wide, tinged violet; perianth segments greenish, 8–9 mm long; hypochile dark olive-brown inside; epichile pink along the edges and at the base. **Habitat**: shady mixed woodland at the montane level, 1,100–1,400 m. **Flowers**: June, July. **Photo**: origin Cr (Nomos Iraklion 22.6.79).

Distribution: Crete. The species was described in 1980 and up to now is only known from a few sites in the Ida and Lasithi mountains ● **Floristic element**: e-mediterranean. **Country**: Eur: SE Cr.

Cyprus Helleborine   *Epipactis troodi* H. Lindb. fil.

Synonym: *E. helleborine subsp. troodi* (H. Lindb. fil.) Sundermann

Synonym: *E. helleborine subsp. troodi* (H. Lindb. fil.) Sundermann
Similar to *E. cretica* in appearance; perianth segments green and, especially the lateral petals, often running into pale purple; hypochile greenish-brown inside; epichile greenish, along the edge and at the base and also the outside of the hypochile pink to intense purple. Self-pollinating. **Habitat**: pine woods, deciduous woodland alongside streams; 800–2,100 m. **Flowers**: June, July. **Photo**: origin Cy (Troodos region, 17.6.79). **Distribution**: Cyprus; possibly southern Turkey. ● **Floristic element**: e-mediterranean. **Countries**: Asi: Cy ?An. **Problem**: Whether *E. troodi* and *E. persica* can always be separated has to be tested.

31

Large White Helleborine *Cephalanthera damasonium* (Miller) Druce

Synonym: *C. alba* (Crantz) Simonkai, *C. grandiflora* S. F. Gray, *C. pallens* I. C. M. Richard

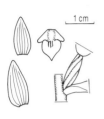

Plant with short creeping rhizome. Stem 15–60 cm high, bare, with 2–3 basal scale leaves and 2–5 foliage leaves. Lower leaves short, ovate; upper larger, 4–7 (–10) cm long and 1.8–3.5 cm wide, (narrow) elliptical, held at an angle or horizontally, folded lengthwise or flat. Inflorescence lax, 3–20 flowers; bracts gradually becoming smaller towards the top are similar to the foliage leaves. Flowers whitish-cream. Sepals ovate–lanceolate 15–20 mm long (rarely longer) and 4–8 mm wide, blunt; lateral petals somewhat shorter; labellum 10–14 mm long, 2-jointed, without spur; hypochile 4–6 mm long, concave, with upright, obliquely triangular lateral lobes, with a yellow mark inside; epichile triangular, heart-shaped, with wavy, slightly turned-up edges, turned down at the point, with 3 (5) orange longitudinal stripes on the surface.

Habitat: woods; up to 1,800 m; mostly in shade but also in semi-shade, prefers base-rich soils. **Flowers:** May–July. **Photos:** Ge, Hessen, 25.5.75 (l); Br, Buckinghamshire, 7.6.82 (r).

Distribution: in Europe and the Near East from the meridional as far as the temperate zone, but hardly penetrating into continental eastern Europe. Also in Caucasia eastwards as far as northern Persia.

Floristic element: mediterranean sub-mediterranean pannonic danubic (pontic) subatlantic centraleuropean (sarmatic).

Countries: Eur: **SE** Cr, Gr, Tu, Al, Ju, Bu, Rm, RK, **S** Si, It, Sa, Co, **SW** B1, Hs, Lu, **W** Ga, Be, Ho, Br, **C** He, Au, Hu, Ge, Da, Cz, Po, RB, **E** RW, RC; **Asi:** ?Cy, An; **Afr.**

Kotschy's Helleborine *Cephalanthera kotschyana* Renz & Taubenheim

Synonym: *C. damasonium subsp. kotschyana* (Renz & Taubenheim) Sundermann

Similar to *C. damasonium*, but generally more robust. Plant 30–60 cm high. Leaves 6–10 cm long and 2–5 cm wide, often folded lengthwise. Inflorescence 10–20 flowered. Flowers white. Sepals elliptic–lanceolate, with narrowing stem-like base, 20–30 mm long and 7–11 mm wide; labellum 13–16 mm long. Ovaries similar to *C. damasonium*, relatively short and robust.

Habitat: deciduous woods and scrub; in the montane zone; 700–1,800 m

Flowers: May–July **Photos:** An, Vil., Ordu 26.6.82.

Distribution: species endemic in asiatic Turkey, centred in eastern Anatolia.

● **Floristic element:** e-mediterranean oriental e-submediterranean. **Country: Asi:** An.

Key to the *Cephalanthera damasonium* group:

1 Ovaries held up at an angle of about 30° to the stem, the flowers remain closed or open only slightly and are held at the same angle as the ovaries; because of this the inflorescence appears narrow and open; sepals up to 20 mm long . . . . *C. damasonium*

1* Ovaries held out at an angle of about 45° to the stem, flowers open wide and are inclined outwards, making the inflorescence appear wider and denser; sepals more than 20 mm long . . . *C. kotschyana*

Red Helleborine *Cephalanthera rubra* (L.) L. C. M. Richard

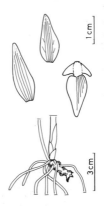

Plant with an elongated descending rhizome. Stem 20–60 cm high, the upper part with glandular hairs, several scale leaves at the base and 2–6 foliage leaves, lanceolate to linear-lanceolate up to 14 cm long and 3 cm wide. Inflorescence lax, up to 15 flowers; bracts become gradually smaller towards the top of the inflorescence, the lower one(s) longer than the flowers, glandular. Flowers pale – deep lilac-red, open wide. Sepals ovate – lanceolate, 17–25 mm long and 6–8 mm wide, pointed; outer surface pubescent; lateral petals 15–20 mm long, glabrous; labellum paler than the other perianth segments, 17–23 mm long, 2-jointed, without spur; hypochile barely a third of the total length, concave with vertical lateral lobes; epichile ovate-lanceolate, with 7–15 brownish longitudinal stripes. Ovaries slim, glandular. **Habitat**: semi-shaded and shaded woods; up to 2,000m; on base-rich soils, mainly on limestone. **Flowers**: May – July. **Photos**: Ge, Südwurttemberg 2.7.66 (l); Ge, Südbaden 18.5.72 (u/r); He, Kt. Zürich 23.6.78 (l/r).

Distribution: in Europe, North Africa and the Near East from the temperate to the meridional zone, only rarely in the atlantic and pontic floristic regions. Also in Caucasia and further to the south-east as far as northern and western Persia. Very rare in Britain.

Floristic element: meridional/montane submeridional temperate.

Countries: Eur: **SE** Cr, Gr, Tu, Al, Ju, Bu, Rm, RK, **S** Si, It, Sa, Co, **SW** Hs, Lu, **W** Ga, Be, + Ho, Br, **C** He, Au, Hu, Ge, Da, Cz, Po, RB, **N** Su, No, Fe, **E** RW, RE, RC; **Asi**: LS, Cy, An, AE; **Afr**: Ag, Ma.

Sword-Leaved Helleborine *Cephalanthera longifolia* (L.) Fritsch

Synonyms: *C. ensifolia* (Murray) L. C. M. Richard, *C. xiphophyllum* (L. fil.) Reichenb. fil.

This species somewhat resembles *C. damasonium* but differs from it in the following: stem with 4–12 foliage leaves, lanceolate to linear-lanceolate, up to 18cm long and 4 cm wide. Bracts small, up to 5 mm long, very different in size from the foliage leaves, but occasionally the lowest one or two bracts are more leaf-like. Flowers white, half opening. Sepals 14–18 mm long and 4–6 mm wide, pointed; labellum 7–10 mm long; hypochile 3–4 mm long; epichile with 4–7 orange stripes and an orange, papillose point. Ovary relatively long and slim.

Habitat: open woodland, in grass along woodland edges; up to 2,000 m; generally in semi-shade on base-rich soils.

Flowers: April – July **Photos**: Su, Öland 11.6.78 (l); Ga, Dept. Var 19.4.71 (r).

Distribution: in Europe, North Africa and the Near East from the temperate to the meridional zone, dying out in continental eastern Europe. Also in Caucasia and in the meridional zone through Persia to the western Himalayas. **Floristic element**: meridional/montane submeridional temperate.

Countries: Eur: **SE** Cr, Gr, Tu, Al, Ju, Bu, Rm, RK, **S** Si, It, Sa, Co, **SW** Bl, Hs, Lu, **W** Ga, Be, Ho, Br, Hb, **C** He, Au, Hu, Ge, Da, Cz, Po, RB, **N** Su, No, Fe, **E** RW, RC; **Asi**: IJ, LS ?Cy, An, AE; **Afr**: Tn, Ag, Ma.

Related species: a close relative is *C. caucasica* (Kranzlin) with wider ovate – lanceolate leaves and larger flowers; endemic in the mountains along the southern coast of the Caspian Sea.

Cephalanthera

35

Spurred Helleborine *Cephalanthera epipactoides* Fischer & C. A. Meyer

Synonym: *C. cucullata subsp. epipactoides* (Fischer & C. A. Meyer) Sundermann

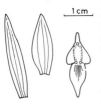

Closely related to *C. kurdica* but differs in the following (*see also* the key): stem up to 1 m high, often several close together arising from a single rhizome. Inflorescence fairly dense. Flowers generally held up at an angle, most open wide, larger than in the other species. Sepals 25 – 36 mm long and 4 – 7 mm wide; lateral petals 18 – 25 mm long; lateral lobes of the hypochile truncate; epichile with (6 –) 7 – 9 yellowish-brown ribs.

Habitat: open woodland and macchi, garrigue; up to 1,200 m; mostly in semi-shade on base-rich soils. **Flowers**: March – June. **Photo**: Tu, Vil. Çanakkale 28.5.81.

Distribution: a species of the eastern Mediterranean region; mainly in western and south-western Anatolia, north-westwards to Greek Thrace, eastwards in the pontic mountains as far as Kastamonu, appears to be absent further east. ● **Floristic element**: e-mediterranean e-submediterranean

Countries: Eur; SE Gr, Tu; **Asi**: An, AE.

Hooded Helleborine *Cephalanthera cucullata* Boiss & Heldr.

Stem 10 – 30 cm high. Leaves up to 6 cm long, rolled into a cone shape. Flowers white to pale pink, held up at an angle. Lateral petals 12 – 16 mm long; lateral lobes of the hypochile rounded; epichile heart-shaped with 3 – 6 yellowish longitudinal ridges.

Habitat: open woodland in the montane zone; up to 1,500 m on damp base-rich soils. **Flowers**: May, June. **Photo**: Cr. Prov. Iraklion 21.5.75.

Distribution: endemic to the island of Crete. ● **Floristic element**: e-mediterranean. **Country**: Eur: SE Cr.

Kurdish Helleborine *Cephalanthera kurdica* Bornm.

Synonyms: *C. cucullata subsp. kurdica* (Bornm.) Sundermann *C. floribunda* Woronow, *C. cucullata subsp. floribunda* (Woronow) Sundermann

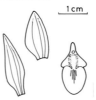

Plant with short rhizome. Stem 10 – 70 cm high, with 1 – 3 basal scale leaves and 2 – 4 foliage leaves, up to 5 cm long, ovate (elliptical), all cone-shaped or the largest with a flatter spreading blade. Inflorescence lax, usually to much more than half way down the stem; bracts get gradually smaller towards the top. Flowers generally deep pink, partly or fully opening, held horizontally. Sepals lanceolate, 20 – 25 mm long and 5 – 8 mm wide; lateral petals 16 – 18 mm long; labellum 14 – 16 mm long, in 2 parts, spurred; hypochile pink, 5 – 6 mm long, concave, with wide triangular upright lateral lobes; epichile whitish, with 6 (7) brownish-yellow longitudinal ridges.

Habitat: open woodland and scrub, particularly oak; 800 – 1,500 m, on base-rich soils. **Flowers**: April – June. **Photos**: An, Vil. Icel 14.5.83. **Distribution**: from the western part of south Turkey eastwards through Turkish and Iraqui Kurdestan to western Persia and into north-eastern Turkey, in the east links up with that of *C. epipactoides*; the two species are geographical variants. **Floristic element**: e-mediterranean oriental (e-submediterranean).

Countries: Asi: LS, An.

Key for species in *Cepipactoides* group:

1   Spur 1 – 2 mm long; sepals 14 – 20 mm long . . . . *C. cucullata*

1* Spur 3 – 4 mm long; sepals 20 – 26 mm long 2

2   Flowers whitish-cream to (greenish) yellowish; front part of the labellum (epichile) triangular – lanceolate . . . . *C. epipactoides*

2* Flowers pink, rarely whitish; epichile ovate heart-shaped . . . . *C. kurdica*

Cephalanthera

Violet Limodore   *Limodorum abortivum* (L.) Swartz

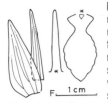

Plant with a short rhizome with fleshy roots. Stem without foliage leaves with numerous sheathing scale leaves, all a violet colour, scarcely any chlorophyll. Inflorescence fairly lax; flowers short-stalked, pressing against the stem. Stem to 80 cm high, up to 25 flowers. Flowers usually violet, opening wide. Sepals ovate – lanceolate, 16 – 25 mm long and 5 – 11 mm wide; lateral petals obviously shorter, narrow lanceolate. Labellum 14 – 22 mm long, 2-jointed; hypochile 4 – 7 mm long and wide with upright edges making it appear like a stalk; epichile 10 – 15 mm long and 7 – 12 mm wide with concave, turned-up, wavy edges, lengthwise convex, on the upper side paler to yellowish in the centre with dark longitudinal veins; spur at least half as long as the ovary, 15 – 25 mm directed downwards.

Habitat: open woodland, scrub, also in poor grassland; to 2,300 m; often, though not exclusively, on base-rich soils. **Flowers**: April – July. **Photos**: It, Prov. Triente. 8.6.68 (u/l); AE, Rhodes, 14.4.73 (r); An, Vil. Hatay 7.5.72 (l/l).

Distribution: Mediterranean area, northwards as far as Central Europe, outside this area eastwards from Caucasia to southern Persia.

Floristic element: mediterranean sub-mediterranean pannonic danubic s-atlantic s-subatlantic s-centraleuropean. **Countries**: Eur: SE   Cr, Gr, Tu, Al, Ju, Bu, Rm, RK, **S**   Si, It, Sa, Co, **SW**   Bl, Hs, Lu, W   Ga, Be, **C**   He, Au, Hu, Ge, Cz; **Asi**: IJ, LS, Ly, An, AE; **Afr**: Tn, Ag, Ma.

Variation: a striking blood-red colour variant is known from Turkey and Cyprus (photo. l/l). Departing more strongly from the normal type is *L. a subsp. gracile* B. & E. Willing: plant delicate, 10 – 30 cm high; inflorescence with 3 – 6 (– 9) flowers; flowers white or very pale violet; so far only in Arcadia (Peloponnes).

Trabut's Limodore   *Limodorum trabutianum* Batt.

Synonym: *L. abortivum subsp. trabutianum* (Batt.) Rouy

In general appearance, similar to the previous species (*see* that description). Stem up to 55 cm high, up to 20 flowers. Flowers violet, scarcely opening; petals pointing forward, narrower than in the other species. Differs from this especially in the form of the labellum: this is not 2-jointed but narrow spatulate, up to 18 mm long and 5 mm wide, bent outwards at the point; spur short, up to 4 mm long. Column with a tooth-like projection on the ventral side (absent in the other species).

Habitat: Open oak and pine woods and scrub; up to 2,000 m; on base-rich soils; often found growing with *L. abortivum*. **Flowers**: April – June, at about the same time as the other species. **Photos**: Hs, Prov. Malaga 10.5.80

Distribution: south-western Europe and western North Africa, northwards as far as the Dept. Charente-Maritime and Deux-Sèvres on the French Atlantic coast, eastwards to the Italian island of Pantelleria off the Tunisian coast.

Floristic element: w + c-mediterranean w-submediterranean s-atlantic.

Countries: Eur: S Si, SW Bl, Hs, Lu, W Ga; **Afr**: Ag, Ma.

Key to the *Limodorum* species:

1   Spur   15 – 25 mm   long;   labellum constricted near the broadened base, the forward part (epichile) ovate, 7 – 12 mm wide . . . . *L. abortivum*
1*   Spur   1 – 4 mm   long;   labellum not constricted, spatulate, 3 – 5 mm wide . .
. . . . *L. trabutianum*

Ghost Orchid   *Epipogium aphyllum* Swartz

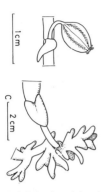

Plant with coral-like branched rhizome covered in scale leaves, without roots, with thin runners, without foliage leaves or chlorophyll, glabrous. Stem 5–30 cm high, 1–8 flowered, brown scale leaves at the base. Flowers short-stalked, pendulous, not twisted, labellum uppermost. Sepals and lateral petals about the same length 8–15 mm, pale yellow to reddish. Labellum whitish, 6–9 mm long, 2-jointed; hypochile with 2 broad triangular lateral lobes; epichile heart-shaped, concave, with 4–6 rows of papillae on the upper surface, often flecked or shaded red; spur thick, 3–5 mm long often bent.

Habitat: shady woods especially in the montane zone; up to 1,700 m; on nutrient- and base-rich soils. **Flowers**: July, August; often flowers below ground and cannot be seen where it is growing. **Photos**: Ge, Südbaden 21.8.65 (l); An, Vil. Kastamonu 23.7.83 (r). **Distribution**: in a large part of Europe and the Near East, absent from the Mediterranean and Continental regions. Eastwards through temperate Asia to Japan, Korea, Kamtschatka; southwards into Caucasia and in the Himalayas. Extremely rare in Britain. **Floristic element**: submediterranean c-atlantic sub-atlantic centraleuropean karpatic sarmatic c-siberian scandinavian. **Countries**: Eur: SE   Gr, Al, Ju, Bu, Rm, RK, S   It, W   Ga, Be, Br, C   He, Au, Hu, Ge, Da, Cz, Po, RB, N   SU, No, Fe, E   RW, RC; **Asi**: An. **Related species**: another species belonging to this genus, *E. roseum* (D. Don) Lindley, grows in the tropics and sub-tropics of the Old World.

Bird's Nest Orchid   *Neottia nidus-avis* (L.) L. C. M. Richard

Plant with a short creeping rhizome densely covered with unbranched fleshy roots and having the appearance of a bird's nest, without foliage leaves, (yellowish-)brown, only traces of chlorophyll (principally in the inflorescence) which are insufficient for nutritional needs. Stem 20–45 cm high with sheathing scale leaves. Inflorescence many-flowered, less dense towards the base, glabrous or slightly glandular. Flowers (yellowish-)brown, short-stalked, twisted, fragrant. Sepals and lateral petals similar, 4–6 mm long, obovate, bending towards each other; labellum up to 12 mm long, boat-shaped at

the base, deeply divided at the tip into two lobes spreading outwards and broadening out at the tips. **Habitat**: shady deciduous woods (often with beech), also in mixed pine woods; up to 2,000 m; on nutrient- and base-rich soils. **Flowers**: May–July; occasionally flowers below ground when self-pollination takes place. **Photos**: Ge, Allgäu, 2.6.81 (u/l); Ge, Südbaden 1.6.66 (l/l); Ge, Südwürttemberg 13.6.70 (r). **Distribution**: widely in Europe, North Africa and the Near East from the temperate to the meridional zones, in the boreal zone (north European coniferous woodland area) only rare occurrences. Eastwards in the temperate zone to central Siberia, also in Caucasia and north-western Persia. **Floristic element**: meridional/montane submeridional temperate (boreal). **Countries**: Eur: SE   Gr, Tu, Al, Ju, Bu, Rm, RK, S   Si, It, Sa, Co, SW   Bl, Hs, Lu, W   Ga, Be, Ho, Br, Hb, C   He, Au, Hu, Ge, Da, Cz, Po, RB, N   Su, No, Fe, RN, E   RW, RE, RC; **Asi**: An; **Afr**: Ag.

Epipogium

Neottia

41

Twayblade *Listera ovata* (L.) R. Br. -

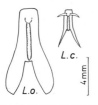

Stem 20−60 cm high, very hairy, 2−3 brown basal scale leaves and 1−3 green scale leaves below the inflorescence. Foliage leaves mostly 2 almost opposite, 4−13 cm long and 3−8 cm wide. Inflorescence 20−80 flowers. Flowers yellowish-green. Perianth segments bend forwards, of about ˌequal length (4−5 mm), sepals about 2 mm, lateral petals about 1 mm wide; labellum 7−15 mm long with blunt lobes, basal nectary bounded at the sides by ridges, continuing in a groove down as far as the middle of the labellum. **Habitat:** woodland, scrub, meadows, poor grassland, fenland; up to 2,000 m; on deep base-rich damp to wet soils; a species with a wide habitat spectrum. **Flowers:** May − July. **Photos:** Su, Öland, end of 5.73 (l); Ge, Oberbayern 18.5.64 (r). **Distribution:** widely in Europe and the Near East from the boreal to the meridional zones, rarer in the Mediterranean region. In Asia eastwards through the temperate zone as far as central Siberia, also from the Caucasus through the meridional zone to the western Himalayas. **Floristic element:** meridional submeridional temperate boreal. **Countries: Eur: SE** Cr, Gr, Al, Ju, Bu, Rm, RK, **S** Si, It, Sa, Co, **SW** Hs, **W** Ga, Be, Ho, Br, Hb, **C** He, Au, Hu, Ge, Da, Po, RB, **N** Su, No, Fe, RN, Is, **E** RW, RE, RC; **Asi:** An, AE.

Key for the *Listera* species:

1 Plant strong, stem higher than 20 cm and some 3 mm thick; leaves ovate (elliptical), more than 4 cm long; labellum without teeth at the base, both lobes blunt . . . . *L. ovata*

1* Plant delicate, stem seldom more than 15 cm and about 1 mm thick; leaves wide, heart-shaped up to 3 cm long. labellum with a pair of horn-shaped teeth at the base, both lobes pointed . . . *L. cordata*

Lesser Twayblade *Listera cordata* (L.) R. Br.

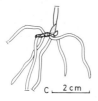

Plant with a slim creeping rhizome bearing thin roots. Stem 5−15 (−25) cm high, glabrous below, sparsely hairy above, 1−2 brown scale leaves at the base. The 2 foliage leaves are almost opposite, 1⇁3 cm long and wide, upper surface shiny. Inflorescence lax, up to 25 flowers; bracts shorter than the stalks of the club-shaped ovaries. Flowers have a green ground-colour generally shading to brown (as is the stem). Perianth segments spreading, elliptical − lanceolate, and of about equal length (1.5 − 2.5 mm); labellum wedge-shaped, 3.5 − 4.5 mm long, divided into two up to half its length, with pointed spreading lobes; horn-shaped outgrowths of the basal nectary 0.5 − 0.7 mm long. **Habitat:** coniferous woodland generally in damp or wet places, also in dune slacks and fenland; up to 2,200 m; on nutrient-deficient acid soils; sometimes removed as a weed in coniferous plantations. **Flowers:** May − August. **Photos:** An, Vil. Artvin 17.7.76 (l); Au, Salzburg 31.5.71 (r). **Distribution:** centred in northern Europe, dying away in the continental regions; southwards into the submeridional zone, but virtually confined to the mountains. A species with circumpolar area of distribution predominantly boreal-temperate, but here and there advancing into the arctic and submeridional zones, large gaps in Siberia (Jakutien)? Yukute **Floristic element:** sub-meridional/montane temperate boreal (arctic). **Countries: Eur: SE** Ju, Bu, Rm, **S** It, SW, Hs, **W** Ga, Ho, Br, Hb, Fa, **C** He, Au, Hu, Ge, Da, Cz, Po, RB, **N** Su, No, Fe, RN, Is, **E** RW, RC; **Asi:** An.

Variation: A species with little variation. In western North America there is a relative growing with somewhat larger leaves and flowers: *L. c. var. nephrophylla* (Rydberg) Hulten (*see* Luer 1975).

Listera

43

Summer Lady's Tresses   *Spiranthes aestivalis* (Poiret) L. C. M. Richard

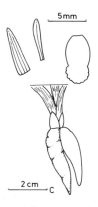

Plant with 2–6 fleshy narrow cylindrical or spindle-shaped roots 5–8 cm long. Stem 10–40 cm high, slightly glandular upper part, 1–2 brown scale leaves at the base; basal foliage leaves 3–6 linear-lanceolate up to 12 cm long and 1 cm wide, upright; stem leaves getting smaller towards the top. Inflorescence 3–10 cm long, fairly lax, with 6–20 flowers in 1 spiral row; bracts 6–9 mm, somewhat longer than the ovaries. Flowers white, scented, held horizontally. Perianth segments stay together turning up slightly at the ends; sepals 6–7 mm long, glandular on the outside; lateral petals 5–6 mm long; labellum 6–7 mm long, tongue-shaped, front edge notched and turned dowards, upper side yellowish at the base.

Habitat: fenland; up to 1,400 m; mostly on calcareous soils and often associated with limestone tufa; because of the special demands dispersed or rare. **Flowers**: June – August. **Photos**: Ge, Allgau 23.7.72 (l); He, Kt, Schwyz 30.7.78 (r).

Distribution: concentrated in the western and central Mediterranean areas, northward as far as western and central Europe, eastwards to Yugoslavia. Extinct in Britain (last recorded in the New Forest, Hampshire). ● **Floristic element**: w + c mediterranean w + c sub-mediterranean s + m atlantic s-subatlantic s-centraleuropean. **Countries**: **Eur**: **SE** Ju, **S** It, Sa, Co, **SW** Hs, + Lu, **W** Ga, Be, Ho, Br, **C** He, Au, Hu, Ge, Cz; **Afr**: Ag, Ma.
Key to the *Spiranthes* species, p46

Autumn Lady's Tresses   *Spiranthes spiralis* (L.) Chevall

Synonym: *S. autumnalis* L. C. M. Richard

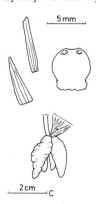

Plant with 2–3 (–5) elongated egg-shaped roots from 1.5 to 4 cm long. Stem 6–40 cm high, glandular above, with 3–7 sheathing scale leaves. The rosette of leaves for the following season's flowering stem already develops alongside this year's flowering stems; leaves ovate to elliptical, over-wintering, withering before the flowers. Inflorescence 3–15 cm long with 6–30 blossoms in 1 spiral row. Flowers (greenish-) white, scented, held horizontally. Perianth segments 4–7 mm long; sepals glandular outside, the lateral ones spreading, the central one forming a tube with the lateral petals, labellum yellowish-green with a white edge, 4–7 mm long, rounded, 2 small warts at the base, notched in front with well turned-up edges. **Habitat**: poor meadows and pastures, open coniferous woodland, garrigue, more rarely damp meadows, dunes; to 1,200 m; on acid, lime-free as well as on neutral and calcareous soils. **Flowers**: August – October. **Photos**: Ge, Südwürttemberg, 3.9.82 (l); An, Vil. Hatay 9.9.78 (u/r); Ge, Hessen 8.9.66 (l/r).

Distribution: widely in Europe with main concentration in south-west of sub-continent and in North Africa; absent from northern Europe in boreal zone and in eastern Europe in continental part of the temperate zone. **Floristic element**: mediterranean sub-mediterranean s + m atlantic subatlantic centraleuropean. **Countries**: **Eur**: **SE** Cr, Gr, Tu, Al, Ju, Bu, Rm, **S** Me, Si, It, Sa, Co, **SW** Bl, Hs, Lu, **W** Ga, He, Ho, Br, Hb, **C** He, Au, Hu, Ge, Da, Cz, Po, **N** Su, **E** RW; **Asi**: IJ, LS, Cy, An, AE; **Afr**: Tn, Ag.

Spiranthes

Pink Lady's Tresses *Spiranthes sinensis* (Pers.) Ames

Synonym: *S. amoena* (Bieb.) Sprengel

This species is related to *S. aestivalis* and resembles it, the obvious difference being the red flowers. Stem up to 50 cm high.

Inflorescence 2−15 cm, 5−30 flowers. Sepals 4−7 mm long, lateral petals the same or slightly shorter; labellum 4−7 mm long, tongue-shaped or violin-shaped − constricted in the middle, 2 small warts at the base (absent from the other species) − papillose in the centre, front whitish.

Habitat: damp meadows, bogs. Flowers: July, August. Photos: origin Japan, cult. 28.8.77 (r) 5.10.79 (l).

Distribution: in Europe only in the region of the central Urals (Kama) on the north-western edge of its range, in the whole temperate zone in Asia, southwards to the mountains of the meridional zone (Himalayas); also in the southern hemisphere (New Guinea, Australia, New Zealand). Floristic element: sarmatic. Country: Eur: E RC.

Key to the *Spiranthes* species:

1   Flowers arranged in 3 spiral rows; flower bracts 10−22 mm long; sepals 8−12 mm long .... *S. romanzoffiana*
1* Flowers in 1 spiral row; bracts 5−9 mm, sepals 4−7 mm 2
2   Flowering stem, next to the leaf rosette for the following year, has only scale leaves; rosette leaves ovate to elliptical .... *S. spiralis*, p44
2* Flowering stem has no adjacent leaf rosette, has foliage leaves at the base and gradually getting smaller up the stem; leaves narrow lanceolate 3
3   Flowers white .... *S. aestivalis*, p44
3* Flowers red .... *S. sinensis*

Irish Lady's Tresses *Spiranthes romanzoffiana* Cham.

Synonym: *S. gemmipara* (Sm.) Lindley, *S. stricta* (Rydb.) A. Nelson

Plant with 2−6 narrow, cylindrical, fleshy roots. Stem 12−50 cm high, upper part sparsely glandular.

Lower leaves linear to narow-lanceolate, up to 25 cm long and 1.5 cm wide, upright; upper leaves small, bract-like. Inflorescence 2.5−8 cm long, 20−60 flowers; flowers arranged in 3 spiral rows; bracts larger than in the other species, 10−22 mm long. Flowers whitish-cream held upwards at an angle; perianth segments come together to form a tube bent upwards at the tip, of about equal length 8−12 mm; labellum 8−11 mm long, violin-shaped (narrow above the centre and wider in front), 2 small warts at the base, front part crenate and turned down.

Habitat: damp meadows, fens, in North America also in open woodland, raised bogs and stony, poor grassland; on base-rich soils. Flowers: July, August. Photos: Hb, Antrim, 11.8.84 (r); Hb, Kerry 27.7.84 (l)

Distribution: In Europe at the eastern edge of its range, only on the western part of the British Isles (western and northern Ireland, western Scotland, south-west England). Mainly in North America; in the boreal and temperate zones of the whole continent westwards as far as the Aleutians and penetrating southwards along the Rocky Mountains into the meridional zone. Floristic element: m-atlantic Countries: Eur: W Br, Hb.

Variation: the European population shows some variation in the form of the leaves (linear; elongated-lanceolate) and in the inflorescence (short and compact; elongated and more lax), but this is no more than is to be seen in that of North America.

Spiranthes

Creeping Lady's Tresses   *Goodyera repens* (L.) R. Br.

Plant with long surface runners. Stem 10–30 cm high with basal foliage leaves, scale leaves up the stem, glandular. Basal leaves cordate to ovate with a short wide stalk, reticulate venation. Inflorescence 5–15 flowered, vaguely spiral. Flowers white to cream, pendulous, scented. Perianth segments tending to come together, 3–5 mm long; sepals glandular on the outside; labellum 2.5–4 mm long in two parts; hypochile hemispherical hollowed, papillose inside; epichile triangular, flat. The new leaf rosettes grow in the autumn and overwinter.
Habitat: coniferous woods rich in mosses, often growing in half-shade; up to 2,000 m; on fairly dry to damp, base-rich soils; is spread by afforestation along with the conifers. **Flowers:** June–September. **Photos:** Au, Kärnten

24.7.81 (l); Ge Südwürttemberg 29.7.81 (r).
Distribution: In Europe and the Near East from the boreal to the submeridional zones, only occasionally in oceanic western Europe. Total distribution circumpolar, boreal-temperate, penetrates further south in the mountains. **Floristic element:** submeridional/montane temperate boreal.
Countries: Eur: SE Ju, Bu, Rm, RK, S It, SW, Hs, W Ga, Be*, Ho, Br, C He, Au, Hu, Ge, Da, Cz, Po, RB, N Su, No, Fe, RN, E RW, RC; Asi: An.
Key for the *Goodyera* species:
1 Lower leaves up to 3.5 cm long; flowers 3–5 mm long .... *G. repens*
1* Lower leaves longer than 5 cm; flowers 12–13 mm .... *G. macrophylla*
Madeiran Lady's Tresses *G. macrophylla* Lowe is a little known endemic of the island of Madeira. The plants are robust, 20–60 cm high, more than 30 flowers. **Habitat:** damp, shady woodland. **Flowers:** September – November. • **Floristic element:** madeiran.

Musk Orchid   *Herminium monorchis* (L.) R. Br.

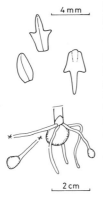

Plant with a single spherical tuber. Stem 7–30 cm high with 1–2 scale leaves at the base, 2 (rarely 3–4) foliage leaves at ground level and 0–2 scale leaves up the stem; rosette leaves lanceolate – elliptical, 2–12 cm long and 0.6–2 cm wide. Inflorescence 1.5–10 cm, slender, lax; bracts somewhat shorter than the ovaries. Flowers pendent, yellowish- or whitish-green, honey-scented. Sepals ovate – lanceolate, 2.5–3 mm long and 1–1.5 mm wide conical, directed forwards; lateral petals 3.2–3.9 mm long, tongue-shaped, the rear third toothed or lobed, tip turned backwards; labellum 3.5–4.5 mm long, 2 narrow lateral

lobes in the rear third, a dish-shaped depression at the base. **Propagation:** the plant forms several new tubers on long runners; flowering stems are thus often in groups. **Habitat:** poor grassland and meadows, fenland; up to 2,000 m on base-rich soils, mostly on limestone. **Flowers:** May–August. **Photos:** Ge, Oberbayern 18.6.67 (l); Au, Liechtenstein 22.6.74 (r). **Distribution:** centred in the temperate zone in Europe; spreading into the submeridional zone along the Appenines and the Balkan peninsula and a little way into the boreal zone in Scandinavia. Also in Caucasia and in the temperate zone eastwards to . Japan; from there through the Chinese mountains as far as the Himalayas. **Floristic element:** (w) + c + (e)-submediterranean pannonic carpatic (s) + m-atlantic subatlantic centraleuropean sarmatic (scandinavian). **Countries:** Eur: SE Ju, Bu, Rm, S It, W Ga, Be, Ho, Br, C He, Au, + Hu, Ge, Da, Cz, Po, RB, N Su, No, Fe, RN, E RW, RE, RC.

Goodyera

Herminium

49

Two-Leaved Gennaria *Gennaria diphylla* (Link) Parl.

Synonyms: *Orchis diphylla* (Link) Samp.,
Coeloglossum diphyllum (Link) Fiori & Paol.

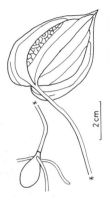

Plant with 1 ellipsoidal tuber. Stem 10 – 50 cm high with 1 – 2 sheathing scale leaves at the base and 2 alternate foliage leaves on the stem; lower leaf wide, cordate 3 – 12.5 cm long and 2.2 – 8 cm wide clasping the stem; upper leaf similar but smaller. Inflorescence up to 13.5 cm long, 10 – 45 flowers, dense, one-sided. Perianth segments of about equal length, 3.5 – 4 mm; sepals green pointing straight forward with cowl-shaped points; lateral petals yellow-green, rhombic, points curved backwards; labellum yellow-green, wide tongue-shaped with three lobes, the central lobe triangular, side lobes shorter and about half the width, tips turned downwards; spur pouched, grooved, 1.5 mm long. **Propagation:** new tubers form at the tips of thin runners which produce a long-stalked leaf from time to time over several years before flowering.

Habitat: broad-leaved evergreen woods, coniferous woods, garrigue, shady rock clefts; up to 1,000 m. **Flowers:** January to April. **Photos:** Cl, Tenerife 1.4.79 (l); Lu, Prov. Estramadura 31.3.71 (r).

Distribution: From Sardinia and Corsica throughout the Mediterranean region to the Atlantic islands but only near the coasts; on the islands of Madeira and Porto Santo; on the western part of the Canary archipeligo, but not known from Lanzarote or Fuerteventura.

● **Floristic element:** c + w-mediterranean madeiran canarian c-submediterranean. **Countries:** Eur: S Sa, Co, **SW** Bl, Hs, Lu; **Afr:** Ag, Ma, Ml, Cl.

Three-Lobed Habenaria *Habenaria tridactylites* Lindley

1 cm

Plant with 2 ellipsoidal tubers. Stem 10 – 30 (– 60) cm high, generally with 3 leaves at the base, bare above, lowest leaf scale-like, the 2 upper ones flattish, almost opposite, narrow to ovate-elliptical (1.5 –) 5 – 18 cm long (1 –) 1.5 – 7 cm wide, sharply pointed. Inflorescence lax, slender, cylindrical 2 – 12 (– 24) flowered; bracts ½ – ¾ the length of the ovaries. Flowers yellowish-green, scented; lateral sepals directed somewhat downwards and backwards, linear to elliptical, sickle-shaped, 5 – 7 mm long and 1 – 2.5 mm wide; centre sepal wide ovate, 4 – 6 mm long forming a helmet-shape with the 2 lateral petals which are of similar length and shape, the latter have a tooth at the base of the front edge; labellum 7 – 9 mm long, deeply divided into 3 linear spreading lobes of about equal length; spur 9 – 14.5 (– 17) mm long, slender cone-shaped, pointing down and curving forwards.

Habitat: probably a species associated with laurel woods. Today, because of widespread disturbance, it has been banished to humid rocky slopes; the species has also been able to occupy the vegetation which has replaced the woodland, in tree-heather scrub and in the cultivated areas (on old terrace walls in neglected fruit gardens) in shady places; on slightly acid mostly damp soils; up to 800 m.

Flowers: November – April. **Photos:** Cl, Tenerife 5.4.79 (l) 3.1.81 (r).

Distribution: a species endemic to the Canary islands, particularly to the western side of the group; rare (Lanzarote) or not reported (Fuerteventura) on the drier islands to the east.

● **Floristic element:** canarian. **Country: Afr:** Cl. **Relationship:** the genus has several hundred species distributed in the tropics and sub-tropics.

Gennaria

Habenaria

51

Algerian Butterfly Orchid *Platanthera algeriensis* Batt. & Trabut

Synonym: *P. chlorantha subsp. algeriensis* (Batt. & Trabut) Emberger

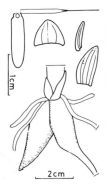

Plant with 2 elongated ovate tubers. Stem 25 – 70 cm high, 1 – 2 scale leaves at the base with 2 large and 4 – 6 small foliage leaves spaced out on the stem, lower leaves held up at an angle, broadly lanceolate, 9 – 30 cm long and 2 – 5 cm wide. Inflorescence up to 25 cm long, dense many-flowered, appears slender (flowers spread only slightly); bracts often large, longer than the flowers. Flowers yellow-green, smaller than in *P. chlorantha*; central sepal wide heart-shaped, 6 – 8 mm long and wide; lateral petals are of the same length but lanceolate, 2 – 2.5 mm wide, come together with the central sepal to form a helmet; lateral sepals ovate 8 – 11 mm long and 4 – 6 mm wide, somewhat concave, spreading, turning forward only slightly if at all; labellum narrow tongue-shaped, 8 – 12 mm long and 1.7 – 3.4 mm wide, often bent strongly back-wards; spur 18 – 24 mm long, the rear half is laterally compressed and appears broader from the side; anthers inclined at an angle to one another.

Habitat: wet meadows; up to 2,100 m; habitats on the plains have probably all been destroyed through drying out so the species is now mainly found at the montane level.

Flowers: May, June. **Photos**: Ma, Central Atlas, 20.5.80 (l) 23.5.81 (r).

Distribution: western Mediterranean area, mainly in north Africa in Morocco, eastwards as far as the region of Algiers; also known from the Sierra Nevada (Prov. Granada) in Europe.

● **Floristic element**: w-mediterranean.
Countries: Eur: SW Hs, Afr: Ag Ma.

Holmboë's Butterfly Orchid *Platanthera holmboei* H. Lindb. fil.

Synonym: *P. chlorantha subsp. holmboei* (H. Lindb. fil.) J. J. Wood

Very similar to *P. algeriensis* differing more in quantitative than qualitative characteristics; plants on the whole less strong with shorter leaves, inflorescence more lax and with fewer flowers; perianth segments of the same length are somewhat narrower, lateral sepals often more srongly twisted; spur compressed laterally in the same way, but not broadened (whether never?).

Habitat: coniferous woodland, also garrigue; in the montane zone; up to 2,000m; on soils from damp to varying degrees of wetness.

Flowers: May – July. **Photos**: Cy, Troodos area 6.5.80 (l), cult. 11.4.84 (r).

Distribution: eastern Mediterranean area; Cyprus and the coastal mountains from southern Turkey to Israel. For a long time the species was thought of as endemic to Cyprus and has only been found on the mainland in recent years. Its exact distribution remains to be clarified.

● **Floristic element**: e-mediterranean.
Countries: Asi: IJ, LS, Cy, An. Key for the species of the *Platanthera algeriensis* group:
1   Spur, as seen from the side, somewhat wider in the rear half; lateral sepals ovate, 8 – 11 mm long and 4 – 6 mm wide . . . .
. . . . *P. algeriensis*
1* Spur slender, not broadening; lateral sepals narrowly ovate, 7 – 10 mm long and 3 – 4 mm wide . . . . *P. holmboei*
Problem: whether two species can be distinguished must be clarified by comparative investigation; the indications point towards them being subspecies. It is possible that the differences noted depend on the habitat (even the shape of the spur may be correlated with the size of the plant). If this were so then the status of subspecies may even be too high.

Greater Butterfly Orchid   *Platanthera chlorantha* (Custer) Reichenb.

Synonym: *P. montana* Reichenb. fil.

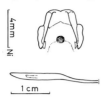

Plant with 2 elongated ovate tubers. Stem 20 – 80 cm high with 1 – 3 sheathing scale leaves at the base, 2 (3) larger foliage leaves near the ground and 1 – 4 small leaves above them. The lower leaves elliptical to ovate, 6 – 20 cm long and 2.5 – 8 cm wide. Inflorescence up to 25 cm long, fairly lax, many-flowered, appears wide (flowers spreading); bracts little longer than the flowers. Flowers white, often pale greenish or yellowish; central sepal broad heart-shaped 6.5 – 10 mm long and wide, forming a helmet shape with the 2 lateral petals, these are about the same length, but narrower, 2 – 3 mm; lateral sepals lop-sided ovate, 9 – 12 mm long and 5 – 6 mm wide, generally twisted, wavy-edged, spreading; labellum tongue-shaped, 9 – 18 mm long and 2.3 – 4 mm wide, bent downwards or backwards, intensely coloured in front; spur 18 – 40 mm long, laterally compressed and broadened in the lower half; anthers held at an angle to each other. **Habitat:** damp open woodland, damp and wet meadows, fenland, also poor grassland, up to 2,200 m, on base-rich soils, often over limestone. **Flowers:** May – August, some 2 weeks before *P. bifolia* **Photos:** Ge, Pfalz 29.5.66 (u/l); Ge, Allgäu 27.5.81 (l/l); Ge, Oberbayern 3.7.83 (r). **Distribution:** In Europe, north Africa and the Near East from the meridional to the temperate zones, in oceanic Scandinavia, also in the boreal zone, spreading eastwards in the sarmatic region, also in Caucasia and western Persia. **Floristic element:** meridional/montane submeridional temperate (boreal). **Countries:** Eur: **SE** Gr, Tu, Al, Ju, Bu, Rm, RK, **S** Si, It, Sa, Co, **SW** Hs, **W** Ga, Be, Ho, Br, Hb, **C** He, Au, Hu, Ge, Da, Cz, Po, RB, **N** Su, No, Fe, **E** RW, RC; **Asi:** ?IJ, ?LS, Cy, An, AE; **Afr:** Ma.

Lesser Butterfly Orchid   *Platanthera bifolia* (L.) L. C. M. Richard

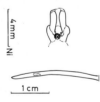

Similar to *P. chlorantha* on average slimmer and with somewhat smaller, more sweetly-scented flowers; lateral sepals often less twisted or flat; spur not widened; stamens parallel and closer together.

Habitat: open woodland, poor meadows, heaths; up to 2,300 m; on dry to wet soils over various substrates. **Flowers:** May – August. **Photos:** Ge, Südwürttemberg 2.7.66 (l); He, Kt. Schaffhausen, 25.6.78 (r).

distribution: in Europe, North Africa and the Near East but rarer in the meridional zone. Eastwards in the temperate zone as far as central Siberia, also in Caucasia and northern and western Persia. **Floristic element:** meridional/montane submeridional temperate boreal. **Countries: Eur: SE** Gr, Tu, Al, Ju, Bu, Rm, RK, **S** Si, It, Sa, Co, **SW** Bl, Hs, Lu, **W** Ga, Be, Ho, Br, Hb, Fa, **C** He, Au, Hu, Ge, Da, Cz, Po, RB, **N** Su, No, Fe, RN, **E** RW, RE, RC; **Asi:** An; **Afr:** Tn, Ag.

Problem: the species is very variable. It has still to be tested whether the following subspecies can be distinguished:

1. *P. b. subsp. graciliflora* Bisse. Dense flowering, flowers in the centre 2 – 6 mm apart; spur 12 – 23 mm long; labellum 6 – 12 mm long. On poor acid soils in the lowlands round the North Sea and the Baltic (m-atlantic n-subatlantic; Ho Br Ge Da Su No); flowers 3 weeks later than the following subspecies.

2. *P. b. subsp. latiflora* (Drejer) Løjtnant Lax inflorescence; flowers 5 – 10 mm apart; spur 20 – 41 mm long; labellum 10 – 16 mm long. Corresponds to the widely distributed type (habitat and area of distribution as given for the species). Probably *P. Kuenkelei* H. Baumann from North Africa belongs here; it is similar but very tall, up to 90 cm).

Northern Butterfly Orchid *Platanthera hyperborea* (L.) Lindley

Synonyms: *Habenaria hyperborea* (L.) R. Br., *Limnorchis hyperborea* (L.) Rydb., *P. convallariifolia* (Fischer) Lindley.

Plant with turnip-shaped swollen roots. Stem 8 – 40 cm high with 1 – 2 scale leaves at the base and 4 – 8 foliage leaves above; largest leaves lanceolate up to 13 cm long and 2 cm wide.

Inflorescence 2 – 9 cm long, dense and many-flowered; flowers yellowish-green to greenish, scented. Central sepal 3 – 5 mm long, ovate, together with the lateral petals (which are of similar length but narrower and sickle-shaped) form a helmet shape; lateral sepals 4 – 6 mm long, spreading downwards, twisted; labellum 4 – 7 mm long, lanceolate, with a somewhat shorter and often curved spur.

Habitat: mainly in damp and wet meadows, also in drier poor grassland; outside Europe in addition in wet woodland, rough grazing and heather moors, fens and raised bogs. Flowers: July, August. Photos: USA, Wisconsin 14.7.77 (l); USA, Vermont 30.7.72 (r) Distribution: In Europe only in Iceland at the eastern boundary of the main area of distribution – which is centred in North America from the arctic to the temperate zones, in the Rocky Mountains penetrating into the meridional zone; westwards to eastern Asia (Kamchatka, Japan) Floristic element: n-atlantic. Country: Eur: N Is.

Variation: the species contains several very variable types differing in such things as the number and shape of the leaves, the shape of the labellum and the spur length. In each case they are classified as varieties of a single species or as separate species according to an evaluation of the degree of relationship. If the wider concept is employed, then the Icelandic plants belong to *P. hyperborea var. hypoborea*.

Azores Butterfly Orchid
Plantanthera azorica Schlechter

Synonym: *Habanaria longibracteata* Hochst.

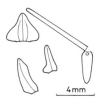

Similar to *P. micrantha* in the vegetative organs but more robust; stem and leaves larger. Flowers whitish-green. Central sepal and lateral petals about 3 mm long, widely triangular, connivent to form a hood; lateral sepals about 4 mm, longish inverted-ovate, pointing almost vertically downwards; labellum 3.3 mm long, narrow tongue-shaped, turned up, with spur 7 – 9 mm long. Habitat: grassy heaths in the trade wind cloud zone, 500 – 1,000 m. Flowers: June, July. Photo: Az, Sao Miguel 16.6.80. Distribution: species endemic to the Azores, known from the islands of Santa Maria, Sao Miguel, Sao Jorge, Pico and Flores. ● Floristic element: azorian. Country: Eur: W Az.

Small-Flowered Butterfly Orchid
Platanthera micrantha (Hochst.) Schlechter

Synonym: *Habenaria micrantha* Hochst. Resembles *P. hyperborea* (roots, foliage, inflorescence, layout of perianth). Stem to 50 cm high. Leaves to 23 cm long and 5 cm wide. Flowers yellow-green, scented. Sepals 2.5 – 4 mm long, broad ovate, the lateral ones spreading and pointing down at an angle; lateral petals and labellum somewhat shorter; labellum broad tongue-shaped, bent downwards; spur 2 – 3 mm long, curved. Habitat: grassy heaths; 200 – 1,300 m; on acid damp soils. Flowers: May – July. Photo: origin Az, (Sao Miguel 14.6.80). Distribution: species endemic to the Azores. ● Floristic element: azorean. Country: Eur: W Az.

One-Leaved Butterfly Orchid
Platanthera obtusata (Pursh) Lindley *Subsp. oligantha* (Turcz.) Hulten

Synonyms: *P. oligantha* Turcz., *Lysiella oligantha* (Turcz.) Nevski, *P. parvula* Schlechter

Plant with fleshy roots, scarcely thickened or not at all. Stem 6–20 cm high, at the base 1–2 scale leaves and 1 foliage leaf, ovate–lanceolate 4–7.5 cm long and 1.2–2.1 cm wide, above this sometimes a further small narrow leaf. Inflorescence 2–9 flowered, fairly dense; bracts about as long as the ovaries; flowers greenish-white; central sepal 2–2.3 mm long and wide conniving to form a hood with the lateral petals which are of similar length but narrower; lateral sepals 2.5–3 mm long, lanceolate, spreading; labellum 3–3.5 mm long, triangular tongue-shaped, spur 2.5–3 mm long.

Habitat: the subspecies grown in Europe on dwarf shrub heaths in the subalpine zone on lime-rich soils, in Asia also in damp birch and pine woods. *

Flowers: July. Photos: No, Troms, 4/5.7.76.

Distribution: in Europe only found in a few localities in the northern Scandianavian mountains (Prov. Troms, Finnmark and Torne Lappmark); main distribution area in boreal and arctic Asia reaching southwards into the temperate zone in the central Siberian mountains. Floristic element: scandinavian.

Countries: Eur: N Su No.

Relationship: *P. obtusata subsp. obtusata* (Syn: *Lysiella obtusata* (Pursh) Rydb., *Habenaria obtusata* (Pursh.) Richardson) occurs in North America (submeridional/montane temperate boreal, arctic); flowers are larger (sepals up to 6.5 mm, labellum to 10 mm long). As intermediate forms occur, the two races are not always recognized as independent subspecies.

Dwarf Alpine Orchid   *Chamorchis alpina* (L.) L. C. M. Richard

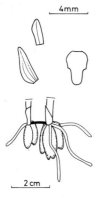

Plant with ellipsoidal tubers. Foliage leaves 4–10 in a basal rosette surrounded by 2–3 scale leaves, grass-like, folded into a groove, as long as, or longer than, the inflorescence. Stem 5–15 cm long. Inflorescence 2–12 flowered, fairly dense; lower bracts longer than the flowers; flowers yellow-green often tinged with brownish-purple. Perianth segments curved to form a hood; sepals ovate, 3.5–4.2 mm long; lateral petals slightly narrower, 2.3–3 mm long; labellum tongue-shaped, 3–4 mm long, the edges turned backwards, generally with 2 tooth-like lateral lobes; no spur. Pollinia with separate viscidia in a common bursicle.

Propagation: the plants are able to produce additional daughter tubers (2 rather than 1 each year) and short runners, so that several flowering stems are often found growing close together.

Habitat: in stony and rocky poor grassland in exposed places with only a slight covering of snow in winter; in the subalpine and Alpine levels above the tree line; up to 2,700 m; on shallow dry soils on calcareous rocks.

Flowers: July, August. Photos: He, Kt. Tessin 17.7.71 (l); He, Kt. Graubünden 20.8.83 (r).

Distribution: the species is confined to the high mountains in Europe; throughout the Alps, in the northern and southern Carpathians as well as in the Scandinavian mountains north-eastwards as far as the Kola peninsula. ●

Floristic element: alpine carpatic scandinavian lapponic.

Countries: Eur: SE Ju Rm, S It, W Ga, C He Au Ge Cz Po, N Su No Fe RN.

Relationship: a monotype genus with only one species and no near relatives.

Platanthera

Chamorcis

59

Frog Orchid *Coeloglossum viride* (L.) Hartman *subsp. viride*

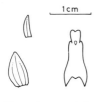

1cm

Plant with tuber, shaped like a hand. Stem 5 – 30 cm high. Foliage leaves 3 – 7, lower ones ovate, near the base of the stem, held upright at an angle, up to 10 cm long and 5 cm wide, upper leaves lanceolate. Inflorescence 5 – 25 flowered; bracts scarcely to clearly longer than the flowers; flowers (yellow-) green often tinged brownish-red. Perianth segments of similar length curved to form a hood 3.5 – 7 mm long; sepals ovate 2 – 3 mm wide, lateral petals linear-lanceolate 0.7 – 1.5 mm wide; labellum tongue-shaped, 5 – 9 mm long, widening in front, 3-lobed with parallel lateral lobes and a shorter, tooth-like central lobe; spur grooved, 2 – 3 mm long, shaped like a small sack. **Habitat**: poor pastures and meadows, heather moors, open woodland; up to 2,900 m mainly on acid soils. **Flowers**: May – August. **Photos**: Au, Osttirol 16.7.83 (I); It, Prov. Verona 19.6.70 (r). **Distribution**: In Europe and the Near East southwards to the submeridional zone, absent from the pontic region, rare in the Mediterranean area; subspecies with a circumpolar distribution principally boreal temperate; in Asia still further south in the Caucasus and Himalayas.
Floristic element: (meridional/montane) submeridional/montane temperate boreal arctic. **Countries**: Eur: SE Gr Al Ju Bu Rm RK, S It, SW Hs, W Ga Be Ho Br Hb Fa, C He Au Hu Ge Da Cz Po RB, N Su No Fe RN Is, E RW RC; Asi: An. **Variation**: in the north and high in the mountains, low-growing variants occur with fewer leaves and flowers; these correspond to *C. v. var. islandicum* (Lindley) M. Schultze. The other subspecies *C. v. subsp. bracteatum* (Willd.) K. Richter grows in North America and east Asia; characteristics: more robust, up to 80 cm high; leaves stick out horizontally, up to 18 cm long; labellum does not widen out in front.

Hooded Orchid *Neottianthe cucullata* (L.) Schlechter

Synonym: *Gymnadenia cucullata* (L.) L. C. M. Richard

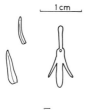

1cm

2cm

Plant with 2 spherical to ellipsoidal tubers. Stem 10 – 30 (– 40) cm high, with 1 – 2 sheathing scale leaves and 2 foliage leaves at the base as well as 1 – 2 (– 5) scale leaves further up; the lowest foliage leaf longish elliptical to circular, 2.5 – 9 cm long and 1.5 – 5 cm wide, held up at an angle, the upper smaller and narrower. Inflorescence 3 – 8 cm long, 6 – 20 flowered, fairly lax, often more or less one-sided; bracts scarcely longer than the ovaries, flowers purplish-pink, hanging over, scentless. Perianth segments 6 – 8 mm long and 1 – 1.5 mm wide, curved into a turned-up hood; labellum 7 – 9 mm long, directed downwards, paler towards the base with 2 – 8 dots, divided into 3 lobes for more than half its length, middle lobe longish and straight, side lobes ⅔ the length and ½ the width, spreading; spur 5 – 6.5 mm long, pointing downwards, bent into an S-shape, wider at the tip. **Habitat**: coniferous and deciduous woodland, generally growing in the semi-shade, also in scrub and on mountain meadows; probably on acid soils. **Flowers**: June – August, in eastern Central Europe mostly before the end of July. **Photos**: Po, Wojewod. Bialystok 7.8.74 **Distribution**: east Europe and eastern central Europe, western limit in Poland. The abundant occurrences end at the western limit of the sarmatic floristic retion, isolated outposts lie further west. Eastwards in the temperate zone in Asia, in China and Japan also in the submeridional zone. **Floristic element**: (n-centraleuropean) sarmatic c-sibirian. **Countries**: Eur: C Po RB, E RW RC.

Coeloglossum

Neottianthe

61

Small White Orchid   *Leucorchis albida* (L.) E. H. F. Meyer

Synonyms: *Gymnadenia albida* L. C. M.
Richard, *Pseudorchis albida* (L.) A. & D. Löve.

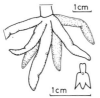

Plant with 2 tubers which are forked almost their whole length. Stem 10 – 40 cm high with 2 – 3 basal scale leaves and 3 – 7 foliage leaves, lower leaves elongated-ovate, 2.5 – 8 cm long and 1 – 2.5 cm wide; inflorescence 2 – 10 cm long, dense and many-flowered; perianth segments curved to form a hood; front third of labellum comb-like with 3 lobes of equal length; spur 2 – 3 mm long, swelling at the end.

Habitat: poor grassland, heather moors; up to 2,500 m; on acid soils. Flowers: May – August. Photos: He, Kt. Graubünden 19.7.74 (l); Au, Osttirol 7.8.78 (r).

Variation: the species comprises two subspecies, the authenticity of which has still to be confirmed:

1. *L. a. subsp. albida* central sepal 20 – 28 mm long, lateral sepals and labellum 24 – 32 mm long; flowers greenish-white to pale yellow; bracts shorter to longer than the flowers.
Distribution: in Europe from the submeridional to the boreal zones in areas with an oceanic climate.
Countries: Eur: SE Gr Al Ju Bu Rm, S It Co, SW Hs, W Ga Be + Ho Br Hb Fa°, C He Au Ge Da Cz Po, N Su No Fe RN°, E RW. In the areas marked ° perhaps also the following subspecies.

2. *L. a. subsp. straminea* (Fernald) A. Löve.
Syn: *L. a. var. subalpina* (Neuman) Hyl. Central sepal 27 – 40 mm long, lateral sepals and labellum 33 – 45 mm long; flowers pale yellow; bracts always longer than the flowers. Distribution: northern Europe, the Alps; eastern North America.
Floristic element: alpine n-atlantic scandinavian/montane lapponian.
Countries: Eur: C He, N Su No Fe Is.

Frivald's Orchid   *Gymnadenia frivaldii* Griseb.

Synonyms: *Leuchorchis frivaldii* (Griseb.) Schlechter, *Pseudorchis frivaldii* (Griseb.) P. F. Hunt

Plant with 2 tubers which are forked to about half their length to look like a hand. Stem 10 – 30 cm long with maximum 2 brown scale leaves at the base and 3 – 5 foliage leaves above them; lower leaves elongated-lanceolate up to 9 cm long and 1 (1.5) cm wide; inflorescence ovate 1.5 – 3 cm long, dense; bracts as long as the ovaries; flowers a whitish-cream, often with a pink tinge or pale red; central sepal 3 – 3.5 mm long, ovate, curved to form a hood with the scarcely shorter lateral petals; lateral sepals slightly longer, obliquely rhomboid, spreading horizontally; labellum 3.5 – 4 mm long, 3-lobed with tooth-like lateral lobes, occasionally almost undivided, front bent downwards; spur 1.5 – 3 mm long, slim, not swelling at the tip, slightly curved.

Habitat: wet meadows; subalpine and Alpine levels, occasionally at the montane level; down to 1,200 m; over silicate rock. Flowers: June – August. Photos: Ju, Kosovo and Metohija 19.6.82.

Distribution: mountains in the Balkan peninsula from Montenegro to northern Greece, eastwards as far as the central Balkans in Bulgaria; western southern Carpathians. ●

Floristic element: c + e-submediterranean/ alpine carpathian.

Countries: Eur: SE Gr Al Ju Bu Rm.

Leucorchis

Gymnadenia

63

Fragrant Orchid   *Gymnadenia conopsea* (L.) R. Br.

Synonyms: *G. c. subsp. densiflora* (Waglenb.) K. Richter, *G. c. subsp. montana* Bisse, *G. c. var. alpina* Reichenb. fil *G. C. var. lapponica* Zett.

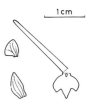

Plant with 2 tubers which are forked to about half their length to look like a hand; stem with 2−3 scale leaves at the base and 3−9 foliage leaves, lower leaves 5−25 cm long and 0.5−4 cm wide, linear−lanceolate; flowers pink to lilac-red; sepals 4−7 mm long, elliptical, the lateral ones spreading horizontally, the central one curving to form a hood with the somewhat shorter ovate lateral petals; labellum 3.5−6 mm long, lateral lobes half to almost as long as the central lobe; spur 10−20 mm long, slender, curved downwards.

Habitat: damp and wet meadows, fens, poor grassland, mountain meadows, open woodland; up to 2,800 m; on fairly dry to wet, acid to basic soils. Flowers: May − August. Photos: Hb, Clare 5.8.84 (l); Hs, Prov. Huesca, 22.5.82 (u/r); Ge, Hessen, 16.6.60 (l/r); *see also* p271.

Distribution: in Europe and the Near East but less common in the Mediterranean floristic area; eastwards through the temperate and boreal zones to eastern Asia; in mountains as far as the meridional zone (Caucasus, northern Persia, through China to the Himalayas).

Floristic element: meridional/montane submeridional temperate boreal (arctic). Countries: Eur: **SE** Gr, Al, Ju, Bu, Rm, RK, **S** Si, It, Co, **SW** Bl, Hs, Lu, **W** Ga, Be, Ho, Br, Hb, **C** He, Au, Hu, Ge, Da, Cz, Po, RB, **N** Su, No, Fe, RN, **E** RW, RE, RC; **Asi:** An, AE.

Variation: rich in forms regarding plant size, leaf width, flower size, colour and scent, spur length. It has not been established whether several subspecies can be distinguished. Obvious types: 'conopsea', to 50 cm high, leaves 0.5−1.5 cm wide, scentless, early flowering; 'alpina' and 'lapponica', compact, intensively-coloured flowers, labellum often spotted; 'densiflora', to 1 m high, leaves 1−3 (−4) cm wide, scented, late flowering (photo 1); 'montana' is similar but scentless.

Key for the *Gymnadenia* species:

1 Spur longer than 10 mm; labellum deeply 3-lobed, acute angle between the central and lateral lobes .... *G. conopsea*
1* Spur shorter than 6 mm; labellum with shallow lobes, obtuse angle between the central and lateral lobes 2
2 Spur 3.5−6 mm long; inflorescence more than 2.5 × as long as broad .... *G. odoratissima*
2* Spur 1.5−3 mm long; inflorescence up to twice as long as broad . *G. frivaldii*, p62

Short-Spurred Fragrant Orchid   *Gymnadenia odoratissima* (L.) L. C. M. Richard

Resembles a slender example of *G. conopsea*; stem up to 30 (50) cm tall; leaves linear, up to 8 mm wide; flowers deep pink to white in all intermediate shades, occasionally pale yellow, strongly scented; lateral sepals 3−4 mm long, longer than the remaining perianth segments and the labellum; spur 3.5−6 mm long, slender, slightly curved. Habitat: poor pastures and meadows, open pine woods, fens; to 2,500 m; prefers soils of varying dampness, only on calcareous rocks.

Flowers: May − August. Photos: Ge, Allgäu 19.7.71 (r); He, Kt. Graubünden 18.7.71 (l).

Distribution: in the submeridional and temperate zones in Europe, especially in the mountains; from southern Sweden and the Baltic to northern Spain, central Italy and northern Greece, penetrating only a little way eastwards into the sarmatic region of Russia.

● Floristic element: submediterranean/montane pannonic karpatic s + (m)-atlantic s-subatlantic centraleuropean (sarmatic).
Countries: Eur: **SE** Gr, Ju, Rm, **S** It, **SW** Hs, **W** Ga, Be, ?Br, **C** He, Au, Hu, Ge, Cz, Po, RB, **N** Su, **E** RW, RC.

densiflora

Gymnadenia

Vanilla Orchid   *Nigritella nigra* (L.) Reichenb. fil.

Synonyms: *N. angustifolia* L. C. M. Richard, *Gymnadenia nigra* (L.) Reichenb. fil.

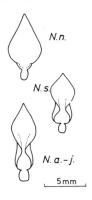

N. n.

N. s.

N. a. - j.

5 mm

Inflorescence spherical to ovate; labellum 6 − 7 mm long, about 4 mm wide, concave, exceptionally constricted to a saddle shape; spur 1.1 − 1.5 mm long; reproduces sexually (Alps) and asexually (Scandinavia). **Variation:** striking bright colour variations generally growing with the darker normal type, occasionally without these in large stands in south Tyrol. **Habitat:** poor pastures and meadows; mostly over 1,500 m, in Scandinavia up to 1,300 m; on basic to weakly acid soils. **Flowers:** June − August. **Photos:** lt, Prov. Bozen 21.7.73 (u/l, c/l); He, Graubünden 10.7.82 (u/r), 17.7.75 (c/r). **Distribution:** higher mountains in southern and central Europe also central and northern Scandinavia. • **Floristic element:** e-mediterranean submediterranean s-subatlantic alpine karpatic scandinavian. **Countries: Eur: SE** Gr, Al, Ju, Bu, Rm, **S** lt, SW, Hs, **W** Ga, C, He, Au, Hu, Ge, Cz (not Britain), **N** Su, No, **E** RW.

Key for the *Nigritella* species:

1 Flowers reddish-brown, rarely yellow, orange, very rarely pink; labellum concave, also occasionally constricted to a saddle-shape . . . . *N. nigra*
1* Flowers ruby or pink; labellum concave and almost always constricted in the lower third to a saddle 2
2 Flowers ruby . *N. rubra p68*
2* Flowers pink 3
3 Flowers remain half-closed, only the lateral sepals spreading . . . . *N. archiducis-joannis*
3* Flowers open fully 4
4 Perianth segments bi-coloured, lilac-pink with white point . . . . *N. stiriaca*
4* Perianth segments a single colour (although the flowers often vary in colour) or if 2-coloured then darker at the tip   5
5 Rear half of labellum bulging, wider than the front part . . . . *N. widderi*, p234
5* Front half of the labellum wider than the slightly bulging rear part 6
6 Saddle-shaped narrowing of the labellum about a third of the length from the base; flowers deep pink (warmer colour) . . . . *N. corneliana*, p68
6* Saddle-shaped narrowing near the base of the labellum; flowers lilac pink (colder colour) . . . . *N. lithopolitanica*, p68

Salzkammergut Vanilla Orchid
Nigritella stiriaca (K. Rech.) Teppner & E. Klein

Infloresence cylindrical slightly to clearly longer than wide; labellum 5.5 − 6.5 mm long and 3.5 − 4 mm wide, saddle-shaped 1.5 − 3 mm from the base; lateral sepals triangular-ovate, somewhat wider than the central one and significantly wider than the lateral petals; spur 1 − 1.3 mm long; asexual reproduction. **Habitat:** alpine poor calcareous grassland; 1,800 to 2,000 m. **Flowers:** June − August. **Photo:** Au, Steiermark 10.8.84. **Distribution:** north-eastern limestone Alps; endemic in the Salzkammergut. • **Floristic element:** alpine. **Country: Eur: C** Au.

Toten Vanilla Orchid   *Nigritella archiducis-joannis* Teppner & E. Klein

Inflorescence spherical; flowers light to dark flesh-coloured; labellum, central sepal and lateral petals point directly forward, not spreading; labellum 8 mm long, 2 − 4 mm from the base constricted to saddle-shape; lateral sepals slightly wider than the lateral petals; spur 1.4 mm long; asexual reproduction. **Habitat:** poor Alpine calcareous grassland; 1,800 to 2,000 m. **Flowers:** July, August. **Photo:** Au, Steiermark 3.8.84. **Distribution:** north-eastern limestone Alps; endemic in the Toten mountains. • **Floristic element;** alpine. **Country: Eur: C** Au.

Nigritella

Cornelias Vanilla Orchid *Nigritella corneliana* (Beauverd) Gölz & Reinhard

Synonyms: N. nigra subsp. corneliana Beauverd. *N. lithopolitanica subsp. corneliana* (Beauverd) Teppner & E. Klein

Inflorescence spherical to somewhat elongated, cylindrical; buds coloured more intensively than the open flowers, pink to vermillion; labellum 8 – 9.5 mm, usually with a saddle-shaped, narrowing 1.5 – 3 mm above the base, rarely nearer the base or not at all; lateral sepals only slightly wider than the lateral petals; spur 0.9 – 1.2 mm; sexual reproduction.

Habitat: calcareous Alpine poor grassland; above 1,800 m. **Flowers:** July, August, earlier than *N. nigra*. **Photo:** It, Prov. Turin 13.7.77. **Distribution:** south-western Alps; from Savoy to the Alpes Maritimes. • **Floristic element:** alpine. **Countries; Eur:** S It, W Ga.

Steineralp Vanilla Orchid *Nigritella lithopolitanica* Ravnik

Inflorescence spherical; buds more intensively coloured than the open flowers; bluish-pink; labellum 6.5 – 8.5 mm long, usually saddle-shaped close to the base (rarely further away); lateral sepals a little to markedly wider than the lateral petals; spur 0.9 – 1.2 mm long; sexual reproduction.

Habitat: calcareous alpine poor grassland above 1,500 m. **Flowers:** July, August, earlier than *N. nigra*. **Photo:** Au, Kärnten 10.7.81. **Distribution:** south-eastern limestone Alps; known from the Steiner Alps, Ostkarawanken and the Koralp; probably more widely distributed. • **Floristic element:** alpine. **Countries: Eur:** SE Ju, C Au. *See also* the addendum p234

Red Vanilla Orchid *Nigritella rubra* (Wettst.) K. Richter

Synonyms: N. nigra subsp. rubra (Wettst.) Beauverd, *Gymnadenia nigra subsp. rubra* (Wettst.) Sundermann, ? *N. miniata* (Crantz) Janchen (the allocation of this name is in dispute; if it belongs to this species then it has priority over *N. rubra*.)

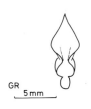

(This general description applies to all the species in the genus). Plant with 2 hand-like tubers. Stem 5 – 30 cm tall, with 2 – 3 sheathing scale leaves at the base, 5 – 12 foliage leaves forming a rosette and 2 – 8 further up the stalk; ground leaves grass-like with a shallow furrow; upper stem leaves flat, not sheathing. Infloresence short, dense and many-flowered; bracts somewhat shorter than or as long as the flowers; flowers sessile, not twisted (resupinate), consequently the labellum is uppermost. Inflorescence often elongated, cylindrical but also ovate-spherical; flowers ruby red (an intense warm red); labellum 7 – 8 mm long and 4 – 4.5 mm wide, concave with a narrow saddle 1.5 – 2.5 mm above the base; lateral sepals slightly wider than the central sepal and the lateral petals; spur 1.3 – 1.7 mm long; asexual reproduction. **Habitat:** poor calcareous Alpine grassland; over 1,500 m; on limestone and calcareous slate. **Flowers:** June – August, some 2 weeks before *N. nigra*. **Photos:** Ge, Oberbayern, 20.6.72 (l); He, Kt. Tessin 6.7.73 (r). **Distribution:** Alps and Carpathians; from Tessin and Toggenburg eastwards to lower Austria, east Rumania and south Carpathians. • **Floristic element:** Alpine Carpathian. **Countries: Eur:** SE Rm, S It, C He, Au, Ge.

Hybrids: *Nigritella* and *Gymnadenia* species not infrequently produce hybrids; similar in appearance to Nigritella but possess twisted flowers (labellum placed sideways, variable) and spur length 3 mm or more.

Nigritella

Roman Orchid   *Dactylorhiza romana* (Sebastiani) Soó

Synonyms: *Orchis romana* Sebastiani, *O. pseudosambucina* Ten., *O. mediterranea* Klinge, *D. sulphurea* Franco, *D. sulphurea* subsp. *pseudosambucina* (Ten.) Franco, *D. sambucina* subsp. *pseudosambucina* (Ten.) Sundermann

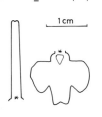

1 cm

Plant with 2 ovate-spherical tubers forked to, at most, ⅓ their length; stem 15 – 35 cm high, with 2 – 3 basal scale leaves, 3 – 7 foliage leaves in a basal rosette and 1 – 3 smaller leaves on the stem; leaves linear-lanceolate, up to 15 (20) cm long and 1.5 (3.5) cm wide. Inflorescence ovate-cylindrical, dense and mostly many-flowered; bracts somewhat longer than the flowers; lateral sepals erect and turned outwards, broadly ovate, 6 – 10 mm long and 3.5 – 7 mm wide; central sepal slightly shorter and inclined over the very wide lateral petals; labellum 7.5 – 12 mm long and (8 –) 10 – 18 mm wide, fairly flat, 3-lobed with raised middle lobe; spur bent, cylindrical 1 – 1.5 mm thick.

Variation: the species appears in several colour variants: flowers yellow, flesh-coloured, violet-red, cream and mixed. The variants are often found growing together, but in many regions appear alone (e.g. in Cy only yellow).

Habitat: open woodland and maqui; up to 2,000 m on fairly dry, often stony, weakly acid to basic soils. Flowers: March – June. Photos: Si, Prov. Messina, 7.4.67 (l); It, Prov. Grosseto 12.4.71 (r).

Distribution: eastern and central Mediterranean area, Black Sea region; absent from southern Levant, and from the northern sub-mediterranean region in Yugoslavia and in Italy (northwards as far as Hvar, Prov. Grosseto).

● Floristic element: e + c-mediterranean e + c-submediterranean.

Countries: Eur: SE   Cr, Gr, Tu, Al, Ju, Bu, RK, S   Si, It; Asi: LS, Cy, An, AE.

Georgian Orchid   *Dactylorhiza flavescens* (C. Koch) Holub

Synonyms: *Orchis flavescens* C. Koch, *O. georgica* (Klinge) Lipsky *D. sambucina* subsp. *georgica* (Klinge) Sundermann, *D. romana* subsp. *georgica* (Klinge) Renz & Taubenheim, *D. ruprechtii* Averyanov

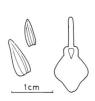

1 cm

Stem (5 –) 10 – 40 cm high; (3 –) 5 – 12 cm radical foliage leaves, narrow lanceolate, up to 18 cm long and 1.5 cm wide; inflorescence dense, few to many-flowered, ovate-cylindrical; bracts as long as or often shorter than the flowers; flowers whitish-yellow with lemon-yellow lip, or red, frequently in the same population, in general, yellow flowers are more numerous; size and position of sepals and lateral petals as in *D. markusii*; spur 7 – 11 mm long, curved, often held almost horizontally.

Habitat: open woods and scrubland, mountain meadows; up to 2,000 m; on fairly dry to wet soils. Flowers: April – June. Photos: An, Vil. Gümüshane 3.6.74 (l); An Prov. Artvin 26.6.76 (r). Distribution: mountains of eastern Anatolia, westwards as far as the Anatolian Diagonal. Also in Caucasia, northern and western Persia, Turkomania. Floristic element: oriental e-submediterranean. Country: Asi: An. Key for the species in the *Dactylorhiza romana* group:

1   Spur (13 –) 17 – 25 mm long, longer than the ovary, generally held vertically
    D. romana

1* Spur 7 – 15 mm, often shorter than the ovary, held up at an angle – 2

2   Labellum (spread out) mostly obviously broader than long, 7 – 10 × (8 –) 10 – 14 mm, 3-lobed
    D. markusii, p72

2* Labellum only a little broader than long or longer than broad, 5 – 9 × 5 – 9 (– 11), 3-lobed or undivided
    D. flavescens

Dactylorhiza

Sicilian Orchid *Dactylorhiza markusii* (Tineo) H. Baumann & Künkele

Synonyms: *Orchis markusii* Tineo, *D. sambucina* subsp. *siciliensis* (Klinge) Sundermann, *D. sulphurea* subsp. *siciliensis* (Klinge) Franco, *Orchis sicula* Tineo, *O. sulphurea* Link

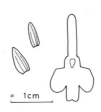

Plant with 2 ovate-spherical tubers, slightly forked at the tip; stem 15 – 45 cm high with 2 – 3 scale leaves at the base, 5 – 7 foliage leaves forming a rosette and 2 – 4 smaller leaves above, radical leaves narrow lanceolate, up to 18 cm long and 1.6 cm wide; inflorescence dense, many-flowered, ovate-cylindrical; bracts about as long as the flowers; flowers whitish-yellow, the labellum light lemon yellow without any red markings; lateral sepals erect and turned outwards, ovate, 5.5 – 10 mm long and 2.5 – 4 mm wide, the middle sepal somewhat smaller and inclined over the lateral petals; labellum convex, domed 3-lobed with a raised middle lobe; spur 9 – 13 (– 15) mm long and mostly about 2 mm thick, sometimes thinner, curved, often flattened, rounded or notched at the point, held up at an angle.

Habitat: open woodland, mostly in semi-shade, also mountain meadows; up to 1,900 m on moist to fairly damp acid soils. **Flowers:** March – June. **Photos:** Si, Prov. Palermo 17.4.80 (l); Hs, Prov. Jaén 4.6.70 (r).

Distribution: western Mediterranean basin; southern focus in the meridional zone, eastwards to Calabria. ● **Floristic element:** c + w-mediterranean w-submediterranean.

Countries: Eur: S Si, It, Sa, SW Bl, Hs, Lu; Afr: Ag, Ma.

Problem: the boundaries between relatives of the *D. romana* group need to be investigated more exactly; plants with intermediate characteristics between *D. romana* and *D. flavescens* have been recorded for Anatolia; the similarity between *D. markusii* and *D. flavescens* is very obvious.

Barton's Orchid *Dactylorhiza insularis* (Sommier) Landwehr

Synonyms: *Orchis insularis* Sommier, *D. sambucina* subsp. *insularis* Soó, *D. romana* subsp. *bartonii* Huxley & P. F. Hunt, *D. insularis* var. *bartonii* (Huxley & P. F. Hunt) Landwehr

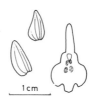

Plant with 2 ovate tubers, slightly forked at the tip; stem 20 – 50 cm high; foliage leaves 6 – 8 light green spread out up the stem, not in a definite basal rosette, longish-lanceolate up to 15 cm long and 2 cm wide, unspotted; inflorescence fairly lax, cylindrical, up to 20-flowered; bracts as long as or shorter than the flowers; flowers lemon-yellow; lateral sepals spreading horizontally or held up at an angle, ovate, 7 – 10 mm long and 3.5 – 5 mm wide; the middle sepal somewhat shorter and inclined over the lateral petals; labellum 5 – 9 mm long and 5.5 – 11 mm wide, almost flat, 3-lobed, central lobe up to almost as large as the laterals and raised; spur cylindrical 7.5 – 11 mm long, 1.5 – 2 mm thick, straight, held horizontally or nearly so.

Variation: the labellum is marked with red to varying degrees, rarely unmarked; in some plants there are just a few spots, in others these are merged into two bright patches (variant 'bartonii'). **Habitat:** pine and sweet chestnut woods, poor meadows; up to 1,500 m; on fairly dry to fairly damp acid soils. **Flowers:** April – June. **Photos:** Sa, Prov. Sassari 28.4.84 (l); Hs, Prov. Teruel 8.6.67 (r).

Distribution: western Mediterranean basin; similar to *D. markussi*, but with a more northern focus in the submediterranean zone; records furthest east are from the Tyrrhenian islands of Elba and Giglio and from the mainland in the province of Grosseto, furthest north in the Corbières. ● **Floristic element:** c + w-mediterranean c + w-submediterranean.

Countries: Eur: S It, Sa, Co, SW Hs, W Ga.

Dactylorhiza

Elder-Flowered Orchid   *Dactylorhiza sambucina* (L.) Soó

Synonym: *Orchis sambucina* L. (recently the species has sometimes been named '*D. latifolia*')

Plant with 2 ovate tubers forked to not more than half-way from the point; stem 10–30 cm tall, hollow, 2 basal scale leaves, 4–7 foliage leaves arranged along the stem or the lower ones tending to form a rosette, lanceolate, 5–12 cm long and 1–2.5 (–3) cm wide, unspotted; inflorescence ovate, dense and many-flowered; bracts as long as or longer than the flowers; lateral sepals protrude at an angle or upright, narrowly ovate 8–13 mm long and 4–5.5 mm wide; middle sepal somewhat shorter and inclined over the lateral petals; labellum transversely elliptical, 7.5–11 mm long and 11–17 mm wide, mostly weakly, seldom deeply, 3-lobed or undivided, slightly convex; spur cylindrical-tapering, curving downwards 10–15 mm long, about 3 mm thick. **Variation**: the species appears in 2 colour variants which are often growing together in the same population; the elder-scented flowers are yellow or red, labellum with small to larger dots in a horseshoe pattern.

Habitat: open woodland, poor pastures and meadows; up to 2,100 m; on fairly dry to quite damp, base-rich, often slightly, acid soils. **Flowers**: March–July. **Photos**: It, Prov. Cúneo 15.6.84 (r); It, Prov. Fóggia 1.4.74 (l).

Distribution: In Europe from the meridional to the temperate zones, but avoids extreme climates, absent from the pontic, w-mediterranean and atlantic areas, in the sarmatic region only in the west, eastwards as far as the head waters of the Dnieper.

● **Floristic element**: e + c-mediterranean submediterranean pannonic subatlantic centraleuropean sarmatic. **Countries: Eur**: SE Gr, Al, Ju, Bu, Rm, S Si, It ? Co, SW Hs, ?Lu, W Ga C He, Au, Hu, Ge, Da, Cz, Po, RB, N Su, No, Fe, E RW, Rc.

Crimean Orchid   *Dactylorhiza iberica* (Willd.) Soó

Synonym: *Orchis iberica* Willd.

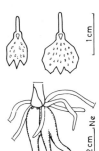

Plant with 2 tubers, narrowly turnip-shaped, whole or forked, up to 6 cm long in autumn; thin subterranean runners (vegetative reproduction); stem 20–60 cm high with 2–3 basal scale leaves and 3–7 foliage leaves, linear-lanceolate up to 25 cm long and 2(3) cm wide, unspotted; inflorescence mostly fairly lax, cylindrical, many-flowered; bracts about as long as the ovaries; flowers light to deep lilac pink; perianth segments tending to come together in a loose, rarely tight, hood; sepals ovate, 5–9 mm long and 2–4 mm wide; lateral petals somewhat shorter and narrower; labellum dotted with red in various forms, 7.5–11 mm long and 6–9 mm wide, narrowing to a stalk-like base, 3-lobed with a small, often tooth-like, middle lobe, rarely undivided, flat; spur cylindrical curving down, 5–7 mm long about 1 mm thick.

Habitat: wet meadows; 600–2,500 m; on calcareous soils. **Flowers**: June–August. **Photos**: An, Vil. Kastamonu 23.7.83 (l); An, Vil. Bolu 22.7.82 (r); *see also* p262.

Distribution: the Near East, Crimea, Greece, Cyprus; widely in Anatolia; as far as Lebanon in the Levant; absent from the Aegean region; further west it occupies an isolated area in the Greek mountains (western Macedonia to the northern Peloponnes) also in Caucasia, northern and western Persia.

Floristic element: e-mediterranean oriental e-submediterranean.

Countries: Eur: SE Gr, RK; **Asi**: LS, Cy, An

Persian Marsh Orchid *Dactylorhiza umbrosa* (Kar. & Kir.) Nevski

Synonyms: *Orchis umbrosa* Kar. & Kir. *O. turcestanica* (Klinge) Klinge, *O. sanasunitensis* H. Fleischm., *D. persica* (Schlechter) Soó, *D. sanasunitensis* (H. Fleischm.) Soó, *D. vanensis* E. Nelson, *D. incarnata subsp. turcestanica* (Klinge) Sundermann, *D. chuhensis* Renz & Taubenheim

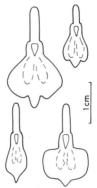

Stem 10–60 (–80) cm tall, hollow, with 4–9 foliage leaves, lanceolate 6–16 (–22) cm long and 1.5–4 (–6) cm wide, widest about the middle; inflorescence dense, many-flowered, (ovate-) cylindrical; flowers purple or magenta, rarely pink; lateral sepals held up at an angle, (ovate-) lanceolate, 6.5–11 mm long and 2.5–5 mm wide; lateral petals narrow-lanceolate, 5–9 mm long; labellum has markings on the paler central area in a horseshoe pattern of very variable form, often longer than broad with a wedge-shaped base, or broader than long with a shortened base, 6–13 mm long and 4–12 mm wide, almost flat, undivided or 3-lobed with a tooth-like projecting central lobe; spur cylindrical, cone-shaped, 7–13 (–15) mm long and 2–3.5 (–5) mm thick, curved downwards. **Habitat:** wet meadows, damp scrub; 1,300–2,800 m. **Flowers:** May–July. **Photos:** An, Vil. Erzurum 2.7.82 (l); An, Vil. Van 15.5.72 (c); An, Vil. Agri 21.5.74 (r). **Distribution:** eastern and southeastern Anatolia from the Prov. Erzincan eastwards, one location further west (Prov. Maras). **Floristic element:** oriental. **Country: Asi:** An. **Variation:** here and there plants appear with one or both sides of the leaves spotted – 'vanensis', 'chuhensis', photo (r).

Osman Marsh Orchid *Dactylorhiza osmanica* (Klinge) Soó

Synonyms: *Orchis osmanica* (Klinge) Lipsky, *O. cataonica* H. Fleischm., *O. cilicica* (Klinge) Schlechter, *D. cataonica* (H. Fleischm.) J. Holub, *D. cilicica* (Klinge) Soó, *D. incarnata subsp. cilicica* (Klinge) Sundermann, *D. elata subsp. anatolica* E. Nelson, *D. osmanica var. anatolica* (E. Nelson) Renz & Taubenheim

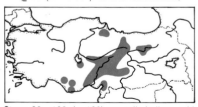

Stem 20–100 (–120) cm tall, hollow, with 4–10 foliage leaves, flat or folded, broadly lanceolate, 10–22 cm long and 2–5 cm wide, widest in the middle; inflorescence dense and many-flowered, cylindrical; bracts longer than the flowers; flowers purplish-red, rarely paler; lateral sepals point upwards at an angle or vertically, ovate–lanceolate, 8–14 mm long and 3.5–5.5 mm broad; lateral petals 6–10 mm long; labellum has a horseshoe pattern on the pale central area, sometimes also with pale washed-out marking round the edge, rounded to transversely elliptical (7–) 9–16 mm long and (8–) 11–16 mm broad, weakly convex, undivided or with a suggestion of 3 lobes; spur cylindrical–conical, slightly curved, 5–11 mm long and 3–4 mm thick. Tall growing plants correspond to the variant 'anatolica'.

Habitat: wet meadows, herbaceous communities alongside streams; 500–2,400 m **Flowers:** May–July. **Photos:** An, Vil. Konya 18.6.76 (l); An, Vil. Samsun 13.6.73 (r). **Distribution:** the species belongs to a distribution type plentiful in Anatolia; it grows in a belt some 250 km wide along the Anatolian Diagonal which runs north-eastwards from the bay of Iskenderun (along the line Adana – Trabzon). ● **Floristic element:** e-mediterranean oriental e-submediterranean. **Countries: Asi:** ?LS, An.

Nieschalk's Marsh Orchid   *Dactylorhiza nieschalkiorum* H. Baumann & Künkele

Synonyms: *D. osmanica* autorum (not Soó, see p76), *D. maculata subsp. osmanica* Sundermann

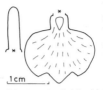

Plant with 2 deeply-forked tubers. stem (20 –) 40 – 70 cm tall, hollow, with 4 – 7 ovate – lanceolate foliage leaves, 8 – 20 cm long and 2 – 6.5 cm wide, widest part slightly higher than the middle; inflorescence very dense and many-flowered (up to 90); bracts somewhat longer than the flowers; flowers (purple)-red; lateral sepals at an angle, upright or inclined forwards, ovate – lanceolate, 11 – 17 mm long and 4 – 6 mm wide; lateral petals 8.5 – 13 mm long; labellum richly marked over the whole surface (generally no horseshoe pattern), broadly elliptical, 10 – 16 mm long and 14 – 23 mm broad, flat with slightly turned-up edges, weakly 3-lobed, central lobe generally much smaller than the sides and extending forwards; spur thick, cylindrical, straight (8 –) 10 – 15 mm long and 3 – 6 mm thick, pointing downwards or almost horizontal.

Habitat: wet meadows, wet places in open woodland; 1,000 – 1,700 m.

Flowers: June – August. Photos: An, Vil. Bolu 18.6.75 (l); An, Vil. Kastamonu 21.7.82 (r).

Distribution: north-eastern Anatolian coastal mountains from the Vil. Bursa (Bithynian Olymp = Ulu dag) as far as the Vil. Ordu, most plentiful in the Vil. Bolu and Kastamonu.

● Floristic element: e-submediterranean. Country: Asi: An. Key for the species in the *Dactylorhiza urvilleana* group:

1 Spur more than 1 ¼ times the length of the labellum; labellum mostly smaller than 10 × 15 mm; leaves usually heavily marked, often the bracts too   *D. urvilleana*
1* Spur about as long as the labellum which is generally larger than 10 × 15 mm; leaves unmarked or marked (often the markings are small and indistinct) . . . . *D. nieschalkiorum*

D'Urville's Marsh Orchid   *Dactylorhiza urvilleana* (Steudel) H. Baumann & Künkele

Synonyms: *Orchis urvilleana* Steudel, *O. triphylla* C. Koch. *O. amblyoloba* Nevski, *D. triphylla* (C. Koch) Czerep., *D. maculata subsp. triphylla* (C. Koch) Sundermann

Plant with 2 deeply-forked tubers; stem (15 –) 30 – 70 cm tall, hollow, with 3 – 9 foliage leaves, ovate – lanceolate, 6 – 20 cm long and 1.5 – 5 cm wide, widest part just above the middle; inflorescence dense and many-flowered; bracts longer than the flowers, occasionally up to several times; flowers purple-red to reddish-violet, occasionally pink; lateral sepals pointing upwards at an angle or inclined forwards, ovate – lanceolate, 8 – 13 mm long and 3 – 4.5 mm broad; lateral petals 6.5 – 9 mm long; labellum richly marked over the whole surface (usually a distinct horseshoe pattern), widely elliptical, 8 – 12 (– 14) mm long and 11 – 17 (– 19) mm wide, flat or slight convex folding, 3-lobed, occasionally almost undivided; middle lobe smaller than the outer ones and protruding; spur thick, cylindrical, straight, 11 – 17 mm long and 2.5 – 5 mm thick, nearly horizontal.

Habitat: wet woodland, wet meadows; up to 2,600 m. Flowers: June – August. Photos: An, Vil. Gümüshane 18.7.82 (l); An, Vil. Artvin 10.7.82 (r).

Distribution: north Anatolia coastal mountains from Vil. Kastamonu eastwards, penetrates into eastern Anatolia southwards as far as the Vil. Erzincan and Erzurum; also in Caucasia. Floristic element: (oriental) e-submediterranean. Country: Asi: An.

Relationships: *D. urvilleana* is close to *D. saccifera D. lancibracteata* (C. Koch) Renz (= *Orchis lancibracteata* C. Koch) from the Caucasus and northern Persia is also similar; on average it has a somewhat shorter spur; sometimes it is classed with *D. urvilleana*.

Dactylorhiza

Caucasian Marsh Orchid   *Dactylorhiza euxina* (Nevski) Czerep.

Synonyms; *Orchis euxina* Nevski, *O. caucasica* (Lipsky) Lipsky, *D. caucasica* (Lipsky) Soó, *D. majalis subsp. caucasica* (Lipsky) Sunderman *D. euxina var. markowitschii* (Soó) Renz & Taubenheim, *D. markowitschii* (Soó)

Averyanov Stem 5 – 25 (– 35) cm tall; 3 – 6 foliage leaves, ovate, spotted or unspotted; flowers (purplish-) red; lateral sepals 8 – 14 mm long and 3 – 5 mm wide;

1cm

labellum 7 – 10 (– 13) long and 8 – 13 (– 15) mm wide, undivided or with a suggestion of 3 lobes, ovate to cordate with coarse teeth along the up-turned margin; spur 6 – 9 mm long and 3 – 4 mm thick. **Habitat**: wet meadows at the upper montane and Alpine levels; 1,700 – 2,800 m. **Flowers**: June, July. **Photos**: An, Vil, Artvin 25.6.78 (l); An, Vil. Kars 6.7.82 (r). **Distribution**: mountains of north-east Ana-

tolia, westwards to Vil. Giresun, south to Vil. Erzurum and Agri. Also in Caucasia. **Floristic element**: (oriental) e-submediterranean. **Country**: Asi: An.
Key for the species in the *D. majalis* group:
1   Spur cylindrical (seen from above) 8 – 14 (often more than 10) mm long; leaves at their widest in the middle or below .... *D. majalis*, p82
1* Spur conical, wider at the point of attachment, 5 – 12 (often less than 10) mm long; leaves at their widest in the middle or above 2
2   Streaks of colour on the labellum in a clear hoseshoe pattern near the centre, but no marks in the outer zone; largest leaves 5 – 15 cm long and 2 – 5.5 cm broad ....*D. cordigera*
2* Labellum mostly without or with an indistinct horseshoe pattern, dots extending into the outer zone (washed out); largest leaves 3 – 6 (– 9) cm long and 1 – 2.5 (– 5) cm broad .. *D. euxina*

Heart-Shaped Marsh Orchid   *Dactylorhiza cordigera* (Fries) Soó

Synonyms: *Orchis cordigera* Fries, *O. bosniaca* (G. Beck) *D. lagotis* (Reichemb. fil.) H. Baumann, *D. cordigera subsp. bosniaca* (G. Beck) Soó, *D. cordigera subsp. siculorum* (Soó) Soó, *D. majalis subsp. cordigera*

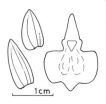

(Fries) Sundermann. Plant with 2 deeply forked tubers; stem 15 – 40 cm tall, hollow, with 2 – 3 basal scale leaves, above these 3 – 7 foliage leaves, these (broadly) ovate to

1cm

broadly lanceolate, heavily or, more rarely, weakly marked, rarely unmarked; inflorescence ovate to cylindrical, up to 12 cm long and 40-flowered; bracts often much longer than the purple (rarely purplish-pink) flowers; lateral sepals held up at an angle or inclined forward, ovate, 10 – 16 mm long and 3.5 – 6 mm wide, the central one bent over the broadly ovate, 8 – 12.5 mm long lateral petals; labellum

8 – 16 mm long and (8 –) 10 – 20 wide, of very variable shape (ovate, rhomboid, broadly cordate), undivided to deeply 3-lobed, mostly with protruding middle lobe, lateral lobes flat or bent up at the sides; spur cone-shaped 5 – 12 mm long and 3 – 5 mm thick at the base, half as long to somewhat longer than the labellum, pointing downwards.
Habitat: wet meadows at the montane and lower Alpine levels, up to 2,400 m; on rich soils. **Flowers**: May – July, **Photos**: Gr, Nomos Serres 10.6.83 (l); Ju, Kosovo and Metohija 19.6.82.
Distribution: northern Balkan Peninsula; from northern Greece to Bosnia and Bulgaria, south- and east-Carpathians.
● **Floristic element**: e + c-submediterranean carpathian. **Countries**: Eur: SE   Gr, Al, Ju, Bu, Rm, **E**   RW.
Variation: the species is very variable in growth and flowers; tall plants with long spurs ('siculorum') approach *D. majalis*.

Dactylorhiza

Broad-Leaved Marsh Orchid *Dactylorhiza majalis* (Reichenb.) P. F. Hunt & Summerhayes

Synonyms: Orchis latifolia L. p.p., *D. latifolia* (L. p.p.) Soó, *D. fistulosa* (Moench) H. Baumann & Künkele.

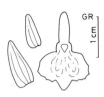

The scientific nomenclature of this species is in dispute. Stem 15–40 (–60) cm tall, hollow, with 3–6 (–9) ovate – lanceolate foliage leaves 6–16 cm long and 1.5–3.5 (–5) cm broad spotted on the upper surface (rarely on both) or, less commonly, unspotted; inflorescence cylindrical up to 10 (16) cm long and 35 (50) flowered; bracts longer than the flowers with pointed teeth along the edges (lens); flowers pale to dark purple or purplish-red; lateral sepals turned up at an angle or vertically, rarely inclined forwards, narrowly ovate, 7–12.5 mm long and 2.5–5 mm wide; lateral petals 5–9 mm long; labellum with horseshoe pattern in paler central area, occasionally also marked in the outer zone, 5–10 mm long and 7–14 mm broad, 3-lobed with protruding middle lobe and spreading to recurved side lobes; spur gently curving downwards.

Habitat: wet meadows, spring bogs; up to 2,500 m; on rich soils. **Flowers**: May – August. **Photos**: Ga, Dept. Moselle 22.5.71 (l); Be, Prov. Luxembourg 30.5.83 (r). **Distribution**: submeridional especially temperate Europe, absent from the east and south-east; south to northern Spain; in Italy not south of the Alps; in the Balkan Peninsula probably only in the north; the pontic region (eastern edge of the Carpathians)? ● **Floristic element**: c + w-submediterranean pannonic (?pontic) s + m-atlantic subatlantic centraleuropean.

Countries: Eur: SE Ju, Rm, S It, SW Hs, W Ga, Be, Ho, C He, Au, Hu, Ge, Da, Cz, Po, RB, N Su, No, E RW. **Variation**: in the Alps there are plants with large, weakly 3-lobed or unlobed labelli (*D. majalis subsp. alpestris* (Pugsley) Senghas.

Kalopissi's Marsh Orchid *Dactylorhiza kalopissii* E. Nelson

Stem 20–60 cm tall, hollow, with 4–9 lanceolate foliage leaves, 9–18 cm long and 2–5.5 cm broad, unspotted or spotted (often dotted); inflorescence cylindrical, dense; bracts about as long as the flowers; flowers pink to pale lilac, rarely darker shades; lateral sepals pointing up at an angle or inclined forwards, narrowly ovate, 8–15 mm long and 3–5.5 mm wide; lateral petals 7–11 mm long; labellum with dots (occasionally also stripes) in the paler central area, arranged in rows or in the horseshoe pattern, 8.5–12 mm long and 9–15 mm broad, 3-lobed to almost undivided, middle lobe protruding, side lobes flat or slightly recurved; spur cylindrical 8–12.5 mm long and 2.5–4 mm thick.

Habitat: wet meadows, fenland; up to 1,200 to 1,600 m, on rich soils probably poor in lime.

Flowers: May, June. **Photos**: Gr, Nomos Ioannina 7.6.83 (l, c) **Distribution**: north-west Greece; Pindus mountains in the general area of the Katara pass.

● **Floristic element**: e-submediterranean. **Country**: Eur: SE Gr.

Problem: In the higher mountains of northern and north-western Greece similar related species are growing which up to now have received little attention. The characteristic they have in common is the bright red flowers, but there are considerable differences in other characters such as the number of leaves and flowers. One which has recently been described is *D. graeca* (H. Baumann) found growing in wet meadows in the Varvous mountains at 1,500 m; leaves narrow, lanceolate, 13–20 cm long and 1.5–2.5 cm broad; lateral sepals 10–12 mm long and 3–4 mm wide, labellum weakly 3-lobed, 9–10 mm long and 10–11 mm broad; spur 8–9 mm long. **Photo**: Gr, Nomos Serres 2.7.81 (r)

Dactylorhiza

D. kalopissii   *D. graeca*

83

Northern Marsh Orchid *Dactylorhiza purpurella* (T. & T.A. Stephenson) Soó

Synonyms: *Orchis purpurella* T. & T. A. Stephenson, *D. majalis subsp. purpurella* (T. & T. A. Stephenson) D. Moresby Moore & Soó, *D. purpurella subsp. majaliformis* Løjtnant (not E. Nelson, *see* below), *D. purpurella var. pulchella* (Druce) Soó (not to be confused with *D. incarnata* 'pulchella', p90!)

1cm

Plant with 2 deeply forked tubers; stem 10 – 30 (– 40) cm high, hollow with 2 – 3 basal scale leaves, above these 4 – 8 ovate – lanceolate foliage leaves, 5 – 10 (– 16) cm long and (1 –) 1.5 – 3.5 cm broad, mostly unspotted, some spotted ('majaliformis'), none, or at least the uppermost 1 – 2, not sheathing the stem; inflorescence cylindrical, dense, short (up to 7 cm long); bracts shorter than or as long as the flowers, fine teeth along the edges (lens!); flowers mostly dark, occasionally paler, purplish-red to carmine; lateral sepals held up at an angle, narrowly ovate, 6 – 8.5 mm long and 2.5 – 3.5 mm wide, often spotted; lateral petals 5 – 6 mm long; labellum with a horseshoe pattern approaching the edges, sometimes with dots and stripes ('pulchella'), broadly rhomboid, 5 – 8 mm long and 6.5 – 12 mm broad; spur cylindrical (– ?conical), straight, 6 – 10 mm long and 2 – 3.5 mm thick. **Habitat:** wet meadows and spring swamps, often near the coast, dune hollows; up to 500 m; on neutral to weakly acid soils. **Flowers:** June, July 3 – 4 weeks later than *D. kerryensis.* **Photos:** Br, Highlands 9.7.75 (l); Br, Cumbria 13.6.80 (r). **Distribution:** Atlantic Europe and southern Sweden; southwards in the British Isles to Ireland, Wales and northern England, isolated sites in Hampshire, northwards along the Norwegian coast as far as Sør-Trøndelag, eastwards to north Jutland, isolated sites in Schonen. ● **Floristic element:** m + n-atlantic (n-subatlantic). **Countries: Eur: W** Br, Hb, Fa, **C** Da, **N** Su, No.

Western Marsh Orchid *Dactylorhiza kerryensis* (Wilmott) P. F. Hunt & Summerhayes

Synonyms: *Orchis majalis var. occidentalis* Pugsley, *O. kerryensis* Wilmott, *D. majalis subsp. occidentalis* (Pugsley) P. D. Sell, *D. majalis subsp. cambrensis* (R. H. Roberts) R. H. Roberts. *D. majalis subsp. scotica* E. Nelson, *D. purpurella subsp. majaliformis* E. Nelson

1cm

In general appearance resembles *D. purpurella*; stem 8 – 25 (– 35) cm tall with 4 – 10 foliage leaves which are often concentrated near the base of the stem, on average somewhat narrower than *D. purpurella,* mostly weakly to heavily spotted, rarely unspotted; bracts shorter than the flowers, frequently spotted; flowers mostly dark magenta or purplish-red, seldom pale; lateral sepals held vertically upwards or at an angle, 6.5 – 9 mm long and 3 – 3.5 mm wide, often spotted; labellum with markings over the whole surface, with horseshoe pattern, or dots and stripes, broadly elliptical, 6 – 10 mm long and 8 – 13 mm broad, central lobe small often scarcely protruding or not at all; lateral lobes often have 1 (2) deep notches; spur 5 – 10 mm long and 2.5 – 3 mm thick.

Habitat: wet meadows, fenland, dune hollows; up to 200 m; on acid or basic soils. **Flowers:** May, June. **Photos:** Hb, Clare 11.6.79. **Distribution:** British Isles; strongly associated with a maritime climate and at times confined to the coastal areas to the west.

● **Floristic element:** m + n-atlantic. **Countries: Eur: W** Br, Hb.

Key for species of *D. purpurella* group:
1   Labellum clearly 3-lobed, convexly folded with the side lobes turning downwards . . . . *D. kerryensis*
1* Labellum entire or obscurely 3-lobed, flat with the edges turning upwards . . . . *D. purpurella*

Dactylorhiza

Southern Marsh Orchid   *Dactylorhiza praetermissa* (Druce) Soó

Synonyms: *Orchis praetermissa* Druce, *D. majalis subsp. praetermissa* (Druce) D. Moresby Moore & Soó, *D. incarnata subsp. praetermissa* (Druce) Sundermann, *D. praetermissa var. junialis* (Vermeulen) Senghas, *D. majalis subsp. pardalina* (Pugsley) E. Nelson

Plant with 2 deeply-forked tubers; stem 20 – 70 cms tall, hollow, with 2 – 3 basal scale leaves, 4 – 9 foliage leaves above these, 8 – 25 cm long and 1.5 – 4.5 cm broad, broadest about the middle, unspotted or spotted (often ring-shaped as in 'junialis', 'pardalina'); inflorescence cylindrical 3 – 13 cm long with up to 60 blooms; bracts as long as or longer than the flowers; flowers in various shades of purple or purplish-red, mostly paler (pink), rarely dark shades; lateral sepals bending over or held up at an angle, narrowly ovate, 8 – 11 mm long and 3 – 4.5 mm wide, occasionally spotted; lateral petals 6 – 8 mm long and 2.5 – 4 mm wide; labellum with tiny dots (occasionally with lines also) in the centre or over the whole surface, sometimes in a horseshoe pattern, 7 – 10 mm long and 8 – 14 mm broad, entire or obscurely 3-lobed, flat to moderately convex; spur cone-shaped, 5 – 9.5 mm long and 2 – 3.5 mm thick, curving slightly downwards.

Habitat: wet meadows, fenland, dune hollows, large sedge communities; usually on calcareous wet to damp soils. Flowers: June – August. Photos: Ge, Niederrhein 11.6.71 (l); Br, north-east England 22.6.80 (r).

Distribution: Atlantic Europe; British Isles (England, Wales), south to the centre of France (Depts. Cher, Indre-et-Loire), east to the German Rhineland, rare in Jutland, north to south-west Norway, reported from the prov. Reggio (northern Italy). ● Floristic element: s + m-atlantic. Countries: Eur: W   Ga, Be, Ho, Br, C   Ge, Da, N   No.

Sphagnum Moor Orchid   *Dactylorhiza sphagnicola* (Höppner) Soó

Synonyms: *Orchis sphagnicola* Höppner. *D. incarnata subsp sphagnicola* (Höppner) Sundermann, *D. deweveri* (Vermeulen) Soó Should the name *D. wirtgenii* (Höppner) Soó belong to this species it has precedence over *D. sphagnicola*.

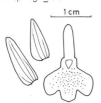

Stem (20 –) 30 – 60 cm tall, with 4 – 8 foliage leaves, 10 – 24 cm long and 1 – 3 (– 3.5) cm broad, unspotted; inflorescence similar to *D. praetermissa*:

flowers pale to dark purplish-pink; lateral sepals drooping or more or less erect and twisted, 9 – 12.5 mm long and 3 – 5 mm wide; labellum dotted over practically the whole surface, sometimes also with short lines and a tendency towards a horseshoe pattern, often rhomboid, 7 – 11.5 mm long and 8.5 – 14 mm broad, 3-lobed with a small protruding middle lobe, more rarely entire; spur 8 – 14 mm long and 2 – 3.5 mm thick, straight or slightly bent.

Habitat: raised and intermediate bogs with sphagnum moss; up to 600 m; on poor, sour and wet peat soils. Flowers: June, July. Photos: Ge, Niedersachsen 24.6.70.

Distribution: coastal regions of western Europe and southern Scandinavia; because of the special habitat demands of the species, distribution is very patchy; mountains of northern France to southern Holland, Rhineland, the north German plain, Schonen in Sweden to Østfold in Norway. ● Floristic element: m-atlantic n-subatlantic. Countries: Eur: W   Ga, Be, Ho, C   Ge, Da, N   Su, No.

Key for species in *D . praetermissa* group:

1   Largest leaf 3.5 – 6 (– 7) times as long as broad; spur usually shorter than the labellum, rarely a little longer . . . . *D. praetermissa*

1*   Largest leaf (6 –) 7 – 14 times as long as broad; spur clearly 1.2 – 1.4 times longer than the labellum . . . . . *D. sphagnicola*

Robust Marsh Orchid *Dactylorhiza elata* (Poiret) Soó

Synonyms: *Orchis elata* Poiret, *O. sesquipedalis* Willd., *O. munbyana* Bois & Reuter, *D. elata subsp. sesquipedalis* (Willd.) Soó, *D. elata subsp. durandii* (Boiss. & Reuter) Soó, *D. elata subsp. brennensis* E. Nelson, *D. incarnata subsp. africana* (Klinge) Sundermann

Stem 30 – 125 cm tall, hollow, 5 – 10 foliage leaves, variable narrow to ovate-lanceolate, up to 25 (45) cm long and 4.5 (5.5) cm broad, at their widest at or below the middle, unspotted or rarely spotted; inflorescence long and many-flowered; bracts longer than the flowers: flowers dark purplish-red to lilac-pink; lateral sepals turned up and twisted, 9 – 18 mm long and 3 – 6 mm wide, often spotted; lateral petals 7 – 14 mm long; labellum has a horseshoe pattern (rich markings, tendency to dots), 9 – 15 mm long and 10 – 22 mm broad, 3-lobed with a small middle lobe, or entire, side lobes spreading to turned down; spur cylindrical, cone-shaped, straight to (strongly) curved downwards 9 – 16 mm long and 2 – 4 mm thick. **Habitat:** wet meadows, fenland, spring communities; up to 2,500 m; on base-rich soils. **Flowers:** April – July. **Photos:** Hs, Prov. Granada 3.6.72 (l); Ga, Dept. Lot 31.5.81 (r). **Distribution:** western Mediterranean basin, northwards in France as far as the Depts. Deux-Sèvres, Vienne, Indre. A claim for Holland requires confirmation. ● **Floristic element:** c + w-mediterranean c + w-sub-mediterranean s-atlantic s-subatlantic.
Countries: Eur: S Co, **SW** Hs, Lu, **W** Ga; **Afr:** Tn, Ag, Ma. **Variation:** the species is very variable. A separation into 3 – 4 subspecies which has been advocated from time to time would be very arbitrary because of the variability of all the characteristics. The population 'brennensis' (Dept. Indre) shows a bigger divergence with its lower growth and smaller flowers.

Baltic Marsh Orchid *Dactylorhiza baltica* (Klinge) Orlova

Synonyms: *Orchis latifolia subsp. baltica* Klinge, *O. baltica* (Klinge) Klinge, *D. majalis subsp. baltica* (Klinge) Senghas, *D. latifolia subsp. baltica* (Klinge) Soó

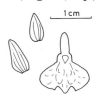

Plant with 2 deeply forked tubers; stem 25 – 70 cm tall, thin (up to 1 cm thick at the base), hollow, 2 basal scale leaves, above these 4 – 7, mostly 5, foliage leaves, upright-projecting, longish-lanceolate, 10 – 25 cm long and 1.5 – 3.7 cm broad, at their broadest in the middle or slightly below, numerous small, often washed-out spots on the upper surface, rarely unspotted, inflorescence ovate to cylindrical, 3 – 9.5 cm long, dense; bracts somewhat longer than the purplish-red flowers; lateral sepals erect, at an angle or vertically, narrowly ovate, 8 – 10 mm long and 3 – 4.5 mm wide, mostly spotted. central sepal bending over the 6.5 – 8 mm-long lateral petals; labellum has a horshoe pattern on the scarcely paler central part, often also marked on the outer part, broad wedge-shaped, horizontally elliptic, 6.5 – 9 mm long and 8 – 13 mm broad, 3-lobed with a small middle lobe, weakly convex lengthwise with turned-up, toothed side lobes; spur cone-shaped, almost straight, pointing downwards, 6 – 9 mm long and 2 – 3 mm thick.
Habitat: wet meadows in the Baltic region, especially near the coast.
Flowers: June, July, later than *D. majalis*. **Photos:** RB Rajon Tukums, 1.7.78 (l); origin. RB, cultiv. 11.6.82 (r).
Distribution: a euroasiatic species, from the east through the temperate and boreal zones in Russia to the Baltic region, here from the island of Aaland to Mecklenburg (Zingst); in Asia eastwards to central Siberia, to Mongolia and north-west China. **Floristic element:** n-centraleuropean sarmatic siberian n-russian.
Countries: Eur: C Ge, Po, RB, **N** Fe, RN, **E** RC.

Dactylorhiza

Early Marsh Orchid   *Dactylorhiza incarnata* (L.) Soó

Synonyms: *Orchis incarnata* L., *O. strictifolia* Opiz, *D. strictifolia* (Opiz) Rauschert, *D. incarnata subsp. punctata* Doll

Problem: the *D. incarnata* group is rich in different forms which makes the taxonomic classification correspondingly difficult.

Key to the species:

1 Flowers pale yellow; labellum darker yellow in the middle, 3-lobed, the side lobes mostly toothed and folded downwards .... *D. ochroleuca*

1* Flowers red, sometimes yellow but in this case uniformly coloured, without the other characteristics ..... *D. incarnata*

1. *Dactylorhiza incarnata*

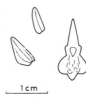

Stem 25–60 (–80) cm tall, hollow, with 4–7 foliage leaves, upright or bent backwards, narrow-lanceolate, up to 20 cm long and 3.5 cm broad, at their widest towards the base, unspotted; inflorescence 4–12 cm long up to 50-flowered; bracts green, longer than the flowers, with an almost smooth edge; flowers flesh-coloured; lateral sepals often upright and twisted, lanceolate, 7–9 mm long and 2.5–4 mm wide; lateral petals 5.5–7.5 mm wide; labellum with a horseshoe pattern in the paler central area, rarely dotted ('punctata'), 4.5–8 mm long and 5–9 mm broad, mostly obscurely 3–lobed with a small protruding middle lobe, side lobes somewhat turned downwards, edges (almost) entire; spurs cone-shaped, 6.5–10 mm long and 2–3 mm thick, almost straight.

Habitat: wet meadows; up to 2,100 m; on base-rich soils. **Flowers:** April–July. **Photos:** variant 2: He, Kt. Aargau 2.6.79 (u/l); Ge, Allgäu 16.6.67 (u/m); Br, Yorkshire 17.6.81 (l/m) variant 3: Br, South Wales 6.7.83 (u/r) – variant 5: It, Prov. Bozen 15.4.80 (l/l).

Distribution: in Europe and the Near East from the submeridional to the boreal zones; also in the boreal and temperate zones eastwards, further into the Caucasus and the mountains of Turkestan.

Floristic element: submeridional/montane temperate boreal. **Countries: Eur: SE** Gr, Al, Ju, Bu, Rm, RK, **S** It, SW, Hs, ?Lu, **W** Ga, Be, Ho, Br, Hb, **C** He, Au, Hu, Ge, Da, Cz, Po, RB, **N** Su, No, Fe, RN, **E** RW, RE, RC; **Asi:** An

Variants: the above description applies to the widespread variant 1. – variant 2 (*D. i. subsp. pulchella* (Druce) Soó); stem 14–40 cm tall; leaves up to 2 cm broad; inflorescence up to 7 cm long, 10–25 (–40) flowered; bracts shaded with lilac; flowers deep purplish-red to reddish-violet; whether this form has colonized its own distribution area has not been clarified. – variant 3 (*D. i. subsp. coccinea*): stem 5–25 cm tall; leaves up to 2 (2.7) cm broad, often clustered at the base of the stem; inflorescence up to 7 cm long; bracts shaded lilac; flowers shining vermillion to crimson (warm red); on coasts of the British Isles in wet dune hollows, also occurs inland; – variant 4 (*D. i. subsp. haematodes*): like variant I; leaves spotted on the upper surface here and there; – variant 5 (*D. i. subsp. hyphaematodes*): like variant 1; leaves spotted on both surfaces here and there (*see also D. cruenta*, p92).

2. *Dactylorhiza ochroleuca* (Boll) Averyanov:

Similar to *D. incarnata* (variant 1); often tall (up to 90 cm, inflorescence to 18 cm); foliage leaves lie close to the stem; flower size on the upper limit of the range of variation in *D. incarnata*. **Habitat:** wet meadows, fenland and intermediate bogs, those over infilled lakes are particularly favoured; up to 600 m; on base-rich soils. **Flowers:** May–July. **Photo:** Ge, Oberschwagen 20.6.68 (l/r). **Distribution:** Central Europe and surrounding areas as far as England, into the Baltic region, to the Carpathian basin and to northern Ukraine.

● **Floristic element:** pannonic m-atlantic subatlantic centraleuropean ?scandinavian. **Countries: Eur: SE** RM, **W** ?Be, Br, **C** He, Au, Hu, Ge, Da, Po, RB, **N** Su, ?No, **E** RW.

D. incarnata: 'serotina'

'coccinea'

Dactylorhiza

'hyphaematodes'

'pulchella'

D. ochroleuca

Lapland Marsh Orchid *Dactylorhiza lapponica* (Hartman) Soó

Synonyms: *Orchis lapponica* (Hartman) Reichenb. fil., *O. pseudocordiger* (Neuman) *O. angustifolia subsp. pycnantha* Neuman *D. pseudocordiger* (Neuman) Soó, D. pycnantha (Neuman) Averyanov *D. trausteineri subsp. lapponica* (Hartman) Soó, *D. cruenta subsp. lapponica* (Hartman) E. Nelson, *D. majalis subsp. lapponica* (Hartman) Sundermann

1 cm

Plant with 2 deeply forked tubers; stem 10 – 30 cm tall, tinged with violet above, with 1 basal scale leaf and 2 – 5 (mostly 3) foliage leaves standing out from the stem, heavily spotted on the upper surface, lanceolate, 3 – 8 cm long and 0.6 – 2 (– 2.5) cm wide, widest in the lower half; inflorescence fairly lax, 5 – 20- flowered, cylindrical; bracts about as long as the flowers; flowers dark purple or magenta; lateral sepals upright and twisted outwards, ovate – lanceolate, 6 – 10 cm long and 2 – 4 mm wide, sometimes spotted; lateral petals 5 – 8 mm long; labellum with horseshoe pattern in the central area, which is scarcely lighter than the margin, variable shape (broader than long to longer than broad), 4.5 – 8 mm long and 6 – 11 mm broad, flat or convex, 3-lobed with a long or short middle lobe or may be undivided; spur cone-shaped 6.5 – 11 mm long and 2 – 3 mm thick, very slightly bent, almost horizontal.

Habitat: fens and wooded mires, wet meadows, streamside gravel; up to 1,000 m (northern Europe) 500 – 2,400 m (Alps) in wet, lime-rich places. **Flowers:** June, July. **Photos:** No, Nordland 18.7.84 (l); Su, Jämtland 12.7.76 (r). **Distribution:** the area is in two parts: the Alps from Kt. Schwyz eastwards, particularly the southern limestone Alps; central and northern Scandinavia including Gotland.

● **Floristic element:** alpine + (n-centraleuropean) scandinavia. **Countries:** Eur: S It, C He, Au, N Su, No, Fe.

Flecked Marsh Orchid *Dactylorhiza cruenta* (O. F. Müller) Soó

Synonyms: *Orchis cruenta* O. F. Müller, *D. incarnata subsp. cruenta* (O. F. Müller) P. D. Sell

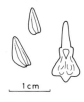

1 cm

Stem 15 – 30 cm tall, hollow, with 3 – 5 ovate – lanceolate foliage leaves, 4 – 10 cm long and 1 – 2.5 cm wide, 2.5 – 6 × (the largest leaf 4 ×) as long as wide, the lower half the widest, mostly with violet spots on both sides, sometimes the whole surface coloured, or spotting may be on one side only, or absent (photo. r); inflorescence 3 – 8 cm long with 10 – 30 dark purplish-red flowers; flower dimensions similar to *D. incarnata*.

Habitat: wet meadows (also along the shore); fenland and pine wood mires; up to 2,400 m (Alps); on wet calcareous soils. **Flowers:** June, July. **Photos:** He, Kt Graubünden 13.7.74 (l), 19.7.76 (r); Su, Jämtland 11.7.76 (c)

Distribution: eastern Europe, northern Europe, northern central Europe (Baltic area), Alps; also in the temperate and boreal zones of Asia. **Floristic element:** alpine ?m-atlantic n-subatlantic n-centraleuropean sarmatic c-siberian scandinavian n-russian n-siberian. **Countries:** S It, SW Ga, W ?Br, ?Hb, C Ge, + Da, ?Po, RB, N Su, No, Fe, RN, E RC.

Problem: the delimitation of the species is yet to be clarified. Difficulties arise above all in the subdividing of *D. incarnata*. *D. cruenta* is distinguished by its relatively shorter and broader leaves and darker flowers. There is controversy, for example, as to how the plants with narrow leaves, spotted on one or both surfaces, should be classified; here they have been shown as variants to *D. incarnata*. The 'cruenta' plants in Ireland and Scotland could be treated in a similar way. Amongst the rest, plants with spotting on both leaf surfaces occasionally turn up in other species (*see D. umbrosa*, p76).

Traunsteiner's Orchid *Dactylorhiza traunsteineri* (Reichenb.) Soó

Synonyms: *Orchis traunsteineri* Reichenb., *O. angustifolia* Reichenb., *D. majalis subsp. traunsteineri* (Reichenb.) Sundermann. For plants of the British Isles: *O. francis-drucei* Wilmott, *O. majalis subsp. traunsteinerioides* Pugsley, *D. traunsteineri subsp. francis-drucei* (Wilmott) Soó, *D. traunsteinerioides* (Pugsley) Landwehr, *D. majalis subsp. traunsteinerioides* (Pugsley) Bateman & Denholm, *D. traunsteineri subsp. hibernica* Landwehr

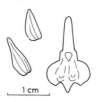

1 cm

Stem 10–40 cm tall, thin, pith core or hollow with 2–5 foliage leaves held at an angle or spreading, linear-lanceolate, 5–16 cm long and 0.5–1.9 cm wide, spotted or not. inflorescence cylindrical (lax, up to 15-flowered, Alpine) or ovate (dense up to 25-flowered, England); bracts shorter than or often longer than the flowers; flowers purplish-red; lateral sepals erect at an angle, narrowly ovate, 8–11 mm long and 2.5–4 mm wide; middle sepal mostly not inclined over the 6–8.5 mm long lateral petals; labellum has a paler central area with horseshoe pattern 6–10 mm long and 6.5–13 (–14.5) mm broad, 3-lobed with a small projecting middle lobe, side lobes slightly or strongly curved downwards, sometimes with up-turned edges; spur cone-shaped to cylindrical, 9–12.5 (England 7–11) mm long and 2–3.5 mm thick. **Habitat:** fenland and spring bogs, also poor meadows with fluctuating water content; up to 1,900 m; on lime- or base-rich soils. **Flowers:** May–July. **Photos:** Au, Tirol 25.6.77 (u/l); Ge, Oberbayern 15.6.64 (u/r); Br, Oxfordshire 24.6.84 (l/l, l/r).

Distribution: scattered in the temperate and boreal zones in Europe, penetrates into the Alps and Pyrenees in the submeridional zone. Also in the temperate zone in Asia as far as central Siberia.

Floristic element: pyrenean alpine m+n-atlantic subatlantic centraleuropean sarmatic scandinavian n-rossian. **Countries:** Eur: **SE** Ju, S, It, **W** Ga, Ho, Br, Hb, **C** He, Au, Ge, Cz, Po, RB, **N** Su, No, Fe, RN, **E** ?RW, RC.

Problem: the *D. traunsteineri* group is very variable.

One type, which perhaps deserves an independent status, is *D. russowii* (Klinge) J. Holub, (**Syn:** *Orchis russowii* (Klinge) Klinge, *D. majalis subsp. russowii* (Klinge) Sundermann) **Photos:** Ge, area Rostock, 16.7.75 (p96 u/l, u/r); Su, Västernorrland 30.6.84 (p97 u/l). Stem height, leaf number and size and the flower measurements all lie within the range of variation of *D. traunsteineri*. Differences are: stem always hollow, somewhat thicker; leaves spreading widely or bent back; inflorescence mostly dense and many-flowered, ovate (but occasionally low in flower number, lax and cylindrical); flowers pink-red, with or without a faint purple component; alleged differences in leaf spotting and labellum shape are not available. The type is described from the Baltic region (Ge Po RB Su Fe RN; reported +Cz), it is also reputed to occur in continental Europe as far as central Siberia to the east. The characteristics given also turn up singly or together in *D. traunsteineri*; for example, the red flower colour in the Alps or the many-flowered ovate inflorescences in England.

It is not clear how the plants with sickle-shaped, bent back leaves should be evaluated. They are more plentiful in boreal Europe. Sometimes they are given the status of species or subspecies, *D. curvifolia* (F. Nyl.) Czerep. (**Syn:** *Orchis curvifolia* F. Nyl., *D. traunsteineri subsp. curvifolia* (F. Nyl.) Soó). Possibly the position of the leaves, although certainly striking, should be evaluated as an insignificant extreme. Plants resembling *D. traunsteineri* have been described as subspecies of *D. majalis*:

1. *D. m. subsp. brevifolia* Bisse, **Photo:** Ge, area Suhl 25.6.84 (p.97 u/r). calcareous fenland (Ge, Su).

2. *D. m. subsp. turfosa* Procházka, acid intermediate mires (Cz, Böhmerwald, Erz mountains). Characteristic of both are a stem 20 (25) cm tall, narrow leaves (turfosa: 6–9.5 × 0.9–1.4 cm); inflorescence 5 (6.5) cm long.

Dactylorhiza

'traunsteinerioides'

Bauman's Orchid *Dactylorhiza baumanniana* Hölzinger & Künkele

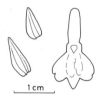

1 cm

Plant with 2 deeply forked tubers; stem 15–40 cm tall with 1–2 basal scale leaves, above these (3–) 4–6 lanceolate foliage leaves 7–12 (–15) cm long and 0.8–3 (–4.2) cm wide, widest in the centre or below, strong or washed-out spots. inflorescence narrow cylindrical rather lax 5–12 cm long with 8–15 (–35) flowers; bracts about as long as the flowers; flowers purplish-red, mostly a dark shade; lateral sepals erect, at an angle to almost vertical, and twisted, narrowly ovate, 8–12.5 mm long and 3.4.5 mm wide; lateral petals 6–10 mm long; labellum with a horseshoe pattern in the lighter central area, sometimes only faint stripes and dots, 7.5–10 (–12) mm long and 7.5–12 (–15) mm broad, mostly 3-lobed, the middle lobe small often protruding, occasionally with almost no divisions, lateral lobes turned down to varying degrees, sometimes with deep notches along the edges; spur cylindrical, slightly wider in the middle (as seen from above), 8.5–12.5 mm long and 2–3 mm thick, straight or slightly curved, pointing downwards.

Habitat: wet meadows, fenland; 1,000–1,800 m; on rich soils probably short of lime.

Flowers: May, June. **Photos**: Gr, Nomos Grevena, type population, 16.5.83.

Distribution: north-west Greece, northern Pindus mountains, known from the Nomi Grevena and Ioannina. The species is in the mountains of Greece which up to now have been little explored for the *Dactylorhiza* species; probably more widely distributed; could be in the Vermion mountains and possibly also further south in Fthiotis and Achaia.

● **Floristic element**: e-submediterranean.
Country: Eur: SE   Gr.

'russowii'

D. majalis subsp. brevifolia

Dactylorhiza

Wedge-Lipped Orchid *Dactylorhiza saccifera* (Brongn.) Soó

Synonyms: Orchis saccifera Brongn., O. gervasiana Tod., O. macrostachys Tineo, O. maculata subsp. saccifera (Brongn.) K. Richter, O. maculata subsp. macrostachys (Tineo) Rohlena, D. gervasiana (Tod.) H. Baumann & Künkele, D. maculata subsp. saccifera (Brongn.) Diklić, D. bithynica H. Baumann

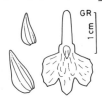

Plant with 2 deeply forked tubers; stem 25 – 90 cm tall, mostly full of pith, with 4 – 12 spotted foliage leaves, the lowest short ovate, the middle ones lanceolate, 10 – 20 cm long and 2 – 6 cm wide, widest in the middle or above (or below), spreading to turned back, upper ones small and bract-like; inflorescence 6 – 22 cm long, many-flowered; bracts much longer than the flowers; flowers purplish-pink or red; lateral sepals inclined forwards, lanceolate, 7 – 14 mm long and 2.5 – 5 mm wide; lateral petals 5.5 – 10 mm long; labellum with clear or washed-out markings arranged in a fan-shaped pattern, 7 – 11 mm long and 8.5 – 16 mm broad, flat, deeply 3-lobed with protruding middle lobe and toothed side lobes, surface area of middle lobe about (⅓) ½ as large as that of one of the side lobes; spur cylindrical, slightly curved, 9 – 15 mm long and 2 – 4.5 mm thick.

Habitat: damp woods, wet meadows, concentrated in the montane level; up to 2,000 m on moist to wet base-rich soils. **Flowers:** May – July. **Photos:** Al, Prov. Vlorë 26.5.83. **Distribution:** east and central Mediterranean region, northwards as far as the Carpathian Siebenbürgens, eastwards to Turkish Kurdestan. The records for the Iberian Peninsula are probably mixed up with D. maculata (fuchsii). ● **Floristic element:** e + c-mediterranean (oriental) e + c-sub-mediterranean karpatic. **Countries: Eur: SE** Gr, Tu, Al, Ju, Bu, Rm, **S** Si, It, Sa, Co; **Asi:** LS, An.

Madeiran Orchid *Dactylorhiza foliosa* (Vermeulen) Soó

Synonym: Orchis maderensis Summerhayes

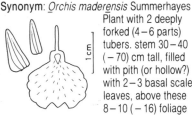

Plant with 2 deeply forked (4 – 6 parts) tubers. stem 30 – 40 (– 70) cm tall, filled with pith (or hollow?) with 2 – 3 basal scale leaves, above these 8 – 10 (– 16) foliage leaves, getting smaller towards the top, the uppermost ones bract-like, lower leaves longish-lanceolate up to 20 cm long and 6 cm wide, widest about the middle, spreading wide or overhanging, unmarked or rarely faint spotting; inflorescence 5 – 13 cm long, dense; bracts often shorter than the pale to deep purplish-red flowers; lateral sepals inclined forwards, ovate – lanceolate, 8 – 11 mm long and 2.5 – 4 mm wide; central sepal held upright at an angle and not leaning over the lateral petals; the latter 7.5 – 9 mm long and sometimes spreading; labellum with faint fan-shaped markings over the whole surface, horizontally elliptic, 8 – 17 mm long and 9.5 – 20 mm broad, flat, weakly 3-lobed with a small middle lobe which mostly does not protrude beyond the side lobes, these are often sinuate and toothed; spur narrow-cylindrical, 5 – 11 mm long and about 1 mm thick, bent downwards; stigma ringed dark purple.

Habitat: damp woods, wet meadows, rock walls; 400 – 1,000 m on wet acid soils in shady moist air sites, also on drier soils. **Flowers:** May – July. **Photos:** Ml, cult. 20.6.80 garden hybrid? (l); 12.5.83 (r).

Distribution: species endemic on the island of Madeira; has been cultivated in gardens since 1828, especially in England. ● **Floristic element:** madeiran. **Country: Afr:** Ml.

Relationship: the position of the isolated island type has been assessed in different ways; there is much to be said in favour of a close relationship with the D. maculata group; possible connections with D. elata are also a subject for discussion.

Heath-Spotted Orchid *Dactylorhiza maculata* (L.) Soó

Synonym: *Orchis maculata* L.

GR *Index:*
$$\frac{2A}{B+C}$$

Stem 15–60 (– 100) cm tall, filled with pith or rarely hollow; foliage leaves 3–9 (– 12) the lower ones concentrated in a rosette, narrow lanceolate to spatulate, 3–13 (– 20) cm long and 0.5–3 (– 4.5) mm wide, pointed or rounded, spotted or unspotted, the upper (1 –) 2–4 (– 6) not sheathing and bract-like; inflorescence short to elongated, dense-flowered; bracts generally shorter than the flowers; flower colour variable, purple to white; lateral sepals inclined forwards, ovate – lanceolate 5 – 11 mm long and 1.5 – 4 mm wide; central sepal held up at an angle, not over the 3.5 – 8 mm long lateral petals; labellum generally with the horseshoe pattern, also dotted or unmarked, 5 – 11 mm long and 6.5 – 15 mm broad, 3-lobes with spread-out side lobes; spur cylindrical, 4 – 12 mm long and 0.5 – 2.5 mm thick.

Habitat: woodland, heaths, poor grassland, fenland and intermediate mires; up to 2,200 m; on acid to basic, fresh to wet soils. **Flowers:** May – July. **Distribution:** in Europe from the submeridional to the arctic zones, absent from the pontic area, isolated sites in the Atlas mountains. Also in the temperate zone as far as central Siberia. **Floristic element:** w-mediterranean submeridional temperate boreal arctic. **Countries: Eur: SE** Ju, Rm, **S** It, Co, **SW** ?Bl, Hs, Lu, **W** Ga, Be, Ho, Br, Hb, Fa, **C** He, Au, Hu, Ge, Da, Cz, Po, RB, **N** Su, No, Fe, RN, Is, **E** RW, RE, RC; **Afr:** Ag, Ma.

Problem: the *D. maculata* group offers a bewildering variety of types. With our present state of knowledge it is not possible to produce a satisfactory classification. While it is true that some types can be well separated there are numerous populations which cannot easily be arranged. A division into two groups according to the shape of the labellum still seems to be the best initial step: **Type 1:** labellum with shallow divisions into 3 lobes, middle lobe appreciably smaller and mostly shorter or as long as the side lobes; labellum index less than 1.2. **Type 2:** labellum deeply 3-lobed, middle lobe large, protruding, its area more than half as large as one side lobe; labellum index over 1.2.

Type 1: *D. maculata* in the 'strict' sense; western, northern and northern central Europe. **A.** Tall-growing types: 1. *D. m. subsp. ericetorum* (E. F. Linton) P. F. Hunt & Summerhayes, **(Syn:** *D. m. subsp. rhoumensis* [H.-Harrison] Soó); **Photos:** Ga, Dept. Pyrénées-Orientales 11.7.78 (p.103 (l/l/r); Ga, Dept. Hautes-Pyrénées 22.6.84 (u/r); Br, E. Lothian 24.7.80 (p.102 u/l); Br, Argyll 27.7.80 (p. 102 u/r). – 2. *D. m. subsp. caramulensis* Vermeulen; Portugal. **B.** Low-growing types; *D. m. subsp. elodes* (Griseb.) Soó. **Type 2:** 'fuchsii' type: Europe (southern concentration), Asia **A.** Tall-growing types: 1. *D. m. subsp. meyeri* (Reichenb. fil.) Tournay **(Syn:** *Orchis fuchsii* Druce, *D. fuchsii* (Druce) Soó, *D. m. subsp. fuchsii* [Druce] HYL.); **Photos:** He, Kt. Graubünden 8.7.71 (p.103 l/l), 23.7.71 (u/l); Ge, Südbaden 1.8.65 (p.103 l/u/r); atypical: Au, Vorarlberg 25.6.70 (l/l). – 2. *D. m. subsp. transsilvanica* (Schur) Soó; leaves unspotted; flowers yellowish-white, without markings; Carpathians to Erz mountains. **Photo:** Rm, Judet Brasov 6.7.78 (l/r). – 3. *D. f. subsp. sooana* (Borsos) Borsos; leaves spotted; flowers white, marked purple; Hungary. **B.** Low-growing types: 1. *D. M. subsp. sudetica* (Reichenb. fil.) Vöth **(Syn:** *D. f. subsp. psychrophila* (Schlechter) Holub); montane level. – 2. *D. f. subsp. okellyi* (Druce) Soó; flowers white, scented; Ireland, Scotland. **Photo;** Hb, Clare 5.8.84 (p.103 u/r). – 3. *D. m. subsp. hebridensis* (Wilmott) E. Nelson; west coast of British Isles; **Photos:** Hb, Donegal 9.8.84 (p.102 u/l u/r).

Types with an intermediate labellum shape:
1. Scandinavian types; **Photo:** Su, Norbotten 21.6.76 (p.103 u/l); *D. m. subsp. deflexa* Landwehr, *D. m. subsp. montellii* (Vermeulen) Landwehr.
2. Atlas types: *D. m. subsp. baborica* Maire & Weiller; Kabylie. *D. m. subsp. maurusica* (Emberger & Maire) Maire & Weiller; Rif.
3. Carpathian types: *D. m. subsp. schurri* (Klinge) Soó; resembles *'elodes'*.

'meyeri'

'maculata'

Dactylorhiza

'meyeri' (over-colouring)

'transsilvanica'

101

scandinavian type

'okellyi' (maculata type)

Dactylorhiza

'meyeri'

'maculata', above: 'meyeri'

103

Hooded Orchid *Steveniella satyrioides* (Sprengel) Schlechter

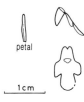

petal

1 cm

Plant with 2 ovoid-spheroid tubers. Stem 15–40 (+60) cm tall with 2 basal sheathing scale leaves; 1 large foliage leaf at the base and 2 forming long sheaths round the stem, large leaf longish-lanceolate, 6–20 cm long and 1.5–6.5 cm wide, bent down, often, as is the whole plant, tinged with brownish-purple; inflorescence up to 13 (18) cm long with 20 (30) upright flowers; bracts much shorter to as long as the ovaries; sepals growing together to form a 3-toothed hood, 7–10 mm long, olive green and brownish purple mixture; lateral petals 4–7 mm long and 0.4–0.5 mm wide; labellum olive-green to greenish-yellow with purple base, finely papillose, 6–7 mm long, 3-lobed, middle lobe ovate, side lobes short, rounded; spur 2–4 mm long and equally wide at the base, cone-shaped with a cleft tip.

Habitat: open coniferous and broad-leaved woodland, grassy woodland edges, scrub, hazelnut plantations; from the plains to the montane level, up to 1,300 m (2,100 in Persia); on calcareous soils.
Flowers: April, May.
Photos: An, Vil. Bolu 5.5.74 (l), 9.5.83 (r)
Distribution: mountains bordering the Black Sea in northern Anatolia and in the Crimea; also in Caucasia and in north and west Persia.
Floristic element: e-submediterranean.
Countries: Eur: SE Rk, **Asi:** An.
Relationship: the genus is isolated and has only the one species.

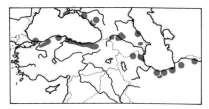

Komper's Orchid *Comperia comperiana* (Steven) Ascherson & Graebner

Synonyms: *Orchis comperiana* Steven, *C. taurica* C. Koch, *C. karduchorum* Bornm. & Kranzlin

1 cm

Plant with 2 ovoid tubers; stem 25–60 cm tall, with 2 basal sheathing scale leaves, 2–4 foliage leaves on the lower half and 2–3 long scale leaves sheathing the stem above; foliage leaves elongated-elliptical up to 15 cm long and 4 cm wide, upright; inflorescence up to 25 cm long, up to 30-flowered; bracts membranous, the lower ones longer than the flowers; sepals grow together to form a hood for about ¾ of their length, 13–20 mm long, greenish with lilac-brownish shading; lateral petals 14–16 mm long, narrow-lanceolate with 1–2 pointed teeth on each side: point extended to short curved thread; labellum 3-lobed, pale lilac, triangular with a wedge-shaped base, up to 1.5 cm long, lateral lobes

and point of middle lobe drawn out into thread-like extensions 3–8 cm long; spur curving downwards, 12–18 mm long, whitish-lilac.
Habitat: open coniferous and broad-leaved woodland at the montane level; up to 1,800 m.
Flowers: May – July. **Photos:** An, Vil. Denizli 24.5.74.
Distribution: in Europe only in the Crimea; mainly in Asia Minor, westwards as far as the eastern Aegean islands with higher mountains (Lesbos, Samos, Kos, Rhodes), eastwards through Iraqi Kurdestan as far as western Persia. **Floristic element:** e-mediterranean oriental e-submediterranean. **Countries: Eur: SE** RK; **Asi:** LS, An, AE.

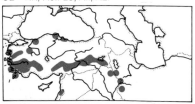

Steveniella

Comperia

105

Dense-flowered Orchid *Neotinea maculata* (Desf.) Stearn

Synonym: *N. intacta* (Link) Reichenb. fil.

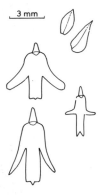

Plant with 2 ellipsoidal tubers; stem 10 – 30 (– 40) cm tall, with 1 – 2 brown scale leaves at the base and 4 – 6 foliage leaves, of these 1 – 3 form a basal rosette, the upper ones sheathing the stem; leaves elongated-elliptical, 3 – 12 cm long and 1 – 4.5 cm wide, bluish-green, spotted or unspotted; inflorescence 2 – 8 cm long, dense and many-flowered; bracts shorter than the ovaries; flowers small, scented, of various shades, pink to brownish-red, or greenish-white to pale yellow; sepals 3 – 4 mm long, lanceolate, forming a hood with the somewhat shorter lateral petals; lip 3 – 5 mm long, mostly marked with red, pointing downwards at an angle, 3-lobed, middle lobe narrow rectangular, 3-toothed at the end, side lobes linear, shorter, usually spreading; spur conical 1 – 2 mm long. **Habitat:** coniferous woods, garrigue, poor grassland with scrub; up to 1,600 m; on dry to fresh soils, often over limestone. **Flowers:** March – May (June in Ireland). **Photos:** Cy, Limassol region 20.3.84 (l); AE, Rhodes 4.4.81 (r). **Distribution:** Mediterranean region, Atlantic islands (Madeira and the Canaries, however not on Lanzarote and Fuerteventura); isolated locations in western Ireland (Burreu) and on the Isle of Man. ● **Floristic element:** mediterranean, canarian madeirian submediterranean m-atlantic (absent from s-atlantic). **Countries: Eur: SE** Cr, Gr, Ju, **S** Me, Si, It, Sa, Co, **SW** Bl, Hs, Lu, **W** Ga, Br, Hb); **Asi:** IJ, LS, Cy, An, AE; **Afr:** Tn, Ag, Ma, MI, Cl. **Relationship:** the single species genus is related to the militaris group of *Orchis* and to *Aceras*.

Man Orchid *Aceras anthropophorum* (L.) Aiton fil.

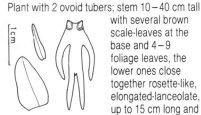

Plant with 2 ovoid tubers; stem 10 – 40 cm tall with several brown scale-leaves at the base and 4 – 9 foliage leaves, the lower ones close together rosette-like, elongated-lanceolate, up to 15 cm long and 2.6 cm wide, unspotted, the upper ones sheathing the stem; inflorescence narrow cylindrical, dense and many-flowered; bracts shorter than the ovaries; flowers, background colour is greenish-yellow with tints of brownish-red of varying intensity; sepals 5 – 8 mm long and 2.5 – 5 mm wide, ovate, forming a hood with the somewhat shorter lanceolate lateral petals; lip 12 – 15 mm long, pendent with 2 lateral swellings at the base, deeply 3-lobed, middle lobe 2-pointed and with a middle tooth, all parts linear; differs from the *Orchis* subsp. in having no spur and two viscidia very close together or fused.

Habitat: poor and semi-arid grassland; light scrub and woodland; woodland edges; up to 1,500 m; on dry to fairly fresh, mostly calcareous soils. **Flowers:** March – June. **Photos:** Br, Cambridgeshire, June 1981 (l); It, Prov. Grosseto 19.4.82 (r).

Distribution: in the Mediterranean region, concentrated in the western and central parts, fairly rare in the eastern part; spreads northwards in the parts under the oceanic influence in western and central Europe. In Britain restricted to southern counties.

● **Floristic element:** mediterranean c + w-submediterranean s + m-atlantic s-sub-atlantic. **Countries: Eur: SE** Cr, Gr, Al, Ju, **S** Si, It, Sa, Co, **SW** Bl, Hs, Lu, **W** Ga, Be, Ho, Br, **C** He, Ge; **Asi:** LS, Cy, An, AE, **Afr:** Tn, Ag, Ma.

Relationship: the single species genus is closely related to the militaris group of the genus *Orchis*. Hybrids are not uncommon and at times will form swarms with large numbers of individuals (e.g. with *Orchis simia*).

Neotinea

Aceras

107

Pink Globe Orchid   *Traunsteinera globosa* (L.) Reichenb.

Synonym: *Orchis globosa* L.

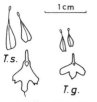

Plant with two ellipsoidal to ovoid tubers; stem 20–60 cm tall, with 2–3 brown scale leaves at the base and 4–6 upright foliage leaves arranged equidistant up the stem; lower leaves longish-lanceolate, 5.5–13 cm long and 1–3 cm wide, higher ones gradually getting smaller; inflorescence dense, at first pyramidal-spherical then lengthening as the flowers fade, 1.5–6 cm long and 1.5–3 cm wide; bracts membranous about as long as the ovaries; flowers purplish-pink, lip and sometimes the petals with purple dots; sepals 4.5–8 (–9) mm long, ovate, extended into a narrow point with a swollen club-shaped tip, inclined slightly forwards; lateral petals 3.5–6 (–7) mm long obliquely ovate; lip wide, wedge-shaped, 3.5–5 (–6) mm long, 3-lobed up to about half the length, lobes triangular to rhomboid; spur 2.5–3 mm long, slim.

Habitat: mountain meadows, poor grassland; mainly at the montane and subalpine levels; up to 2,500 m; on fresh to damp, deep base-rich soils.

Flowers: May–August. **Photos**: It, Prov. Brescia 14.6.71 (r), 12.6.74 (l).

Distribution: in the submeridional zone in Europe and south-west Asia and in the temperate zone in central Europe, particularly on the high mountains and the higher central mountains, seldom getting down to the lower levels; also in Caucasia. It is not clear whether the plants of the Bithynic Olympus near Bursa belong to this species or the following.

Floristic element: submediterranean pannonic (pontic) alpine carpatic s-subatlantic s-centraleuropean. **Countries**: Eur: SE ? Al, Ju, Bu, Rm, RK, S It, SW Hs, W Ga, C He, Au, Hu, Ge, Cz, Po, E RW; Asi: ?An.

Yellow Globe Orchid   *Traunsteinera sphærica* (Bieb.) Schlechter

Synonyms: *Orchis sphaerica* Bieb., *T. globosa subsp. sphaerica* (Bieb.) Soó

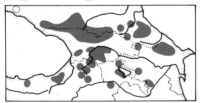

In appearance resembles *T. globosa* (tubers, stem height, spacing shape and size of leaves, shape of inflorescence, size of bracts); the sepals also are extended into the club-shaped tips; the main differences are the colour and size of the flowers: flowers cream-coloured to pale yellow, no spots; sepals 8–12.5 mm long; lateral petals 4.5–7.5 mm long; lip 5–9 mm long, middle lobe has a thread-like tip, side lobes often toothed; spur 3–5 mm long.

Habitat: mountain meadows, open coniferous woodland; in the montane and subalpine levels; 1,600–2,400 m; probably occupies similar sites to the other species. **Flowers**: June, July. **Photos**: An, Vil Trabzon 13.7.82 (l); An, Vil. Giresun 27.6.82 (r).

Distribution: widespread in Caucasia and spreading westwards into the pontic coastal mountains (northern Turkey); the Turkish area is not sufficiently well known since the species has been rather ignored; the most westerly report to date is in the Vilayet Giresun, but it may occur further to the west.

Floristic element: e-submediterranean.

Country: Asi: An.

Relationship: the genus comprises the two species described, it is rather isolated without close relatives.

Key to the *Traunsteinera* species:

1   Flowers pink to pale lilac; petals and lip with purple spots, sepals 4.5–9 mm long . . . . *T. globosa*

1*   Flowers pale yellow, without spots; sepals 8–12.5 mm long . . . . *T. sphaerica*

Traunsteinera

Bug Orchid Orchis coriophora L.

Synonyms: O. c. subsp. fragrans (Pollini) K. Richter, O. c. subsp. martrinii (Timb.-Lagr.) Nyman

Stem 15 – 60 cm tall with 1 – 2 scale leaves at the base; 3 – 4 (– 10) foliage leaves at soil level and a few sheathing the stem, basal leaves linear to lanceolate, 5 – 15 cm long and 0.5 – 4 cm wide; inflorescence dense and many-flowered; flowers brown, red, pink or greenish, smelling of bed bugs or vanilla; perianth segments growing together to form a beaked hood, lateral sepals 6.5 – 10 mm long, ovate – lanceolate, the middle one somewhat shorter; lateral petals 4 – 6 mm long linear; lip 3-lobed, 5 – 7 (– 10) mm long, side lobes toothed, shorter than the middle lobe; spur 4 – 9 mm long, cone-shaped, curving downwards.

Habitat: poor meadows, open woodland and scrub, occasionally in damp meadows; up to 2,500 m, on dry to damp base-rich soils.

Flowers: April – June. Photos: IJ, Golan 16.4.81 (l); Ge, Oberbayern 17.6.83 (c); Cy, Larnaca area 31.3.70 (r).

Distribution: in Europe, North Africa and the Near East from the meridional to the temperate zones; absent from the m-atlantic and n-subatlantic floristic regions. Also in Caucasia, Iraqi Kurdestan and northern and western Persia.

Floristic element: meridional submeridional temperate. Countries: Eur: SE Cr, Gr, Tu, Al, Ju, Bu, Rm, RK, S Me, Si, It, Sa, Co, SW Bl, Hs, Lu, W Ga, Be, +Ho, C He, Au, Ge, Hu, Cz, Po, RB, E RW, RE, RC; Asi: IJ, LS, Cy, An, AE; Afr: Li, Tn, Ag, Ma.

Variation: lip size, length of middle lobe, spur and beaked hood, leaf width and scent vary noticeably; extreme forms are obviously different; but with so many intermediates it is hardly possible to separate out subspecies.

Holy Orchid Orchis sancta L.

Synonym: O. coriophora subsp. sancta (L.) Hayek

Plant with 2 ellipsoid-spheroid tubers; stem 15 – 45 cm tall with 1 – 2 scale leaves at the base, 5 – 12 foliage leaves at ground level (at the time of flowering, these are often already wilting), a few leaves sheathing the stem; the basal leaves are 6 – 12 cm long and 0.8 – 1.3 cm wide; inflorescence more lax than that of O. coriophora; flowers pale purple, pink or carmine, outer surface of hood often greenish; perianth segments forming a long-beaked hood; lateral sepals 9 – 15 mm long, ovate, middle sepal slightly shorter; lateral petals 8 – 13 mm long, linear-lanceolate; lip 3-lobed, 8 – 15 mm long, middle lobe longish, narrow, pointed, clearly longer than the relatively larger, wider and large-toothed side lobes; spur 8 – 10 mm long, cone-shaped, pointing downwards and bent forwards.

Habitat: poor meadows and pastures; up to 500 m on dry calcareous soils. Flowers: April – June. Photos: An, Vil. Hatay 7.5.72 (r); IJ, Galilee 26.4.81 (l).

Distribution: eastern Mediterranean area; from the Aegean Islands through western and southern Turkey as far as the Levant.

● Floristic element: e-mediterranean. Countries: Eur: SE Gr; Asi: IJ, LS, Cy, An, AE.

Key to the species in the Coriophora group:

1 Central area of the lip with papillose hairs and purple spots; beak of hood about ¼ to ⅓ as long as the convex hind part (measured at the back along the middle sepal) .... O. coriophora

1* Lip bare and unspotted; beak length about ⅓ to ²/₅ that of the convex part of the hood .... O. sancta

Loose-Flowered Orchid *Orchis laxiflora* Lam.

1 cm

Plant with 2 ellipsoid to spheroid tubers; stem 20 – 60 (– 100) cm tall with 2 – 4 brown scale leaves and 3 – 8 foliage leaves, the latter spaced out up the stem, linear-lanceolate, 7 – 18 cm long and 0.8 – 2 cm wide; inflorescence lax; bracts reddish, somewhat longer than the ovaries; sepals 7 – 12 mm long and 3 – 5.5 mm wide, ovate, the central one pointing forward at an angle, the lateral ones almost vertical and turned outwards; lateral petals 6 – 9 mm long and 3 – 5 mm wide, ovate, inclined together; lip broader than long, 6 – 8.5 × 11 – 17 mm; spur pointing upwards at an angle, 10 – 19 mm long, slightly dilated at the end and often with a shallow bifurcation. **Habitat**: swamp-meadows; up to 1,500 m; in similar places to *O. palustris*. **Flowers**: March – July, some 2 weeks earlier than *O. palustris*.

Photos: Ga, Dept. Var 17.4.68 (r), 18.4.71 (l).
Distribution: Mediterranean region, in western Europe northwards as far as the Channel Islands and to western Switzerland.
● **Floristic element**: mediterranean submediterranean s-atlantic s-subatlantic.
Countries: Eur: SE Cr, Gr, Tu, Al, Ju, **S** Si, It, Sa, Co, **SW** ?Bl, Hs, Lu, **W** Ga, **C** He; **Asi**: Cy, An, AE.
Key to the species in the Laxiflora group:
1 Lip 3-lobed, middle lobe shorter than the side lobes, the latter turned down, intense purplish-red contrasting with the centre of the lip which is white and generally unspotted .... *O. laxiflora*
1* Lip 3-lobed, middle lobe longer than the side lobes, or 2-lobed (divided in the middle) or undivided; lateral lobes spreading out flat or at a slight angle, rarely turned right down; centre of lip a lighter shade of purplish-red than the side lobes, but generally not white, spotted . . .. *O. palustris*

Bog Orchis *Orchis palustris* Jacq.

Synonyms: *O. laxiflora subsp. palustris* (Jacq.) Bonnier & Layens, *O. l. subsp. elegans* (Heuffel) Soó, *O. pseudolaxiflora* Czerniakovska *O. robusta* (T. Stephenson) Gölz & Reinhard, *O. l. subsp. robusta (T. Stephenson) Sundermann, ?O. dinsmorei* (Schlechter) H. Baumann & Dafni

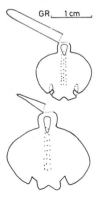

GR 1 cm

Similar in appearance to *O. laxiflora*; very variable in all characters; stem 15 – 100 (– 130) cm tall; leaves linear to lanceolate, 0.5 – 5 cm wide; inflorescence lax to dense; bracts shorter to much longer than the ovaries; sepals 7 – 15 mm long and 3 – 6 mm wide; lip shorter or longer than broad, 8.5 – 17 × 8 – 24 mm; spur may point downwards, horizontally or upwards, (5 –) 7 – 19.5 mm, straight or curved, tip rounded or pointed.
Habitat: swamp-meadows, fens; up to 1,200 m; on base-rich soils, salt tolerant. **Flowers**: April – July. **Photos**: Bl, Mallorca 2.4.75 (l); An, Vil. Eskisehir 26.5.72 (u/r); Ge, Oberbayern, 20.6.64 (l/r).
Distribution: in Europe, the Near East and North Africa from the meridional to the temperate zone, rare in the Mediterranean region and in oceanic Europe. Also in the meridional zone eastwards through Persia and Afghanistan to Turkestan and Saudi Arabia.
Floristic element: meridional submeridional temperate. **Countries: Eur: SE** Cr, Gr, Al, Ju, Bu, Rm, RK, **S** Si, It, Co, **SW** Bl, Hs, **W** Ga, Be, **C** He, Au, Hu, Ge, Cz, Po, **N** Su, **E** RW, RE, RC; **Asi**: IJ, LS, Cy, An, AE; **Afr**: Tn, Ag, Ma.
Variation: several of the variants are looked upon as separate species or subspecies (*see* list of synonyms).

Orchis

Early Purple Orchid   *Orchis mascula* L.

Problem: the classification of the *O. mascula* group with its many types has still not yet been clarified while the distribution of some of the species is uncertain. The key for the species and subspecies can be found on p242 (alternatives 5 – 8).

1.   *Orchis mascula* (in the strict sense)
Synonyms: *O. m. subsp. occidentalis* O. Schwarz, ?*O. m. subsp. wanjkowii* (Wulf) Soó.

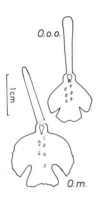

O.o.o.

O.m.

Basal leaves with large spots or unspotted, lanceolate, 1.5 – 3.5 cm wide; lateral sepals turned outwards (!), the front half mostly bent over, 7 – 15.5 mm long, blunt or pointed; lip 7 – 14.5 mm long and 8 – 18 mm wide, usually shorter than the 11 – 21 mm long fairly slim spur.

Habitat: poor grassland, open woodland, mountain meadows; on fresh to fairly dry base-rich (also lime-free) soils. **Flowers:** April – June. **Photos:** Su, Öland, end of 5.73 (u/l); Ge, Hessen 17.6.84 (u/r). **Distribution:** In western Europe and North Africa from the meridional to the boreal zones, Canary Islands (La Palma); the records for eastern and southeastern Europe, Caucasia and Persia unsure. ?

● **Floristic element** (provisional): w + c-mediter-ranean w + c-submediterranean atlantic subatlantic centraleuropean (?e-mediterranean ?e-submediterranean ?sarmatic). **Countries: Eur:** SE ?Gr, ?Al, ?Ju, ?Bu, ?RK, **S** ?Si, It, Co, **SW** Hs, Lu, **W** Ga, Be, Ho, Br, Hb, Fa (not Britain), **C** He, Au, Ge, Da, Cz, Po, RB, **N** Su, No, **E** ?RW, ?RC; **Afr:** Tn, Ag, Ma, Cl.

2.   *O. olbiensis* Barla *subsp. olbiensis*
Synonym: *O. mascula subsp. olbiensis* (Barla) Ascherson & Graebner
Stem 10 – 25 cm tall, 5 – 12 (– 20) flowers; basal leaves with or without spots, linear-lanceolate, up to 2 cm wide; lateral sepals turned outwards (!), 8 – 12 mm long, blunt; lip 7.5 – 12 mm long and 10.5 – 15.5 mm broad.
Habitat: open maquis, garrigue, poor grassland; up to 1,800 m; on dry calcareous soils, especially on rocky slopes. **Flowers:** March – June.
Photos: (p.117) Hs, Prov. Malaga 5.4.71 (u/l, l/l); Hs, Prov. Burgos 31.5.74 (r). **Distribution:** western mediterranean region, eastwards as far as Liguria, Corsica and Tunisia.
● **Floristic element:** w-mediterranean w + c-submediterranean. **Countries: Eur:** S It, Co, **SW** Bl, Hs, Lu, **W** Ga; **Afr:** Tn, Ag, Ma.

3.   *O. olbiensis subsp. ichnusae* (Corrias) Buttler
Synonym: *O. mascula subsp. ichnusae* Corrias
Similar to the subspecies *olbiensis*; differs in having a shorter straight spur.
Habitat: as for the subspecies *olbiensis*; up to 1,300 m. **Flowers:** April, May. **Photo:** (p116) Sa, Prov. Nuoro 20.5.76 (l); Sa, Prov. Cagliari 21.4.80 (r). **Distribution:** endemic on Sardinia; Gennargentu-massif and mountains near Iglesis. ● **Floristic element:** c-mediterranean. **Country: Eur:** S Sa.

4.   *O. signifera* Vest
Synonym: *O. mascula subsp. signifera* (Vest) Soó, *O. speciosa* Host
Stem 20 – 60 cm tall; the lower part, like the leaves, often with tiny dots and dashes; bracts as long as, to much longer than, the ovaries; lateral sepals not twisted (!), about 12 – 15 mm long, narrowly ovate, pointed, point straight or elongated and irregularly bent; lip edge with large teeth, often longer than the fairly thick spur.
Habitat: probably similar to that of *O. mascula*. **Flowers:** April – June.
Photos: It, Prov. Verona 4.6.84 (l/l)
Distribution: eastern Alps, Carpathians and the mountains of central Europe; perhaps also in the western Alps and mountains in the Balkan Peninsula and Corsica.
● **Floristic element** (provisional): alpine pannonic carpatic s-subatlantic s-centraleuropean. **Countries: Eur:** SE Ju, Rm, **S** It, **C** He, Au, Hu, Ge, Cz, ?Po.

O. mascula

Orchis

O. signifera

115

Madeiran Orchid *Orchis scopulorum* Summerhayes

Synonym: *O. mascula subsp. scopulorum* (Summerhayes) Sundermann

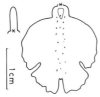

Plant with 2 ovoid-ellipsoidal tubers; stem up to 70 cm tall with 2–3 basal scale leaves, 3–5 foliage leaves forming a rosette and 3–5 sheathing the stem above; rosette leaves unspotted, elongated-elliptical, 9–16 cm long and 3–5 cm wide; inflorescence fairly lax, up to 10 cm long, 8–18 flowered; bracts about as long as the flowers; perianth pinkish-purple, lateral sepals ovate, 10–13 mm long and about 4 mm wide, spreading sideways with the upper surface pointing forwards; central sepal 8–10 mm long, forming a hood with the lateral petals which are of about the same length, but narrower; lip pale pink with dark spots, broadly elliptical to rounded, 14–13 mm long and 13–25 mm wide, almost flat, the edges coarsely toothed, 3-lobed with a narrow gap between the lobes, middle lobe broadly fan-shaped; spur 6–8 mm long, narrow, cylindrical, held horizontally or downwards.

Habitat: in rock clefts or in the small rubble of steep cliffs; on rocky slopes; 800–1,800 m; little is known about the habitat requirements of this species.

Flowers: May, June. **Photos**: MI, Madeira (Botanic Garden) 21.5.75.

Distribution: endemic to the island of Madeira. The species appears to be rare; it has only been found a few times and was first recognized as a separate species in 1959.

● **Floristic element**: madeiran. **Country**: Afr: MI.

Relationship: the species differs from the other members of the mascula group in having a short, horizontal spur. It has most in common with *O. signifera*. It remains to be investigated whether the species is an old relict or a recent development at a later period in the earth's history.

Orchis

Lange's Orchid   *Orchis langei* Lange Ex K. Richter

Synonyms: *O. mascula subsp. laxifloriformis* Rivas Goday, *O. hispanica* A. & C. Nieschalk, *O. mascula subsp. hispanica* (A. & C. Nieschalk) Soó.

Plant with 2 ellipsoidal-ovoid tubers; stem 30−55 cm tall, with 2 basal scale leaves, 2−5 (−10) foliage leaves in a ground rosette and 1−4 sheathing leaves up the stem; rosette leaves lanceolate, 5−15 cm long and 1−2 cm wide; inflorescence lax 10−25 cm long; with 10−35 flowers; bracts about as long as the ovaries; flowers pale purplish-red; lateral sepals ovate- 8−13 mm long and 3−6.5 mm wide, spreading sideways and upwards at an angle spreading sideways and upwards at an angle their upper surface directed forwards; central sepal 7−10.5 mm long, bent over the converging lateral petals which are of about the same length; lip without markings or with fine dots near the base, broader than long 7.5−13.5 × 10−18.5 mm, 3-lobes with a 2-cleft, forward-jutting middle lobe and turned-down side lobes; spur 9−15.5 mm long, slightly bent upwards, somewhat club-shaped at the end, 1−1.5 × as long as the lip.

Habitat: open oak and pine woods; up to 1,500 m on fairly dry, acid sand and slate soils; also in poor stony grassland over limestone.

Flowers: April−June. **Photos:** Hs, Prov. Teruel 30.5.82.

Distribution: western Mediterranean region; from the Pyrenees through the Iberian peninsula as far as the central Atlas mountains.

● **Floristic element:** w-mediterranean w-submediterranean.

Countries: Eur: SW Hs, **W** Ga, **Afr:** Ma

Pinewood Orchid   *Orchis pinetorum* Boiss. & Kotschy

Synonym: *O. mascula subsp. pinetorum* (Boiss. & Kotschy) E. G. & A. Camus & Bergon

Similar to *O. langei* in many qualitative characteristics (lax inflorescence, lateral sepals spreading sideways at an angle, flowers light-coloured, lip only slightly dotted, or not at all, with a protruding middle lobe) and quantitative characteristics (size of the perianth segments, lip and spur) − stem 20−60 cm tall, rosette leaves ovate − lanceolate, 6−15 cm long and 1.6−3.3 cm wide; side lobes of the lip sometimes spreading out flat but could be depressed at an angle, or completely.

Habitat: open broad-leaved and coniferous woods; scrub; woodland edges; up to 2,400 m; on fresh to fairly dry, probably base-rich soils.

Flowers: March−June. **Photos:** An, Vil. Bursa 27.5.72 (l), 9.5.83 (r).

Distribution: Asia Minor and the southern part of the Baltic peninsula; the area is insufficiently well known because the species has often not been distinguished from *O. mascula*; according to present knowledge the area stretches from the east as far as Samos and European Turkey, further west into Yugoslavian Macedonia and in the Pindus mountains. Also in Transcaucasia and Iraqi Kurdestan as well as in northern, western and southern Persia.

Floristic element: e-mediterranean oriental e-submediterranean. **Countries: Eur: SE** Gr, Tu, Ju, ?RK; **Asi:** LS, An, AE.

Key for species in *O. pinetorum* group:

1   Lip bent into the shape of a sheep's nose at an angle of 50−70°; leaves mostly heavily spotted, single plants in a population may be unspotted .... *O. langei*

1*   Lip only weakly bent into the sheep's nose shape − at an angle not more than 30° or not bent at all lengthwise; leaves often unspotted but also with dots or dashes .
.... *O. pinetorum*

Orchis

Pale-Flowered Orchid *Orchis pallens* L.

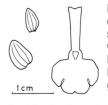

Plant with 2 ovoid-ellipsoidal tubers; stem 15 – 40 cm tall with 2 – 3 basal scale leaves, 4 – 6 foliage leaves forming a ground rosette and 1 – 2 leaves sheathing the lower half of the stem; basal leaves unspotted, elliptic to ovate 6 – 12 cm long and 1.5 – 4 cm wide; inflorescence dense and many-flowered; bracts about as long as the ovaries; flowers pale yellow with a scent of elderflowers; lateral sepals broadly ovate, bent, 6 – 9 mm long and 3.5 – 5 mm wide, held upright vertically or at an angle and turned outwards; centre sepal 5 – 7.5 mm long, bent over the slightly shorter curved lateral petals; lip unmarked, almost flat or folded lengthwise or across, broader than long, 6 – 11 × 7 – 14 mm, 3-lobed with split middle lobe; spur curving upwards, rarely horizontal, 7 – 14 mm long, blunt.

Habitat: mixed deciduous woods, more rarely coniferous woods and poor grassland, at higher elevation also in meadows, mostly in semi-shade; up to 2,400 m; on fresh calcareous soils. Flowers: April – June. Photos: Ge, Südwürttemberg 14.5.81 (l), 2.5.65 (r).

Distribution: In Europe and the Near East in the submeridional and temperate zones; in Greece and Anatolia into the meridional zone; absent from atlantic Europe; also found in Caucasia. Floristic element: e-mediterranean submediterranean pannonic s-subatlantic s-centraleuropean. Countries: Eur: SE Gr, Al, Ju, Bu, Rm, RK, S It, Co, SW ?Hs, W Ga, C He, Au, Hu, Ge, Cz, Po; Asi: An.

Problem: red-flowered plants with the characteristics of *O. pallens* are hybrids. All yellow- and red-flowered species of the mascula group are inter-fertile. Whenever two species are growing together, you have to reckon with hybrids; in these, the red colour is dominant.

Provence Orchid *Orchis provincialis* Lam. & Dc.

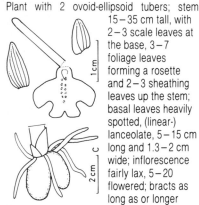

Plant with 2 ovoid-ellipsoid tubers; stem 15 – 35 cm tall, with 2 – 3 scale leaves at the base, 3 – 7 foliage leaves forming a rosette and 2 – 3 sheathing leaves up the stem; basal leaves heavily spotted, (linear-) lanceolate, 5 – 15 cm long and 1.3 – 2 cm wide; inflorescence fairly lax, 5 – 20 flowered; bracts as long as or longer than the ovaries; flowers light yellow; lateral sepals ovate, 9 – 14 mm long and 4 – 6 mm wide, held vertically upwards, most twisted and with a wavy edge; centre sepal 7 – 11 mm long, inclined over the lateral petals which are of about the same length; lip shaped like a sheep's nose (seen from the side the middle lobe is bent downwards at an angle of about 60°), flecked with red, broader than long, 8 – 13 × 11 – 18.5 mm weakly 3-lobed with a split middle lobe and down-turned side lobes; spur curved upwards, 13 – 19 mm long with a blunt end vaguely club-shaped.

Habitat: deciduous and coniferous woods, maquis, also occasionally up in mountain meadows; to 1,700 m; on fresh, fairly acid to fairly basic soils.

Flowers: April, May. Photos: Ga, Dept. Var 17.4.68 (l), 18.4.71 (r).

Distribution: Mediterranean region, concentrated in the submeridional zone; also in Transcaucasia. Floristic element: c + e-mediterranean submediterranean.

Countries: Eur: SE Cr, Gr, ?Tu, Al, Ju, Bu, RK, S Si, It, Sa, Co, SW ?Bl, Hs, Lu, W Ga, C He; Asi: An, AE.

Problem: red-flowered plants with the sheep's nose lip are hybrids.

Orchis

121

Sparse-flowered Orchid *Orchis pauciflora* Ten.

Synonym: *O. provincialis subsp. pauciflora*
(Ten.) E. G. & A. Camus & Bergon

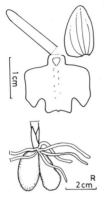

Plant with 2 ovoid-ellipsoid tubers; stem 10–30 cm tall; basal leaves 4–9 unspotted, narrow-lanceolate, 4–7 cm long and 0.8–1.7 cm wide, sometimes sickle-shaped. inflorescence fairly lax, mostly few flowers (3–7 flowers), rarely up to 15 flowers, bracts as long as, or longer than, the ovaries; perianth segments pale yellow; lateral sepals 10–14.5 mm long and 5.5–9.5 mm wide, held up almost vertically and turned outwards; the central sepal 7.5–11.5 mm long inclined over the somewhat shorter lateral petals; lip a darker yellow than the other perianth segments, with small brownish-red spots, broader than long, (9–) 10–14 × (12–) 13–19 mm, weakly 3-lobed with protruding split middle lobe with irregularly toothed edges, slightly or more tightly folded length-wise (then appearing narrow); spur turned upwards, long cylindrical blunt.

Habitat: poor grassland, garrigue; up to 1,700 m on dry, stony, always calcareous soils. Flowers: March, April. Photos: It, Prov. Pisa 16.4.83 (l); Cr, Nomos Rethymnon 31.3.72 (r)

Distribution: central and eastern Mediterranean region; westwards to northern Corsica, eastwards to Thrace and Crete; the records for the eastern Aegean Islands and western Anatolia all appear to belong to *O. provincialis*.
● Floristic element: c + e-mediterranean c-submediterranean. Countries: Eur: SE Cr, Gr, Al, Ju, S Si, It, Co.

Algerian Orchid *Orchis laeta* Steinheil

Synonym: *O. provincialis var. laeta* (Steinheil) Mairer & Weiller

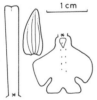

Similar to *O. pauciflora*; the amount of variation within each species is the same regarding stem height, leaf and flower numbers, lip shape and folding, as well as the shape and position of the spur; basal leaves lanceolate, 6–19 cm long and 1.5–2 cm wide; lateral sepals 9–13.5 mm long and 4.5–7 mm wide, vertically upright, sometimes crossing; central sepal 7.5–11 mm long; lip somewhat darker yellow than the pale perianth segments (but less intensively coloured than *O. pauciflora*), with small red dots, 8.5–13 mm long and 11.5–17.5 mm broad.

Habitat: open oak and cedar woods, mountain meadows; up to 1,500 m; on fresh soils over silicate rock. Flowers: February – April.

Photos: Tn, Kroumirie 30.3.72 (l); Ag, Prov. Algiers 7.4.72 (r).
Distribution: Tell-Atlas; from north-western Tunisia to the vicinity of Blida. ● Floristic element: w-mediterranean. Countries: Afr: Tn, Ag.

Key to the species of the *Orchis pauciflora* group:

1   Lateral sepals broadly ovate, 1.5–2 × as long as wide; spur 15–25 mm long, 1.5–2 × as long as the lip; lip a bright yellow to orange-yellow ...*O. pauciflora*

1*   Lateral sepals ovate, 2–2.5 × as long as wide; spur 20–31 mm long, generally more than double the length of the lip; lip pale yellow .... *O. laeta*

Problem: the two species are treated here as independent. Whether they deserve this status is still to be confirmed. Possibly the north African plants should be considered as a subspecies, or even only as variants of *O. pauciflora*.

Orchis

Anatolian Orchid   *Orchis anatolica* Boiss.

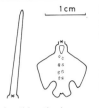

Plant with 2 spheroid-ovoid tubers; stem 10 − 50 cm tall, with 1 − 2 basal scale leaves, 2 − 5 foliage leaves forming a rosette and 1 − 2 sheathing the lower part of the stem; rosette leaves lanceolate to narrowly ovate, (3 −) 8 − 13 cm long and (0.8 −) 1.5 − 3 cm wide, mostly spotted; inflorescence lax, 2 − 15 flowered; flowers pink to purplish-red; sepals ovate (− elliptic), 8 − 10 mm long and 4 − 5 mm wide, the lateral ones often with a green centre, spreading sideways at an angle, the central one bent over the 6 − 8 mm long curving lateral petals; lip with a paler, dotted central band, somewhat broader than long, 8 − 17 × 8 − 22 mm, deeply 3-lobed with a split middle lobe, folded lengthwise; spur 15 − 25 mm long, straight or curved, mostly pointing steeply upwards, rarely horizontal, slightly flattened at the entrance, evenly thinning towards the back, rarely with a somewhat club-shaped tip.

Habitat: open woodland and garrigue, prefers growing in semi-shade; up to 1,700 m on dry, base-rich soils. **Flowers:** March − May. **Photos:** An, Vil. Icel 5.5.72 (c); An, Vil. Izmir 21.3.78 (l); Cy, Troodos region 1.4.70 (r).

Distribution: eastern Mediterranean region and in neighbouring southern Anatolia; the species has its western boundary in the Aegean islands; also joining with the Turkish presence in Iraqi, Kurdestan and western Persia. **Floristic element:** e-mediterranean oriental e-submediterranean. **Countries: Eur:** SE Cr, Gr; **Asi:** IJ, LS, Cy, An, AE.

Variation: the species shows a good deal of variation. Tall, many-flowered plants with wide leaves and large flowers are described from Crete as *O. a. subsp. sitiaca* Renz and from Cyprus as *O. a. subsp. troodi* Renz. These may be variants with a local distribution.

Fan-Lipped Orchid   *Orchis collina* Banks & Solander

Synonyms: *O. saccata* Ten., *O. fedtschenkoi* Czerniakovska, *O. leucoglossa* O. Schwartz

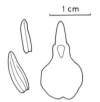

Plant with 2 ovoid tubers; stem 10 − 40 cm tall, strong, with 2 scale leaves at the base, 2 − 6 foliage leaves forming a rosette and up to 4 leaves sheathing and surrounding the stem; rosette leaves broadly lanceolate, 3 − 12 cm long and 1 − 3.5 cm wide, inflorescence lax, narrow-cylindrical, 4 − 20 flowered; bracts broadly lanceolate, the lower ones longer than the ovaries; perianth segments green, mostly tinged with brown (− violet); sepals elongated-lanceolate, 9 − 12 mm long and 3 − 4 mm wide, the lateral ones pointing almost vertically and turned to the outside, the central one forming a hood with the 7 − 10 mm long lateral petals; lip elliptical, 9 − 12 mm long and 8 − 11 mm wide, undivided often crenate in front, the sides finely notched and wavy, brownish-red, lilac-red, pink, occasionally greenish or whitish ('leucoglossa'); spur 5 − 7 (− 10) mm long, pointing downwards at an angle, paler than the lip.

Habitat: open woodland, garrigue, poor grassland; up to 1,300 m; on dry, mostly calcareous soils. **Flowers:** February − April. **Photos:** Cr, Nomos Rethimnon, 10.4.81 (l); Hs, Prov. Malaga 5.4.71 (r).

Distribution: Mediterranean region, concentrated towards the south, less common in the northern submediterranean area, in southeastern Turkey penetrating into the oriental region. Also in Caucasia through northern Persia to Turkomania and to west and south Persia.

Floristic element: mediterranean oriental submediterranean. **Countries: Eur: SE** Cr, Gr, Tu, ?Al, **S** Me, Si, It, Sa, **SW** Bl, Hs, **W** Ga; **Asi:** IJ, LS, Cy, An, AE; **Afr:** Li, Tn, Ag, Ma.

Orchis

125

Spitzel's Orchid *Orchis spitzelii* Koch

Synonyms: *O. viridifusca* Albov. *O. patens subsp. orientalis* (Reichenb. fil.) K. Richter, *O. patens var. atlantica* Batt. & Trabut

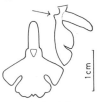

Plant with 2 longish ovoid tubers; stem 20–40 (–60) cm tall; basal foliage leaves 2–7, ovate–lanceolate, 6–12 cm long and 1.6–3.3 cm wide, unspotted; inflorescence usually dense, 10–35-flowered; perianth segments curving to form an open hood, but the lateral sepals may be somewhat raised; sepals a uniform olive-green with a reddish tinge and spotted, ovate 7–11 mm long and 3–5 mm wide; lateral petals 5.5–8 mm long; lip pink to purplish-red, clearly or faintly richly spotted, broader than long, 9–12 × 11–18 mm, deeply 3-lobed with a divided middle lobe, folded lengthwise, the two sides stepped near the spur entrance (seen from the side); spur, cone-shaped, 6–10 mm long and 3–4 mm thick, curving gently downwards, pale colour.

Habitat: open woodland, dwarf mountain pine woods, mountain meadows; mostly between 1,000 and 2,100 m, rare below this; on fresh to damp base-rich (but not always calcareous) soils. **Flowers:** April–July. **Photos:** An, Vil. Denizli 17.5.83 (r); Ga, Dept. Jura 20.6.83 (l).

Distribution: in the meridional and sub-meridional zones of Europe, North Africa and the Near East, further north in the Alps and as a post-Ice Age relict on Gotland; formerly near Nagold (Württemberg). The area is disjuncted, the parts being separated by large holes; somewhat more numerous in the Pyrenees and the Balkans, in the eastern Alps and in outer Anatolia; also in the Transcaucasus.

Floristic element: mediterranean oriental submediterranean alpine (subatlantic) n-centraleuropean. **Countries:** Eur: SE Gr, Al, Ju, Bu, **S** It, **SW** Hs, **W** Ga, **C** Au + Ge, **N** Su; **Asi:** LS, An; **Afr:** Ag, Ma.

Canary Islands Orchid *Orchis canariensis* Lindley

Synonym: *O. patens subsp. canariensis* (Lindley) Sunding & Kunkel

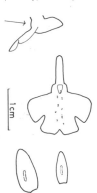

Plant with 2 ovoid tubers; stem 15–40 (–60) cm tall, with 2–3 basal scale leaves, 3–5 foliage leaves in a rosette and 1 or more sheathing the stem higher up; rosette leaves lanceolate, pointed, 5.5–18 cm long and 1.8–4 cm wide, unspotted; inflorescence fairly short, dense, 5–20-flowered; bracts somewhat longer than the ovaries; dimensions of flower parts about the same as those of *O. patens* (*see* p128); sepals ovate with a small central green area surrounded by a wider coloured zone, sometimes without the green, always without spots, the laterals held up at a steep angle, the centre one bending over the lateral petals, which come together in a hood; lip whitish to pale violet-pink with darker markings, deeply 3-lobed with a divided middle lobe, almost flat, the edges toothed to almost smooth, the two sides straight near the spur entrance (seen from the side); spur broad, cone-shaped or sack-like, pointing upwards at an angle extending the plane of the lip, stigma almost parallel with it, not visible from the front.

Habitat: in biotopes with a humid local atmosphere, in pine woods, also enjoys gulleys in steep rock faces on narrow strips of grass; 800–1,400 m, in the trade-wind cloud zone; on slightly acid volcanic rocks. **Flowers:** February–April. **Photos:** CI, Tenerife 1.4.79.

Distribution: the species occupies the west part of the Canary archipelago, it is absent from Lanzarote and Fuerteventura.

● **Floristic element:** canarian.

Country: Afr: CI.

Orchis

Green-Spotted Orchid *Orchis patens* Desf.

Synonym: *O. brevicornis* Viv.

Plant with 2 ovoid tubers; stem 25−45 (−70) cm tall, with 2 basal scale leaves, 3−5 (−9) foliage leaves in a rosette and 1−3 leaves sheathing the stem higher up; rosette leaves linear-lanceolate, 7−20 cm long and 0.8−2.3 cm wide, spotted or unspotted; inflorescence 6−30 (−40) flowered, lax; bracts about as long as the ovaries; sepals ovate with a green spotted centre and a coloured outer zone (8−) 9−11 mm long and 4−5 mm wide, the lateral one held up at a steep angle; lateral petals ovate, 6.5−8 mm long; lip pale to intensive purplish-pink with a paler, spotted central area, broader than long, 9−11 × 11−14 mm, deeply 3-lobed with a divided middle lobe, folded lengthwise, the two sides near the spur entrance stepped (seen from the side); lip base cut with 'V'-shaped notch near spur mouth; spur 6−8 mm long and 4−4.5 mm thick, rounded, held horizontally or downwards.

Habitat: open sweet chestnut, oak and cedar woods; woodland edges; poor grassland; to 1,600 m in the Atlas, up to 600 m in Liguria; on fresh base-rich soils, acid soils too in Liguria.

Flowers: March−June. Photos: It, Prov. Genoa 12.5.73 (l); 11.6.71 (r).

Distribution: Liguria (Prov. Savona, Genoa, La Spezia), Tell-Atlas (Algeria, Tunisia). The unusual distribution area has two centres, one on either side of the Mediterranean sea; none have been reported from the islands between. The 'messinic model' may provide an explanation − a hypothesis, supported by geological factors, according to which the Mediterranean was largely dried out some 5−6 million years ago, thus providing the opportunity for plants to 'wander' across.

● Floristic element: w-mediterranean c-submediterranean. Countries: Eur: S It; Afr: Tn, Ag.

Cretan Orchid *Orchis prisca* Hautzinger

Synonyms: *O. patens* subsp. *nitidifolia* Teschner, *O. spitzelii* subsp. *nitidifolia* (Teschner) Soó, *O. Wildhaber patens* subsp.

falcicalcarata Wildhaber
Plant with 2 ovoid tubers; stem 15−40 cm tall, with 3−7 foliage leaves in a basal rosette and 2−3 sheathing the stem higher up, rosette leaves lanceolate (−elliptic), 6−17 cm long and 1.6−2.9 cm wide, unspotted; inflorescence lax, 5−25 flowered; bracts about as long as the ovaries; flowers a similar colour to those of *O. patens*; lateral sepals 8−13 mm long and 4−5.5 mm wide, held obliquely or steeply upwards; centre sepal 7−11 mm long, lying almost on top of the somewhat shorter lateral petals (not so close in *O. patens*); lip 12−16 mm long, folded lengthwise, the middle lobe exceeds the side lobes by 3−4 mm, the two sides are stepped near the spur entrance; spur 7−11 mm long and 2−3.4 mm thick, directed downwards.

Habitat: open pine woods, mixed pine woods with cypress or maple; 600 − 1,700 m; on dry, thin, base-rich soils over limestone.

Flowers: April, May. Photos: Cr. Nomos Lasithi 25.4.74 (l), 23.5.75 (r).

Distribution: species endemic to Crete, known from the mountains on the western side (White Mountains), in the central part (Ida) and the eastern part (Thriptis).

● Floristic element: e-mediterranean.
Country: Eur: S Cr.

Key to the species of the *Orchis patens* group:

1   Spur straight, saccate to broadly conical, at most 2.5 × as long as thick (vertical cross-section taken close behind the spur entrance), generally though clearly shorter .... *O. patens*

1* Spur curved downwards or, more rarely, almost straight, narrowly conical, 3−4 × as long as thick .... *O. prisca*

129

Pink Butterfly Orchid   *Orchis papilionacea* L.

Synonyms: *O. rubra* Murray, *O. p. subsp. rubra* (Murray) Sundermann, *O. p. var. rubra* (Murray) Brot., *O. p. var. grandiflora* Boiss., *O. caspia* Trautv., *O. p. subsp. bruhnsiana* (Gruner) Soó, ?*O. melchifafii* Hautzinger

Plant with spherical-ovoid tubers; stem 15 – 40 (– 50) cm tall, with 2 – 3 basal scale leaves, 3 – 8 foliage leaves in a basal rosette and 2 – 5 leaves sheathing the stem higher up, rosette leaves linear-lanceolate, 4 – 18 cm long and 0.5 – 1.5 cm wide, unspotted; inflorescence dense to fairly lax, 4 – 14 flowered; bracts coloured, as long as or longer than the ovaries; perianth segments pointing forwards, not forming an enclosed hood, with dark veins; lateral sepals 8 – 22 mm long and 4 – 7.5 mm wide, centre sepal somewhat shorter; lateral petals 6 – 16.5 mm long; lip undivided, usually crenate in front, from a stem-like base ('claw') it broadens out into a wedge-shape or wide fan-shape ('limb'), 9 – 26 mm long and 7 – 23 mm broad; spur 8 – 14 mm long, cone-shaped, horizontal at first, curving downwards.

Habitat: poor grassland, garrigue, open woodland and maquis; up to 1,800 m; on fairly dry, base-rich (but also lime-free) soils.

Flowers: February – May. **Photos:** Co, Dept. Corse du Sud 7.4.81 (u/l); It, Prov. Cosenza 9.4.81 (u/l); It, Prov. Como 19.5.69 (c/l); IJ, Galilee 12.4.81 (l/r); Ga, Dept. Alpes Maritimes 29.4.84 (c/r); An, Vil. Mugla 22.3.78 (l/l).

Distribution: Mediterranean region; northwards as far as the southern edge of the Alps and to the Wallachei. Also in Caucasia.

Floristic element: mediterranean sub-mediterranean danubian. **Countries:** Eur: **SE** Cr, Gr, Tu, Al, Ju, Bu, Rm, **S** Si, It, Sa, Co, **SW** Bl, Hs, Lu, **W** Ga; **Asi:** IJ, LS, Cy, An, AE; **Afr:** Li, Tn, Ag, Ma.

Problem: the species has a large number of different forms and contains several morphological races, each of which seems to have its own area of distribution. At present, it is impossible to decide whether this range of types is differentiated into various subspecies (or even independent species). A reappraisal should take into account the whole of the distribution area. Here the different types are briefly introduced by describing the characters of the 'typical' form. Intermediate forms, which are not uncommon, are not taken into account. Flower characteristics are used in separating the types, especially the shape and colour of the lip and the size of the flower.

1. Type 'papilionacea' in the strict sense ('rubra') (photos u/l, u/r)
Flowers of average size; lateral sepals 14 – 19 mm long; lip (9 –) 12 – 17 (– 22) mm long; limb wide, wedge-shaped, not marked, reddish-violet, whitish near the 'claw'. Occurrence: mainly in the central Mediterranean region; single reports from Algeria, central Greece, Anatolia.

2. Type 'grandiflora' (photo c/l)
Flowers large, lateral sepals 16 – 22 mm long; lip 15 – 26 mm long, limb broad, fan-shaped, often heart-shaped near the base, pink to pinkish-violet, fan-shaped markings. Occurrence: western and southern central Mediterranean region (Iberian Peninsula, southern France, North Africa, Sicily, southern Italy). Similar plants are found in the eastern Mediterranean region (Balkan Peninsula, Aegean, Anatolia), (photo l/l). They possess flowers of similar colour, but of average size corresponding more to those of 'rubra'; limb wide, fan-shaped.

3. Type 'caspia' ('bruhnsiana') (photo l/r)
Flowers small, lateral sepals 8 – 13 mm long; lip 9 – 12 mm long, limb broad, wedge-shaped, pale pink in the middle, pinkish-violet round the edges, with fan-shaped markings. Occurrence: Levant, Caucasia.

Orchis

131

Branciforti's Orchid *Orchis brancifortii* Biv.

Synonym: *O. quadripunctata var. brancifortii* (Biv.) Boiss.

1cm

Similar to *O. quadripunctata*; on average shorter with smaller flowers, flowers open more widely (sepals and lip are all in one plane; in the other species they form an obtuse angle with one another) — stem 10–25 cm tall; lateral sepals 3–5 mm long; lip 3.5–5.5 mm long with 2 spots in front of and 2 to the sides of the spur entrance, these are sometimes fused in pairs; middle lobe rectangular, about twice as long as broad, pointed in front; spur horizontal, bent into a slight S-shape.

Habitat: the species occurs in similar sites to *O. quadripunctata*; 200–1,300 m; mainly over limestone. **Flowers:** April–June. **Photos:** Si, Prov. Palermo 10.4.79 (l); Sa, Prov. Nuoro 20.5.76 (r).

Distribution: endemic to Sicily and Sardinia; the species occupies an approximately 30 km wide strip along the north coast of Sicily and only occasionally penetrates further inland; on Sardinia it is confined to the east coast and a maximum of about 20 km inland. ● **Floristic element:** c-mediterranean. **Countries: Eur: S** Si, Sa.

Key to the species of the quadripunctata group:

1 Side lobes of the lip about the same size (area) or larger than the middle lobe, rounded-ovate to semi-circular, the outside edges curling inwards . . . .
. . . . *O. quadripunctata*

1* Side lobes smaller than the middle lobe, narrowly rectangular (tooth-like), spreading at an angle, with straight edges . . . .
. . . . *O. brancifortii*

Four-spotted Orchid *Orchis quadripunctata* Ten.

Plant with 2 ellipsoidal or spherical tubers; stem 10–30 (–40) cm tall, with 1–2 sheathing scale leaves at the base, 2–6 foliage leaves in a basal rosette and 1–2 long sheathing leaves up the stem; rosette leaves linear to narrow-elliptic, 4–12 cm long and 1–2 (–3) cm wide, spotted or unspotted; inflorescence dense to lax, cylindrical, 8–35 flowered; bracts shorter than or as long as the ovaries; flowers pink to purplish-red; sepals spreading widely, almost arranged on one plane, ovate, the lateral ones 4–7 mm long and 1.5–4 mm wide, the middle one somewhat shorter; lateral petals 2–5 mm long, curved to form a hood; lip 4–7.5 mm long and 6–11 mm wide, very variable, deeply 3-lobed to almost entire, in the centre, white with 2–5 spots in front and 2 (–4) at the sides of the spur entrance; middle lobe longer or shorter than the side lobes, rounded or divided in front; spur 8–14 mm long, turned downwards, often gently turned up at the end, very narrow and scarcely wider at the start.

Habitat: poor grassland, maquis, garrigue; up to 1,500 m; on dry and stony soils, often over limestone. **Flowers:** March–June. **Photos:** Gr, Nomos Attica 10.4.82 (l); Cy, region of Limassol, 1.4.83 (r).

Distribution: eastern and central Mediterranean region, westwards to southern Italy (Apulia, Campania), northwards to Dalmatia, eastwards to western Anatolia and Cyprus. The records for Sicily and Sardinia probably all refer to *O. brancifortii*. ● **Floristic element:** c + e-mediterranean   c-submediterranean. **Countries: Eur: SE** Cr, Gr, Al, Ju, **S** It; **Asi:** Cy, An, Ae.

Orchis

Boryi's Orchid *Orchis boryi* Reichenb. fil.

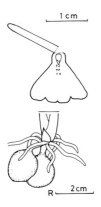

Plant with 2 spherical tubers; stem 10 – 35 cm tall, with 2 – 4 basal scale leaves, 4 – 9 foliage leaves forming a rosette and 2 – 6 leaves sheathing the stem; rosette leaves linear-lanceolate, 5 – 8 cm long and 0.5 – 1 cm wide, unspotted; inflorescence fairly lax, 5 – 15 flowered; bracts tinged with red, rolled around the ovaries and about half as long as them; sepals inclined forward, but not forming a closed hood, broadly ovate, more intensely coloured than the lip, the lateral ones 7.5 – 10 mm long and 4 – 5.5 mm wide, the central one ¹/₅ shorter; lateral petals curving inwards 5.5 – 7.5 mm long; lip with wedge-shaped base, slightly 3-lobed, often with a wavy edge, middle lobe somewhat longer than the sides; lip paler in the centre than around the edges, with 2 rows of 1 – 3 dots; spur narrow-cylindrical, slightly curved, horizontal or pointing downwards.

Habitat: open woodland and maquis, garrigue, poor grassland; up to 1,200 m; on fresh to damp soils, over limestone or slate. **Flowers:** April, May. **Photos:** Cr, Nomos Lasithi 20.4.81 (l); Cr, Nomos Rethimnon 2.4.66 (r). **Distribution:** eastern Mediterranean region; in southern Greece (especially on the Peloponese) and on several islands in the Aegean (Skiathos, Euboea, Kithnos, Crete) ● **Floristic element:** e-mediterranean.

Countries: Eur: SE Cr, Gr.

Israeli Orchid *Orchis israelitica* H. Baumann & Dafni

Stem 10 – 30 cm tall; basal leaves 3 – 6 lanceolate, 5 – 12 cm long and 1.5 – 3 cm wide, unspotted; inflorescence fairly lax, 5 – 20 flowered; bracts tinged with pink, about ²/₃ as long as the ovaries; sepals inclined forward (somewhat wider than in *O. boryi*), concave, whitish to pink, greenish in the middle, the lateral one 6 – 8 mm long and 3 – 4.5 mm wide, the central one and the lateral petals 4.5 – 6.5 mm long; lip clearly 3-lobed, middle lobe longer and mostly also wider than the side lobes, 2 or 4 dark purple dots near the base of the lip; spur narrow-cylindrical, slightly curved, horizontal, pink.

Habitat: garrigue; 400 – 800 m; on calcareous soils. **Flowers:** February – April. **Photos:** IJ, Galilee 12.4.81.

Distribution: discovered in 1978, the species is endemic in Israel. It is found within a small area in Lower and Upper Galilee. ● **Floristic element:** e-mediterranean. **Country: Asi:** IJ.

Key to the species of the Boryi group:
1   Flowers mostly intense lilac-red, rarely pinkish-lilac; lip (flattened out) 8 – 10 mm long and 9.5 – 12 mm wide; spur 13 – 17 mm long . . . . *O. boryi*
1*   Flowers whitish to pale lilac-pink; lip 5 – 8 mm long and 7 – 10 mm wide; spur 11 – 14 mm long . . . .*O. israelitica*

In both species the flowers open from the top downwards.

The species are clearly closely related. A large number of plants must be examined before it can be decided whether they can retain their status as independent species. It may perhaps be preferable to consider them as subspecies (geographical races), as indicated by the overlapping of the range of variation in some characters.

Orchis

135

Green-Winged Orchid *Orchis morio* L.

Problem: The *O. morio* group has numerous forms and requires a thorough reappraisal. The classification is provisional.

Key to the identification of the subspecies:

1   Lip yellowish-white or pale lilac-pink, unspotted; spur lilac-pink
     2. *O. m. subsp. syriaca*

1*   Lip of a different colour, often intense purple; if white or pink then with spots on the central part, or a white spur − 2

2   Lip (spread out) at most 1.4 × as broad as long, 6 − 9 mm wide; spur 6 − 10 mm long
     3. *O. m. subsp. albanica*

2*   Lip at least 1.5 × as broad as long, 9 − 18 mm wide; spur 8 − 14 mm long
     1. *O. m. subsp. morio*

Habitat: open woodland, maquis, garrigue, poor meadows; on dry to variably damp basic soils.

1.   *O. m. subsp. morio* Stem 10 − 50 cm tall; foliage leaves lanceolate, 2.5 − 12 cm long and 0.5 − 2 cm wide; inflorescence 5 − 25 flowered; middle lobe shorter or longer than the side lobe; spur horizontal to pointing upwards. **Variation:** 2 races are often distinguished, but the separation is not clear-cut. 'Morio' variant: lip 6 − 10 mm long and 10 − 18 mm wide; sepals 7.5 − 11 mm long; spur 9.5 − 14 mm long; plants robust, many-flowered; flowers often intense purple, but also lighter; more northerly distribution. 'picta' variant (*O. m. subsp. picta* [Loisel.] K. Richter): lip 4 − 6.5 mm long and 8.5 − 12 mm wide; sepals 6 − 8.5 mm long; spur 8 − 11.5 mm long; plants graceful, few-flowered; flowers often pink to pale violet but may be darker; more southerly distribution.

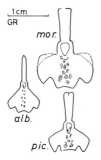

Habitat: to 2,000 m. **Flowers:** February − May. **Photos:** It, Prov. Foggia 11.4.82 (u/u/l); Ga, Dept. Var 12.5.72 (u/l/l); An, Vil. Izmir 21.3.78 (u/r). **Distribution:** in Europe, North Africa and the Near East from the meridional to the temperate zones, to continental eastern Europe.

Floristic element: meridional submeridional temperate. **Countries: Eur:** SE   Gr, Tu, Al, Ju, Bu, Rm, RK, **S**   Me, Si, It, Sa, Co, **SW**   Bl, Hs, Lu, **W**   Ga, Be, Ho, Br, Hb, **C**   He, Au, Hu, Ge, Da, Cz, Po, RB, **N**   Su, No, **E**   RW, RC; **Asi:** An, AE, Cy; **Afr:** Ma.

2.   *O. m. subsp. syriaca* E. G. & A. Camus & Bergon:

Synonyms: *O. syriaca* (E. G. & A. Camus & Bergon) H. Baumann & Künkele, *O. picta subsp. libani* Renz. Stem 10 − 25 cm tall; inflorescence short, 4 − 14 flowered; flower dimensions as 'picta'. **Habitat:** up to 1,300 m. **Flowers:** February up − May. **Photos:** (*see* p139) Cy, Limassol area 15.3.84 (u/l); Cy, Kyrenia area 24.3.83 (u/r). **Distribution:** coastal strip from southern Turkey to the Levant, Cyprus.

● **Floristic element:** e-mediterranean. **Countries: Asi:** ?IJ, LS, Cy, An.

3.   *O. m. subsp. albanica* (Gölz & Reinhard) Buttler:

Synonym: *O. albanica* Gölz & Reinhard Stem 15 − 30 cm tall, graceful; inflorescence 5 − 15 flowered, sepals 5.5 − 8 mm long; lip 4.5 − 7 mm long, mostly pale flowers. **Habitat:** up to 1,500 m. **Flowers:** April − June. **Photos:** Al, Prov. Lushnjë 18.5.80 (l/l); Al, Prov. Vlorë 14.4.82   (l/r).   **Distribution:**   Albania, Montenegro. ● Floristic element (c-mediterranean) c-submediterranean. **Countries: Eur:** SE Al, Ju.

Long-spurred Orchid   *Orchis longicornu* Poiret illustrated on p138

Stem 10 − 35 cm tall, 5 − 15 flowered; lip broader than long, 6 − 8 × 12 − 18 mm; spur 11 − 16 mm long, pointing upwards.

Habitat, flowering times: as *O. m. subsp. morio.* **Photos:** (*see* p138): Si, Prov. Palermo 29.3.67 (l); Bl, Mallorca 7.3.75 (r).

Distribution: western Mediterranean; Balearics to Sicily and Calabria, Corsica (southern part) to North Africa. ● Floristic element: w + c-mediterranean c-submediterranean. **Countries: Eur:** S   Me, Si, It, Sa, Co, SW   Bl, W   ?Ga; **Afr:** Tn, Ag.

'picta'

O. m. subsp. morio

Orchis

O. m. subsp. albanica

137

Champagne Orchid   *Orchis champagneuxii* Barn.

Synonym: *O. morio subsp. champagneuxii* (Barn.) E. G. & A. Camus

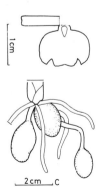

Stem 10 – 25 cm tall; basal foliage leaves 5 – 9, lanceolate, 3 – 8 cm long and 0.7 – 1.5 cm wide; 2 – 3 leaves sheathing the stem; inflorescence lax, 2 – 7 (– 10) flowered; sepals broadly ovate, 6.5 – 10 mm long and 3 – 4.5 mm wide; lateral petals 4.5 – 6.5 mm long; lip broader than long 6 – 8.5 × 11 – 14 mm, middle lobe somewhat longer than the side lobes; spur 10 – 15 mm long, slightly curved, pointing upwards.

Habitat: open woodland and scrub, poor meadows; up to 1,500 m; on dry soils.

Flowers: April – June. **Photos**: Ga, Dept. Var 18.4.71 (l), 17.4.71 (r).

Distribution: western Mediterranean region, concentrated on the Iberian Peninsula and stretching eastwards in southern France along the coast as far as the department of the Alpes-Maritimes. Reports from Morocco need confirmation. ● **Floristic element**: w-mediterranean w-submediterranean.

Countries: Eur: SW Bl, Hs, Lu, W Ga; ?**Afr**: Ma.

Key to the species in the *Orchis-longicornu* group:

1   Middle part of the lip with purplish-red spots, side lobes mostly dark, purplish-red to blackish-purple, rarely pink or red; single plants producing 1 new tuber each year . . . . *O. longicornu*, p136

1* Middle of the lip without spots or, if present, very insignificant; side lobes pink to purplish-pink; plants growing in groups where each plant produces 2 new tubers on long stalks . . . . *O. champagneuxii*

Orchis

Galilean Orchid *Orchis galilaea* (Bornm. & M. Schulze) Schlechter

Synonym: *O. punctulata subsp. galilaea* (Bornm. & M. Schulze) Soó

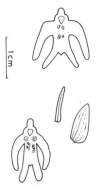

Stem 15–50 cm tall; basal foliage leaves 3–6, unspotted, lanceolate, 6–12 cm long and 2.5–5 cm wide; 1–2 leaves sheathing the stem higher up; inflorescence fairly dense, 4–12 cm long with 15–30 flowers, opening from above downwards (!); bracts 2–3 mm long; for flower colour, *see* Variation; sepals curving to form a hood, ovate 8–10 mm long; lateral petals linear; lip 10–12 mm long, deeply 3-lobed, side lobes and tongues of middle lobe of about the same width, linear, straight or slightly curved, the central tooth of the middle lobe considerably shorter than the tongues; spur 3–4 mm long, cylindrical, slightly curved and pointing down.

Variation: the species occurs in obviously different colour variants which, in the past, have given rise to false identifications. The inner surface of the sepals always has purple veins and the lip is marked with fairly large purple spots; it is the ground colour of the flowers which varies: a) white, b) purplish-pink (purple lip with a paler central area), c) pale yellow to greenish-yellow.

Habitat: open evergreen, broad-leaved and pine woods, garrigue; on hills level from 300 – 900 m; on (fairly) dry, stony and calcareous soils.

Flowers: February – April. **Photos:** IJ, Samaria 11.4.81.

Distribution: species endemic to the Levant and spreading into parts of Lebanon, Israel and Syria. • **Floristic element:** e-mediterranean.

Countries: Asi: IJ, LS.

Punctate Orchid *Orchis punctulata* Lindley

Synonyms: *O. p. subsp. sepulchralis* (Boiss. & Heldr.) Soó. *O. schelkownikowii* Woronow

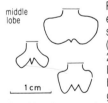

middle lobe

1 cm

Plant with 2 ellipsoidal tubers; stem 25–60 (–85) cm tall, with 2–3 basal scale leaves, 4–8 foliage leaves close to the ground and 1–2 sheathing the stem, lower leaves unspotted, broadly lanceolate, 7–25 cm long and 3–5.5 cm wide; inflorescence dense with up to 100 or more flowers; bracts 1–5 mm long; perianth segments curving to form a hood; segments greenish-yellow on the outside, the inside veined and dotted, 8–15 mm long and 3.5–5 mm wide, lateral petals linear 8–12 mm long; lip yellow with groups of reddish hairs, the points often brownish-red, 7–15 mm long, deeply 3-lobed, the side lobes tongue-shaped and bent inwards, the sides of the middle lobe vary in shape and are only a little longer than the central tooth; spur 3–6 mm long, cylindrical, bent downwards.

Habitat: woods, maquis, garrigue; up to 1,400 m on fairly dry, base-rich soils. **Flowers:** February – May. **Photos:** An, Vil. Antalya 28.3.78 (l); IJ, Galilee 2.4.81 (r).

Distribution: Near East and into Europe in the Crimea and Thrace. Also in Caucasia, Iraqi Kurdestan, northern and western Persia.

Floristic Element: e-mediterranean oriental e-submediterranean.

Countries: Eur: SE Gr, ?Tu, RK; **Asi:** IJ, LS, Cy, An, AE.

Variation: particularly strong large-flowered plants were earlier assigned to a separate subspecies 'sepulchralis'.

Relationship: *O. adenocheila* Czerniakovska is similar (the species has been named erroneously '*O. stevenii*' or '*O. punctulata subsp. stevenii*'). Flowers paler; sepals green; lip greenish-cream. Native to Caucasia, northern and western Persia, Turkomania. One record for Anatolia was actually *O. purpurea*.

141

Conical Orchid *Orchis conica* Willd.

Synonyms: *O. pusilla* Tyteca, ?*O. acuminata* Desf.

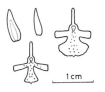

Plant with 2 ellipsoidal tubers; stem 5 – 30 cm tall with 1 – 2 scale leaves and 5 – 8 blue-green foliage leaves, most of them forming a rosette but some may be spread-out up the stem; lower leaves broadly lanceolate 6 – 10 cm long and 1.5 – 2.5 cm wide; inflorescence ovate to long and cylindrical; flowers violet-pink; lateral sepals with a green centre 6 – 8.5 mm long and 1.5 – 3 mm wide with a grooved bent tip; lip with pale or more deeply coloured spots, wider than long 5 – 7 × 5 – 8.5 mm; spur 3.5 – 5 mm long, cylindrical, bent downwards.

Habitat: the requirements of this species seem to be similar to those of *O. lactea*. So far it is known from dry calcareous soils. **Flowers:** February – April. **Photos:** Hs, Prov. Cadiz 3.4.71 (l); Bl, Mallorca 13.3.75 (r).

Distribution: western Mediterranean. Since the species has only recently been separated from *O. lactea* its area of distribution has still not been clearly defined. It is still to be decided whether the records for southern Italy (early-flowering plants) should belong here.

● **Floristic element:** w-mediterranean. **Countries: Eur: SW** Bl, Hs, Lu, W ?Ga; **Afr:** Tn, Ag, Ma.

Key to the species of the *Orchis tridentata* group:

1   Lip 5 – 7 mm long .... *O. conica*
1*   Lip longer than 8 mm, if only 7 – 8 mm then the foliage leaves are narrowly (not broadly) lanceolate and the sepals are without a green centre 2
2   Lip convex; middle and side lobes not turned down; sepals with green centre or entirely green ...... *O. lactea*, p144
2*   Lip concave or flat; middle and side lobes turned up or flat; sepals without green colour .... *O. tridentata*

Toothed Orchid *Orchis tridentata* Scop.

Synonyms: *O. commutata* Tod., *O. tridentata* subsp. *commutata* (Tod.) Nyman

Plant with 2 ellipsoidal tubers; stem 15 – 45 cm tall with 2 – 3 basal scale leaves, 3 – 5 bluish-green unspotted foliage leaves (grouped in a rosette or spaced out on the stem) and 1 – 2 leaves sheathing the stem higher up, lower leaves narrow-lanceolate, 4 – 12 cm long and 1 – 2.5 cm wide; inflorescence usually spherical; bracts 7 – 10 mm long; perianth segments curving to form a hood; sepals purplish-pink with darker veins, ovate, 8 – 13 (– 25) mm long and 3 – 5 mm wide with a short point or extended into a long, grooved, bent point; lateral petals narrow, tongue-shaped 5 – 8 (– 15) mm long; lip pink, heavily spotted in red, 7 – 12 (– 16) mm long and 7 – 13 (– 16) mm wide, deeply 3-lobed, toothed; spur 5 – 10 (– 13) mm long, cylindrical, downward curving.

Habitat: poor meadows, woodland edges, open woodland, garrigue; up to 1,600 m; on fresh to fairly dry base-rich soils. **Flowers:** March – June. **Photos:** An, Vil. Manisa 6.4.78 (l); It, Prov. Triente 16.5.83 (r); *see* p264.

Distribution: south, south-east and central Europe; the closed area extends as far as the southern edge of the Alps and the Carpathians, isolated further north, from Hessen and Thüringen to the lower Oder; also in Caucasia and Iraqi Kurdestan. **Floristic element:** c + e-mediterranean oriental submediterranean pannonic danubic (pontic) subatlantic central-european. **Countries: Eur: SE** Cr, Gr, Tu, Al, Ju, Bu, Rm, RK, **S** Me, Si, It, Sa, Co, **W** Ga, **C** He, Au, Hu, Ge, Cz, Po; **Asi:** IJ, LS, An, AE. **Variation:** flower size, sepal form and lip shape are very variable. Large-flowered plants correspond to the type 'commutata'; it has yet to be decided whether they merit the status of an independent subspecies.

Orchis

Milky Orchid   *Orchis lactea* Poiret

Synonyms: *O. tridentata subsp. lactea* (Poiret) K. Richter, *O. hanrii* Jordan

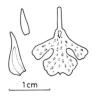

1 cm

Plant with 2 ovoid tubers; stem (5 –) 10 – 20 cm tall with 1 – 3 basal scale leaves, 3 – 8 light green foliage leaves in a rosette with 1 – 3 leaves sheathing the stem, lower leaves ovate – lanceolate, 4 – 7 cm long and 1 – 2.5 cm wide; inflorescence ovoid to elongated, dense; bracts about as long as the ovaries; perianth segments curving to form a hood; sepals whitish-pink, rarely a more intense pink, always with a green centre or even completely green, with dark veins, ovate – lanceolate 9 – 12 mm long and 3 – 4.5 mm wide and extended into a grooved, straight or curved point; lateral petals narrow-lanceolate 5.5 – 8 mm long; lip whitish, heavily spotted, often the lobes are coloured pale to intensive lilac-red or purple (in which case only the centre is whitish) 8 – 11 mm long and 8 – 13 mm broad, deeply 3-lobed with a 2-part middle lobe, lip convex, lobes turn down at the point of attachment (when fully open), middle lobe sometimes sharply bent down; spur 5 – 8 mm long, cylindrical, curving downwards.

Habitat: open woodland, garrigue, poor grassland; up to 1,200 m; on dry calcareous soils. **Flowers:** February – April. **Photos:** AE, Rhodes 10.4.81 (l); Cr, Lasithi 11.4.76 (r).

Distribution: Mediterranean region especially in the meridional zone, only scattered in the submeridional. The species seems to be absent from the Iberian peninsula; records from there, as far as is known, are *O. conica*. The eastern limit is rather vague; it is certainly in western Anatolia, but doubtful in the Levant

● Floristic element: mediterranean submediterranean. **Countries:** Eur: SE   Cr, Gr, Tu, Al, ?Ju, ?Bu, S   Me, Si, It, Sa, Co, W   Ga; Asi: ?LS, An, AE; Afr: ?Tn, Ag, Ma.

Lady Orchid   *Orchis purpurea* Hudson

Synonym: *O. lokiana* H. Baumann *O. caucasica* Regel, *O. fusca* Jacq., *O. moravica* Jacq., *O. Maxima* K. Koch

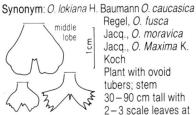

middle lobe

1 cm

Plant with ovoid tubers; stem 30 – 90 cm tall with 2 – 3 scale leaves at the base, 3 – 6 foliage near the ground and 1 – 2 sheathing the stem; lower leaves unspotted, shining, broadly lanceolate, 6 – 20 cm long and 2 – 7 cm wide; inflorescence dense and many-flowered; bracts 1.3 – 3 mm long; flowers with a brownish-red hood and a paler lip marked with numerous brownish-red groups of hairs; sepals ovate, 8 – 13 mm long and 4 – 6 mm wide; lateral petals lanceolate 5 – 8 mm long; lip 9 – 20 mm long and 11 – 22 mm broad, deeply 3-lobed, very variable; spur 3 – 8 mm long, curved downwards, enlarged and often notched at the end. **Habitat:** woods, woodland edges, poor grassland, garrigue; up to 1,800 m; on fairly dry base-rich soils to those of fluctuating dampness. **Flowers:** April – June. **Photos:** Ga, Dept. Moselle 22.5.71 (u/r); An, Vil. Artvin 23.5.74 (l/r); Ga, Dept. Dordogne 23.4.84 (l).

Distribution: in Europe, North Africa, and Asia Minor from the meridional to the temperate zones; fairly rare in the Mediterranean region; in the pontic region only at the eastern foot of the Carpathians, otherwise absent from continental eastern Europe. Also in Caucasia. In Britain mainly confined to Kent. **Floristic element:** mediterranean oriental submediterranean pannonic danubian (pontic) m + s-atlantic subatlantic centraleuropean. **Countries:** Eur: SE   Gr, Tu, Al, Ju, Bu, Rm, RK, S   It, Sa, Co, SW   Hs, W   Ga, Be, Ho, Br, C   He, Au, Hu, Ge, Da, Cz, Po, E   RW; Asi: An; Afr: Ag.

Variation: flower size, form of lip and stem height are variable enough to have encouraged 'splitting' into several species.

Orchis

145

Military Orchid *Orchis militaris* L.

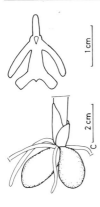

Synonyms: *O. rivinii* Govan *O. cinerea* Schrank

Plant with 2 ovoid-spherical tubers; stem 20–45 (–65) cm tall, with 2–3 basal scale leaves, 3–5 foliage leaves forming a rosette and 1–2 leaves sheathing the lower half of the stem, basal leaves elliptic, 8–18 cm long and 2–5 cm wide, unspotted; inflorescence dense at first, becoming more lax, 10–40 flowered; bracts 2–3 (–5) mm long; perianth segments curving to form a hood; sepals whitish to pale lilac-red on the outside, purplish-red veins and pale spots inside, ovate, pointed, 10–15 mm long and 4–6 mm wide; lateral petals linear, 7–10 mm long and 1–2 mm wide; lip pink to purplish-red with pale centre and groups of dark hairs, deeply 3-lobed, side lobes linear and turned inwards, tip of middle lobe broadly elliptic and spreading; spur 5–7 mm long, cylindrical, curving downwards. **Habitat:** poor grassland and meadows, open woods and scrubland, occasionally also damp meadows; up to 1,800 m on lime-rich, mostly fairly dry soils. **Flowers:** April–June. **Photos:** Ge, Südwürttemberg 31.5.70 (l); Su, Öland 8.6.78 (r). **Distribution:** in Europe in the submeridional and temperate zones, in Spain, rare also in the meridional zone; Mallorca and European Turkey are doubtful. Also in the submeridional and temperate zones through Siberia to Dahuria and Caucasia. Rare in Britain and confined to a few sites in Kent, Sussex and Buckinghamshire. **Floristic element:** (w-mediterranean) submeridional temperate. **Countries:** **Eur:** **SE** ?Tu, Al, Ju, Bu, Rm, RK, **S** It, **SW** ?Bl, Hs, **W** Ga, Be, Ho, Br, **C** He, Au, Hu, Ge, Cz, Po, RB, **N** Su, RN, **E** RW, RE, RC.

Steven's Orchid *Orchis stevenii* Reichenb. fil.

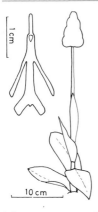

Synonyms: *O. raddeana* Regel *O. simia subsp. stevenii* (Reichenb. fil.) E. G. Camus *O. punctulata subsp. stevenii* (Reichenb. fil.) Sunderm.

Stem 20–50 cm tall; 2–5 basal foliage leaves, broadly lanceolate up to 15 cm long and 4 cm wide, 2–3 leaves sheathing the lower half of the stem; inflorescence generally elongated cylindrical, lax and many-flowered; bracts very short; perianth segments curving to form a hood; sepals pink outside, dark veins inside, narrowly ovate, 15–18 mm long, pointed; lateral petals shorter linear; lip pink to pale violet with groups of dark hairs, deeply 3-lobed, side lobes linear up to 7 mm long, the end of the middle lobe rounded-rhombic; spur 6–7 mm long, cylindrical, pointing downwards. **Habitat:** unmanured rich and damp meadows; 600–1,900 m; on fresh to damp base-rich soils. **Flowers:** May, June. **Photos:** An, Vil. Tunceli 10.6.81 (r); An, Vil. Trabzon 6.6.77 (l). **Distribution:** Asiatic Turkey in the region of the 'Anatolian diagonal'; only a few sites are known in the Trabzon, Tunceli and Nigde Vilayets. Also in Caucasia. **Floristic element:** oriental e-submediterranean. **Country:** Asi: An.

Key to the species in the *Orchis militaris* group:

1 Lip 10–15 mm long, hanging vertically, stem-like part of the middle lobe (measured from the point of attachment to the broadening into the two half lobes) up to 2½ × as long as wide. *O. militaris*

1* Lip 16–20 mm long, held horizontally; stem-like part of middle lobe 3–5× as long as wide . . . . *O. stevenii*

Naked Man Orchid   *Orchis italica* Poiret

Synonym: *O. longicruris* Link

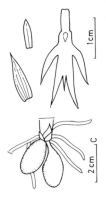

Plant with 2 ovoid or ellipsoid tubers; stem 20–50 cm tall; with 2–4 basal scale leaves, 5–10 foliage leaves in a rosette and 2–4 leaves sheathing the stem; basal leaves elliptic-lanceolate, 5–13 cm long and 1.2–2.8 cm wide, with or without spots, usually with obviously wavy edges; inflorescence dense and many-flowered, spherical to shortly cylindrical; bracts up to 5 mm long; ground colour of the flowers whitish-pink with darker markings on the perianth (veining) and the tips of the lip (indistinct spotting), rarely purple flowers (variant 'purpurea'); perianth segments tending to form a loose hood; sepals lanceolate 8–15 mm long and 3–5 mm wide with long points; lateral petals tongue-shaped, 5–10 mm long with short points; lip 12–19 mm long, deeply 3-lobed, side lobes and the tongues of the middle lobe lanceolate, with long points, curved upwards or randomly; spur 4–8 mm long, cylindrical, curving downwards.

Habitat: poor grassland, garrigue, open woodland; up to 1,300 m; on dry to intermittently damp, base-rich and often stony soils. **Flowers**: March – May. **Photos**: Cr, Nomos Rethimnon 5.4.80 (l); Bl, Mallorca 10.3.75 (r). **Distribution**: Mediterranean region; concentrated in the meridional zone, very scattered in the submeridional zone except in central Italy. ● **Floristic element**: mediterranean submediterranean. **Countries: Eur**: SE   Cr, Gr, Al, Ju, **S**   Me, Si, It, **SW**   Bl, Hs, Lu; **Asi**: IJ, LS, Cy, An, AE; **Afr**: Li, Tn, Ag, Ma.

Monkey Orchid   *Orchis simia* Lam.

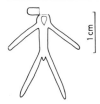

Plant with 2 roundish-ovate tubers; stem 20–45 (–60) cm tall with 2 basal scale leaves, 2–5 foliage leaves in a rosette and 1–2 leaves sheathing the stem, rosette leaves unspotted, elliptic to ovate, 5–20 cm long and 1.5–4.5 cm wide; inflorescence dense and many-flowered, ovate to broadly cylindrical, flowers opening from above downwards (!); bracts 1–4 mm long; perianth segments curving to form a hood, with turned-up points, whitish to pale lilac outside, spotted and veined lilac inside; sepals narrowly ovate, 10–15 mm long and 3–4 mm wide; lateral petals linear-lanceolate, 9–12 mm long; lip 14–20 mm long, deeply 3-lobed with a narrow, rectangular, pale-coloured central part with red dots, side lobes and tongues of the middle lobe narrow lineate, 7–11 mm long and 1 mm, or less, wide, with rounded ends, irregularly curved, intense purple or carmine; spur 4–8 mm long, cylindrical, pointing down. **Habitat**: poor grassland, open woods, garrigue; up to 1,200 m; on fairly dry, rarely on damp, calcareous soils. **Flowers**: March – June. **Photos**: Cy, Troodos area 22.3.70 (u/r); An, Vil. Manisa 6.4.78 (l); It, Prov. Triente 29.4.84 (l/r). **Distribution**: in the meridional and submeridional zones in Europe, North Africa and the Near East, penetrating as far as southern England, southern Holland and south Germany in the regions influenced by the oceanic climate; also in Caucasia from Iraqi Kurdestan through west and north Persia to Turkomania. In Britain, very rare and confined to a handful of sites in Kent and the Chilterns. **Floristic element**: mediterranean oriental submediterranean pannonic danubic s+m-atlantic s-subatlantic. **Countries: Eur**: SE   Cr, Gr, Tu, Al, Ju, Bu, Rm, RK, **S**   It, SW, Bl, Hs, **W**   Ga, Be, Ho, Br, **C**   He, Hu, Ge; **Asi**: IJ, LS, Cy, An, AE; **Asi**: Li ?Tn Ag.

Orchis

Burnt Orchid *Orchis ustulata* L.

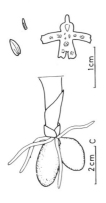

Plant with 2 ovate tubers; stem 10 – 30 (– 45) cm tall, with 2 – 3 basal scale leaves and 5 – 9 foliage leaves which increase in size as they go up the stem, the lower ones tending to form a rosette, the upper closely sheathing the stem for much of their length; lower leaves linear to ovate-lanceolate 2.5 – 10 cm long and 0.5 – 2 cm wide; inflorescence many-flowered, short to long-cylindrical, dense at the top becoming more open below; bracts a little shorter than the ovaries; perianth segments curving to form a hood, red to blackish-brown outside and because of this the buds are strikingly dark; lateral sepals obliquely ovate 3.5 – 4.5 mm long and 1.7 – 2.4 mm wide; the lanceolate central sepal and the linear lateral petals 3 – 3.5 mm long; lip (3.5 –) 5 – 8 mm long, white with red dots, deeply 3-lobed with spreading linear side lobes and a rectangular divided middle lobe; spur 1 – 2 mm long, cylindrical, pointing downwards.

Habitat: poor grassland, poor meadows, rarely in open woodland; up to the subalpine level about 2,000 m; on dry to occasionally moist, base-rich (also lime-free) soils. **Flowers**: April – August, **Photos**: Su, Öland 8.6.78 (l); Ge, Saargebiet 24.5.81 (r).

Distribution: widespread in Europe from meridional to temperate zones, rare in mediterranean floristic region. In Britain, downland in the south and limestones of the Midlands and north of England. **Floristic element**: (meridional/ montane) submeridional temperate. **Countries**: Eur: **SE** Gr, Al, Ju, Bu, Rm, **S** It, SW, Hs, **W** Ga, Be, + Ho, Br, **C** He, Au, Hu, Ge, Da, Cz, Po, RB, **N** Su, **E** RW, RC.

Pyramidal Orchid *Anacamptis pyramidalis* (L.) L. C. M. Richard

Synonyms: *A. p.* var. *brachystachys* (D'urv.) Boiss., *A. p.* var. *tanayensis* Chenevard, *A. urvilleana* Sommier & Caruana Gatto

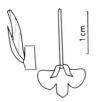

Plant with 2 spherical-ovoid tubers; stem 20 – 80 cm tall, 4 – 10 foliage leaves the lower ones narrow-lanceolate, 8 – 25 cm long and 0.7 – 2 cm wide, upper ones scale-like; inflorescence spherical to ovoid, elongating as the flowers fade, 2 – 10 cm long; flowers light to dark purplish-red, also pink or white; sepals ovate – lanceolate, very slightly turning forwards, the laterals 4 – 8, the central one 3.5 – 6 mm long; lateral petals 3.5 – 6 mm long; lip 6 – 9 mm long with 2 longitudinal ridges near the entrance to the spur, deeply 3-lobed, side lobes shorter or as long as the middle lobe; spur 10 – 15 mm long 0.5 mm thick.

Habitat: poor grassland, open woodland and scrub; up to 2,000 m; on dry to variably damp, base-rich soils. **Flowers**: March – July. **Photos**: Hs, Prov. Navarra 1.6.80 (l); Rm, Judet Brasov 6.7.78 (c); An, Vil. Aydin 4.4.78 (r). **Distribution**: in Europe, North Africa and the Near East from the meridional to the temperate zones, absent from eastern Europe; also in Caucasia and north-west Persia. **Floristic element**: meridional submeridional temperate. **Countries**: Eur: **SE** Cr, Gr, Tu, Al, Ju, Bu, Rm, RK, **S** Me, Si, It, Sa, Co, **SW** Bl, Hs, Lu, **W** Ga, Be, Ho, Br, Hb, **C** He, Au, Hu, Ge, Da, Cz, Po, RB, **N** Su, **E** RW, RC; **Asi**: IJ, LS, Cy, An, AE; **Afr**: Tn, Ag, Ma. **Variation**: the species varies considerably in size, form of inflorescence, shape of lip, spur length and flower colour. For example, 'tanayensis', intensely-coloured flowers, higher altitude in mountains (centre photo).

Orchis

Anacamptis

151

Giant Orchid *Barlia robertiana* (Loisel.) W. Greuter

Synonyms: *B. longibracteata* (Biv.) Parl., *Himantoglossum longibractiatum* (Biv.) Schlechter

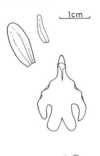

Plant with 2 ovoid tubers; robust stem 25–80 cm tall with 2–4 basal scale leaves and 5–10 foliage leaves, lower leaves ovate to elliptic, fleshy, shining, up to 30 cm long and 10 cm wide; inflorescence 6–23 cm long, dense and many-flowered; bracts leafy, lower ones longer than the flowers; lateral sepals ovate 10–15 mm long and 5–9 mm wide, reflexed at base then curving forwards; central sepal somewhat shorter curving to form a hood with the 7–11 mm long and 1.5–3 mm wide lateral petals; lip 13–20 mm long with a wavy edge, 3-lobed with a divided middle lobe, 2 longitudinal ridges beginning at the spur entrance; spur cone-shaped, 4–6 mm long with a nectary near the tip; pollinia stalks (caudicles) have a common viscid body (viscidium) surrounded by the bursicle. Flowers scented.

Habitat: open woodland, maquis, garrigue, poor grassland; mainly at the planar and colline levels up to 1,700 m; on dry to fresh base-rich soils.

Flowers: January – May. **Photos:** Cr, Nomos Rethimnon 2.4.80 (c); Bl, Mallorca 4.3.75 (l); Hs, Prov. Madrid 12.4.79 (r).

Distribution: in almost all the Mediterranean region, absent from the Levant and the northern Adriatic.

• **Floristic element:** mediterranean w+c-submediterranean. **Countries: Eur:** SE Cr, Gr, Al, Ju, **S** Me, Si, It, Sa, Co, **SW** Bl, Hs, Lu, **W** Ga; **Asi:** Cy, An, AE; **Afr:** Li, Tn, Ag, Ma.

Metlesic's Orchid *Barlia metlesicsiana* Teschner

Similar to the other species but easily distinguished by the characters given in the key; stem 40–60 cm tall; 6–8 foliage leaves, the lower ones ovate – lanceolate, pointed, up to 20 cm long and 7 cm wide; inflorescence 8–16 cm long; lateral sepals 11–13 mm long and 5–7 mm wide; lateral petals 8–9 mm long and 3–4 mm wide; lip 16–22 mm long with relatively less wavy edges, about as broad as long (in *B. robertiana* clearly longer than broad); spur 5–6 mm long.

Habitat: on poor-weathered lava soils among scattered shrubs, also on former cultivated land; 900–1,100 m.

Flowers: December, January.

Photos: Cl Tenerife 29.12.81, type population (l); 28.12.82 (r).

Distribution: endemic to the island of Tenerife; obviously a rare species known from only a few sites; rediscovered in 1979, following a record from the last century.

• **Floristic element:** canarian. **Country: Afr:** Cl. **Relationship:** the genus consists of the species described; it stands isolated but may be related to *Himantoglossum*.

Key to the *Barlia* species:

1 Lower foliage leaves forming a basal rosette, upper ones sheathing the stem without a flat blade; lip has a purple and (grey-) green ground colour – some more purplish, others appearing greener; side lobes lanceolate, sickle-shaped curving inwards and usually turning downwards . . . . *B. robertiana*

1* Leaves spaced-out up the stem, all (including the upper ones) with a flat blade; lip colour purple without a green component; side lobes triangular to rhombic, spreading, not turned down . . . . *B. metlesicsiana*

Barlia

Lizard Orchid   *Himantoglossum hircinum* (L.) Sprengel

2 cm Ne

Stem 20 – 90 (– 120) cm tall, with 2 – 3 scale leaves at the base and numerous foliage leaves becoming smaller as they go up the stem, lower leaves ovate – lanceolate 6 – 15 cm long and 3 – 5 cm wide; inflorescence dense with (20 –) 40 – 120 flowers; bracts membranous 1 – 2 × as long as the ovaries; flowers smell strongly of goat; perianth segments curve to form a hood, greenish- to brownish-white with brownish-red veins on the upper surface; sepals ovate, lateral ones 9.5 – 12.5 mm long and 4 – 6.5 mm wide, central one 7.5 – 10 mm long; lateral petals linear 7 – 9 mm long and 1 – 2.2 mm wide; lip 3-lobed with wavy border at the base, the back part whitish with purplish-red spots in the centre, round the edge and the lobes yellowish-green to pale brownish-lilac; middle lobe 3 – 6 cm long, coiled up when young, later twisted, divided at the tip to a depth of 3.5 (– 7) mm, side lobes 5 – 15 mm long, linear, pointed; spur cone-shaped (2 –) 3 – 6.5 mm long. **Habitat**: poor grassland, edges of scrubland, open woodland, also sand dunes; up to 1,800 m; on calcareous, fairly dry soils. **Flowers**: May – July. **Photos**: Hs, Prov. Santander 7.7.79 (r); Hs, Prov. Palencia 9.7.78 (l). **Distribution**: from the western and central Mediterranean regions northwards to western and central Europe. Rare in Britain with colonies mainly confined to Kent, Sussex and Cambridgeshire. Sporadic appearances are widespread in southern England. • **Floristic element**:   w + c-mediterranean   w-sub-mediterranean s + m-atlantic s-subatlantic s-centraleuropean. **Countries: Eur:** S   Si, It, **SW** Hs, **W**   Ga, Be, Ho, Br, **C**   He, Ge, Cz; **Afr:** Tn, Ag, Ma.

Adriatic Lizard Orchid   *Himantoglossum adriaticum* H. Baumann

Synonym: *H. hircinum subsp. adriaticum* (H. Baumann) Sundermann

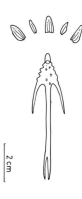

2 cm

In general appearance similar to *H. hircinum*; stem 30 – 95 cm tall; lower foliage leaves lanceolate up to 16 cm long and 3 cm wide; inflorescence lax with fewer flowers (15 – 50) with a faint scent; perianth segments whitish – pale pink with brownish-red veins on the upper surface; sepals ovate, the laterals 8.5 – 11.5 mm long and 4 – 6 mm wide, the central one 7 – 9 mm long; lateral petals linear 6 – 8.5 mm long and 1.5 – 2.5 mm wide; lip brightly coloured – the border, lobes and the spots on the pale central area a strong (brownish-) red to brownish-violet; middle lobe 3.5 – 6 cm long, twisted, divided at the tip to a depth of 5 – 18 mm, side lobes (5 –) 10 – 25 mm long, linear; spur cone-shaped 2.5 – 3.5 (– 5) mm long.

Habitat: poor and steppe grasslands, scrubland edges, open woodland; at the colline and lower montane levels up to 1,300 m; on base-rich dry soils. **Flowers**: May, June. **Photos**: Ju, Istria 2.6.78 (l), 4.6.82 (r).

Distribution: central and northern Italy, Illyria, pannonic basins at the foot of the eastern Alps and the northern Carpathians. Since the species has only recently been distinguished, its areal is not yet known exactly.

• **Floristic element:** c-submediterranean pannonic. **Countries: Eur:** SE   Ju, S   It, **C**   Au, Hu, Cz. **Relationship**: the species is close to *H. caprinum*. It remains to be shown whether the two can always be separated in the northern part of the Balkan peninsula and in the Carpathian region.

Himantoglossum

Balkan Lizard Orchid *Himantoglossum caprinum* (Bieb. Sprengel)

Synonyms: *H. hircinum subsp. caprinum* (Bieb.) K. Richter, *H. calcaratum* (G. Beck) Schlechter, *H. hircinum subsp. calcaratum* (G. Beck) Soó

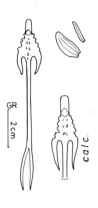

Stem 30–90 cm tall; lower foliage leaves lanceolate up to 17 cm long and 3.5 cm wide; inflorescence fairly lax with 10–45 flowers, faintly-scented, flower colour similar to H. adriaticum; sepals ovate, the laterals 13–18.5 mm long and 6–9 mm wide, the central one 10–15 mm long; lateral petals narrowly lanceolate 9.5–15 mm long and 2–4 mm wide; middle lobe of lip depressed at an angle 4.5–8.5 cm long, twisted, divided at the tip to a depth of 10–50 mm, side lobes 5–24 mm long; spur long, cone-shaped (5–) 6.5–13 mm.

Habitat: open oak-woods, poor grassland, woodland and scrubland edges; up to 1,500 m; on dry calcareous soils. **Flowers**: June–August. **Photos**: An, Vil. Bolu 22.7.82

Distribution: centred in the submeridional zone of south-east Europe and the Near East the species reaches into the meridional zone on the mainland of Greece and on Crete; the northern boundary is indistinct, probably the records from the central mountains of Hungary and Siebenbürgen (parts) are of *H. adriaticum* • **Floristic element**: e-mediterranean e + c-submediterranean pannonic danubean. **Countries**: Eur: **SE** Cr, Gr, Tu, Al, Ju, Bu, Rm, RK, **C** Hu; **Asi**: An.

Variation: the species is very variable in all its characters; a notable variant from southern Yugoslavia with a 9–13 mm spur, more vigorous growth and a large lip with long lobes is known as *H. calcaratum*.

Eastern Lizard Orchid *Himantoglossum affine* (Boiss.) Schlechter

Synonyms: *H. hircinum subsp. affine* (Boiss.) Sundermann, *H. bolleanum* (Siehe) Schlechter

Stem 40–80 cm tall with 2 basal scale leaves and numerous foliage leaves, the lower ones ovate–lanceolate, 8–22 cm long and 2.5–6.5 cm wide; inflorescence lax with 10–35 faintly-scented flowers; perianth segments curving to form a hood, whitish-green tinged with brown; sepals ovate, the laterals 10–14 mm long and 4–7 mm wide, the central one 9–12 mm long; lateral petals narrow lanceolate, 7–11 mm long and 2.5–3.5 mm wide; lip 3-lobed, the inner part with a wavy edge and a pale central area without spots, lip edge and lobes (greenish-) brown, rarely brownish-violet, middle lobe 2.5–5 cm long slightly twisted, when fully open held horizontally or slightly inclined, divided at the tip to a depth of 6–15 mm, side lobes (1–) 3–6 mm long, narrowly triangular; spur cone-shaped, 3–5 mm long.

Habitat: open oak and coniferous woodlands, maquis; at the colline and lower montane levels to 1,300 m; on dry calcareous soils. **Flowers**: May–July. **Photos**: An, Vil. Konya 17.6.76 (l); An, Vil, Maras 20.5.72 (r).

Distribution: in the meridional zone of the Near East from western and southern Anatolia to the Levant, through Iraqi Kurdestan to southern Persia, rare in the Peloponnese (Taigetos). **Floristic element**: e-mediterranean oriental. **Countries**: Eur: **SE** Gr; **Asi**: IJ, LS, An.

Relationship: a similar species is *H. formosum* (Steven) K. Koch, endemic in the eastern Caucasus; it is recognizable by the shorter lip with a middle lobe only 1.2–2 cm long.

Himantoglossum

Scarce Serapias *Serapias neglecta* De Not.

Synonym: *S. cordigera subsp. neglecta* (De Not.) K. Richter

1cm GR

Plant with 2 spherical tubers; stem 10 – 30 cm tall, unspotted, with 1 – 2 basal scale leaves and 4 – 7 narrow to broad lanceolate foliage leaves 5.5 – 11 cm long and 0.7 – 2 cm wide, often folded and bent; inflorescence 2 – 8 (– 18) flowered, short and dense; bracts usually shorter than the upwardly directed sepal hood; sepals 21.5 – 27.5 mm long and 6 – 7.5 mm wide, a dull grey-violet to somewhat greenish on the outside; lateral petals 18.5 – 24 mm long and 6 – 8 mm wide; lip 34 – 43 (– 50) mm long with 2 parallel purple callosities at the point of attachment; hypochile 14 – 18.5 mm long and 22 – 26 mm wide broadly wedge-shaped at the base, the side lobes pink to brownish-purple; epichile broadly ovate 21 – 28 (– 33) mm long, 8 – 11 mm broad at the start increasing to 15 – 19.5 mm at the broadest part often truncate and rounded in front, directed downwards vertically or at an angle, rarely horizontally, ochre to pinkish-brown, seldom intense brownish-red.

Habitat: open pine woods, garrigue, damp meadows, olive groves; up to 600 m; mainly on fairly acid soils. **Flowers:** March – May, some 2 – 3 weeks earlier than *S. cordigera*. **Photos:** Ga, Dept. Var 20.4.75 (l); It, Prov. Genoa 13.4.81 (r).

Distribution: along the coast of the Ligurian Sea from Provence (Dept. Var) to Toscana (Elba), also on Corsica and Sardinia.
● **Floristic element:** c-mediterranean c + w-submediterranean. **Countries: Eur: S** ?Si, It, Sa, Co, **W** Ga.

Ionian Serapias *Serapias ionica* E. Nelson ex H. Baumann & Künkele

Synonym: *Serapias neglecta* De Not, subsp. *ionica* E. Nelson

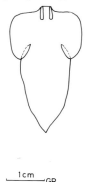

1cm GR

Stem 5 – 15 (– 20) cm tall, unspotted, 3 – 6 basal foliage leaves linear-lanceolate 4 – 9 cm long and 0.6 – 1.2 cm wide folded lengthwise, strongly bent (often almost into a spiral), bluish-green; inflorescence 2 – 8 (– 13) flowered; bracts usually shorter than the almost horizontal sepal hood; sepals 19 – 28 mm long and 5 – 7 mm wide; lip 28.5 – 38 mm long, hypochile 11.5 – 16 mm long and 17 – 21 mm broad, epichile 18.5 – 27 mm long and 11.5 – 16 mm broad, generally, reddish-brown, sometimes rather ochrous, the margins often wavy and turned up. **Habitat:** maquis, garrigue, coniferous woodland; up to 400 m. **Flowers:** April. **Photos:** Gr, Zakinthos 9.4.80 (l); Ju, Brac 6.4.80 (r).

Distribution: islands in the Adriatic and Ionian Seas; known from Kefallinia, Zakinthos (Zante) and Kerkira (Corfu) and from Korcula, Hvar and Brac. A species with an apparent interrupted (disjunct) island distribution; the two parts of the distribution are separated by a gap of 400 km. ● **Floristic element:** c-mediterranean c-submediterranean (disjunct). **Countries: Eur: SE** Gr, Ju.

Key to the subspecies of the *Serapias neglecta* group:

1   Hypochile jutting a long way out of the sepal hood, with side lobes directed sideways at an angle; when the lip is flattened out the epichile and hypochile do not overlap . . . . *S. neglecta*

1*   Hypochile scarcely emerging from the sepal hood, with side lobes held up vertically; epichile and hypochile nearly always overlap . . . . *S. ionica*

Serapias

159

Heart-flowered Serapias   *Serapias cordigera* L.

Synonym: *S. azorica* Schlechter

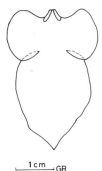

1 cm ⌐GR

Stem 15 – 50 cm tall, unspotted with 1 – 2 basal scale leaves and 5 – 9 lanceolate foliage leaves 7 – 16 cm long and 0.8 – 2.3 cm wide. inflorescence 3 – 10 (– 20) flowered, dense; bracts about as long as the sepal hood which is held up at an angle; sepals 23 – 30 mm long and 6 – 8.5 mm wide, grey-lilac on the outside; lateral petals 19.5 – 26.5 mm long and 6.5 – 8.5 mm wide; lip usually brownish-red to blackish-purple, rarely (Azores) brownish-orange to cream-coloured 31 – 42 (– 48) mm long with 2 blackish (diverging) callosities at the point of attachment, hypochile and epichile overlap (spread out!), hypochile 12.5 – 16 mm long and 19.5 – 26 mm broad, base cordate or occasionally truncate, the side lobes upright and protruding a little way out of the hood, epichile cordate 20.5 – 29 (– 34) mm long 6.5 – 9.5 mm across, at the point of attachment widening to a maximum of (13 –) 16 – 23 (– 26) mm, directed down or backwards, densely hairy towards the centre.

Habitat: open woodland and maquis, garrigue, damp meadows; up to 1,000 m on base-rich (also lime-free) soils. **Flowers:** April, May. **Photos:** Ga, Dept. Alpes Maritimes 1.5.71 (l); Ga, Dept. Var 11.5.83 (r).

Distribution: Mediterranean region eastwards to Crete and western Anatolia; in the temperate zone along the French Atlantic coast as far as the Dept. Finistère; Azores (all the islands except Flores and Corvo).

● **Floristic element:** mediterranean sub-mediterranean azorean s-atlantic. **Countries: Eur: SE**   Gr, Tu, Al, Ju, **S**   Me, Si, It, Sa, Co, **SW**   Bl, Hs, Lu, Az, **W**   Ga; **Asi:** An, AE; **Afr:** ?Li, Tn, Ag, Ma.

Hybrid Serapias   *Serapias olbia* Verguin

Synonyms: *S. cordigera subsp. olbia* (Verguin) Sundermann *S. gregaria* Godfery

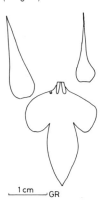

1 cm ⌐GR

Plant with 3 (4) spherical tubers, those of the current year with long stalks (vegetative reproduction); flowering stalks in groups, stem 10 – 20 (– 30) cm tall, the lower part often spotted, with 2 basal scale leaves with 5 – 7 narrow lanceolate foliage leaves 4 – 10 cm long and 0.7 – 1.1 cm wide; inflorescence 2 – 4 (– 5) flowered, lax; bracts much shorter than the vertically angled sepal hood; sepals 19 – 25 mm long and 5.5 – 7.5 mm wide, grey-lilac outside, darker within; lateral petals 16.5 – 21 mm long and 5.5 – 7 mm wide; lip 23.5 – 31 mm long with 2 nearly parallel purple callosities at the point of attachment; hypochile 11.5 – 15 mm long and 15.5 – 19.5 mm broad with truncate base, side lobes blackish-purple; epichile ovate – lanceolate 13 – 18.5 mm long and 4.5 – 6 mm broad at the base and 6.5 – 9.5 mm across the centre, pointed tip, bent strongly backwards, blackish-purple to brownish-red, densely hairy right to the point. **Habitat:** damp meadows, damp dune hollows, also on dry slate slopes; on low ground near the coasts; on acid soils (absent from limestone). **Flowers:** April, May. **Photos:** Ga, Dept. Var 15.4.79 (l), 18.4.71 (r). **Distribution:** southern France; Dept. Var (La Seyne, near Toulon, to Le Lavandou) and Alpes Maritimes (Antibes to Nizza). A record for Asturia (between Belmonte and Ribadsella) is still to be confirmed. ● **Floristic element:** w-submediterranean. **Country: Eur: W** Ga. **Relationship:** the species has probably arisen from a cross between *S. lingua* and *S. cordigera*.

Serapias

161

Plough-Share Serapias *Serapias vomeracea* (Burm. fil.) Briq.

Synonyms: *S. cordigera subsp. vomeracea* (Burm. fil.) Sundermann *S. longipetala* (Ten.) Pollini, *S. pseudocordigera* (Sebastiani) Moric.

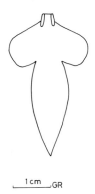

Plant with 2 spherical tubers; stem 20 – 60 cm tall, sometimes spotted, with 2 basal scale leaves, 4 – 7 narrow-lanceolate foliage leaves 6 – 19 cm long; inflorescence 3 – 10 flowered, lax; sepals 23 – 31 mm long and 5 – 8.5 mm wide the hood grey-lilac pointing steeply upwards; lateral petals 20 – 27.5 mm

1 cm GR

long and 6 – 8.,5 mm wide; lip with 2 parallel purple callosities at the point of attachment; hypochile 12 – 17 mm long and 18 – 24 mm wide, broadly wedge-shaped to truncate base, the side lobes upright dark purple scarcely emerging from the sepal hood; epichile lanceolate 20 – 28 mm long 5 – 8 mm broad at the base and 8 – 13 mm across the centre, pointing downwards or curved back, densely hairy as far as the centre; usually rust-red to brownish-violet, rarely ochre colour.

Habitat: open pine and chestnut woodland, garrigue, poor grassland, damp meadows, olive groves; to 1,000 m; on basic to weakly acid soils. **Flowers;** March – June. **Photos:** Ga, Dept. Gard 14.5.81 (l); It, Prov. Como 19.5.69 (r).

Distribution: Mediterranean region northwards to the southern foot of the Alps and in the temperate zone in France as far as the Depts. Charente-Maritime and Corrèze, eastwards as far as the eastern Aegean islands and Cyprus.

● **Floristic element:** mediterranean submediterranean s-atlantic. **Countries:** Eur: SE Gr, Al, Ju, **S** Me, Si, It, Co, SW Bl, Hs, Lu, **W** Ga, **C** He; **Asi:** Cy, AE; **Afr:** ?Li, Ag, Ma.

Eastern Serapias *Serapias orientalis* (Greuter) H. Baumann & Künkele

Synonyms: *S. vomeracea subsp. orientalis* W. Greuter *S. cordigera subsp. orientalis* (E. Nelson) Sundermann, *S. o. subsp. apulica* E. Nelson, *S. o. var. cordigeroides* E. Nelson

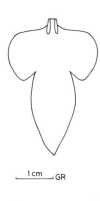

Similar to *S.* . *vomeracea*, on average shorter with a broader lip. Stem 10 – 30 cm tall; hypochile 14 – 19 mm long and 20 – 26 (– 31 mm) broad, base truncate; epichile 18 – 26 (– 33) mm long 7 – 10 (– 15) mm broad at the base and 10 – 14 (– 20) mm across the middle, pale

1 cm GR

ochre-yellow to purplish-red.
Habitat: garrigue, poor grassland, damp meadows, to 1,000 m; prefers calcareous soils. **Flowers:** March – July. **Photos:** An, Vil. Izmir 7.,4.78 (l); An, Vil. Kocaeli 3.6.74 (r).

Distribution: centred in the eastern Mediterranean area, westwards to Apulia; similar plants also in Sicily (Palermo); also in Transcaucasia.

Floristic element: e + c-mediterranean oriental e-submediterranean.

Countries: Eur: SE Cr, Gr, Tu, **S** (Si), It; **Asi:** IJ, LS, Cy, An, AE.

Key to the subspecies of the *Serapias vomeracea* group:

1   Lip 23 – 29 mm long, epichile 13.5 – 18 mm long, sepals 18.5 – 24 mm long. . . . . *S. bergonii*, p164
1* Lip 32 – 42 mm long, epichile 18 – 33 mm long, sepals 23 – 33 mm 2
2   Bracts generally much longer than the sepal hood, 13 – 18.5 mm wide; foliage leaves 0.5 – 1.5 mm wide *S. vomeracea*
2* Bracts scarcely longer than the sepal hood, 18 – 25 mm wide; foliage leaves 1.2 – 2 cm wide . . . . *S. orientalis*

Serapias

Bergon's Serapias *Serapias bergonii* E. G. Camus

Synonyms: *S. vomeracea subsp. laxiflora* (Soó) Gölz & Reinhard *S. parviflora subsp. laxiflora* Soó, *S. cordigera subsp. laxiflora* (Soó) Sundermann, *S. columnae* (Ascherson & Graebner) Lojac.

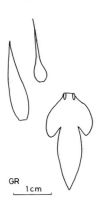

Plant with 2 spherical tubers; stem 15–40 cm tall, often spotted, with 2 basal scale leaves and 6–9 lanceolate foliage leaves 6–14 cm long and 0.9–1.6 cm wide, often curved; inflorescence 4–12 flowered, lax; bracts often longer than the upwardly angled sepal hood; sepals 4–5.5 mm wide, greyish-lilac outside; lip with 2 brownish parallel callosities; hypochile 10–13 mm long and 11.5–14.5 mm wide, wedge-shaped base, side lobes upright, hidden within the hood, blackish-purple; epichile lanceolate 3.5–5 mm wide at the base and 4–7.5 across the middle, bent backwards, almost bare, a dull brownish-red to ochre.

Habitat: grows in similar places to the subspecies *vomeracea*; up to 600 m.

Flowers: March–June. **Photos:** Cr, Nomos Rethimnon 14.4.81 (l); An, Vil. Antalya 28.3.78 (r).

Distribution: centred in the eastern Mediterranean area, only isolated individuals recorded westwards as far as Sicily (Prov. Ragusa) and northern Italy (Prov. Parma, Siena, Grosseto). • **Floristic element:** e + c mediterranean e + c submediterranean. **Countries: SE** Cr, Gr, Tu, Al, Ju, **S** Si, It; **Asi:** Cy, An, AE.

Relationships: the subspecies *vomeracea* and *laxiflora* form mixed populations where the distribution areas overlap (in It, Al, AE, Cy); plants with intermediate characters are not infrequently met with.

Sardinian Serapias *Serapias nurrica* Corrias

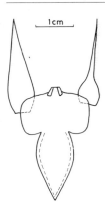

Plant with 2 spherical tubers; stem 20–35 cm tall with 2 basal scale leaves and 6–8 linear-lanceolate foliage leaves 10–18 cm long and 0.8–1.6 cm wide; inflorescence 5–8 flowered, short and dense; bracts shorter than the steeply erect sepal hood; sepals 23–26 mm long and 5–7 mm wide, dull lilac outside, brownish-red veins inside; lateral petals 20–24 mm long and 5.5–6.5 mm wide; lip 25–30 mm long with 2 spreading purple callosities at the base; hypochile 11–13 mm long and 15–18 mm broad, base truncate, side lobes dull lilac, upright and enclosed within the hood; epichile ovate–lanceolate, 14–18 mm long, 5.5–7.5 mm wide at first, widening to 7–10 mm in the centre, pointed, held upright, vertically or at an angle, moderately hairy at the base, 2-coloured with a brownish-red centre and a narrow, dull lilac border. **Habitat:** garrigue; up to about 100 m near the coast; on dry soils over various types of rock (but not limestone). **Flowers:** April–June. **Photos:** Sa, Prov. Sassari, type population 4.5.82.

Distribution: endemic on the islands of Sardinia and Corsica. Discovered in 1974, its distribution is still insufficiently well known. So far it has been found on the south-west coast (island of S. Pietro) and the north coast of Sardinia (Alghero to the island of Caprera) and on the south-east coast of Corsica (Porto-Vecchio). • **Floristic element:** c-mediterranean c-submediterranean. **Countries: Eur: S** Sa, Co.

Relationship: near to *S. vomeracea*, the flower dimensions are closest to those of the subspecies *laxiflora*.

Serapias

165

Small-Flowered Serapias   *Serapias parviflora* Parl.

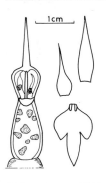

Plant with 2 spherical surface tubers; stem 10 – 30 cm tall, spotted below; foliage leaves 4 – 5, narrow-lanceolate, 6 – 10 cm long and 0.7 – 1 cm wide; inflorescence 3 – 5 (– 8) flowered, lax; bracts shorter to as long as the upwardly-angled sepal hood; sepals 14.5 – 17.5 mm long and 3.5 – 4.5 mm wide, reddish-green to greyish-lilac outside; lateral petals 13 – 15.5 mm long and 3 – 4 mm wide; lip 14 – 19 mm long with two parallel red callosities at the base; hypochile 8 – 10 mm long and 9 – 11.5 mm broad, broadly wedge-shaped base, side lobes brownish-red hidden in the hood; epichile lanceolate 7 – 11.5 mm long, 2.5 – 3 mm broad at the outset up to 3.5 – 4.5 mm across the middle, directed downwards or backwards, sparsely hairy, dull red to yellowish; self-pollinating (*see* the drawing of the column on the left).

Habitat: open pine woods, garrigue, damp meadows; up to 1,000 m; on basic to weakly acid soils. **Flowers:** April – June – later than *S. lingua*. **Photos:** It, Prov. Matera 1.5.81 (l); It, Prov. Bari 13.4.74 (r). **Distribution:** Mediterranean region eastwards as far as the eastern Aegean islands and Cyprus; in the temperate zone along the French Atlantic coast to the Dept. Morbihan; also on the Canary Islands. (Gran Canaria, Tenerife, Hierro and La Palma). Several plants were recently discovered in Britain on the south Cornish coast and its status is under investigation.

• **Floristic element:** mediterranean canarian w + c-submediterranean s-atlantic.
Countries: Eur: SE   Cr, Gr, Al, Ju, **S**   Me, Si, It, Sa, Co, **SW**   Bl, Hs, Lu, **W**   Ga; **Asi:** Cy, AE; **Afr:** Tn, Ag, Ma, Cl. **Relationship:** a similar type occurs in the Algarve (Portugal).

Tongue Orchid   *Serapias lingua* L.

Synonyms: *S. oxyglottis* Willd., *S. stenopetala* Maire & T Stephenson, *S. excavata* Schlechter, *S. mauretanica* Schlechter, *S. lingua subsp. duriaei* (Batt.) Maire

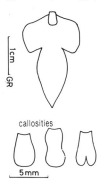

callosities

5mm

Plant with (2) 3 spherical tubers, those of the current year with long stems (vegetative repro-duction); stem 10 – 35 cm tall, sometimes spotted below with 1 – 2 basal scale leaves and 4 – 8 linear-lanceolate foliage leaves 5 – 13 cm long and 0.4 – 1.3 cm wide; inflorescence 2 – 8 (– 14) flowered, lax; bracts shorter than the horizontal sepal hood; sepals 15 – 21 mm long and 4.5 – 6 mm wide, pale to intense greyish-lilac outside; lateral petals 13 – 17.5 mm long and 3 – 4.5 mm wide; lip (16 –) 22 – 29 mm long, a single purple callosity at the base which may be rounded, violin-shaped or crenate in front; hypochile 8 – 12 mm long and 13 – 17 mm broad with purplish-red upright side lobes; epichile (8 –) 13 – 18 mm long, (2.5 –) 4.5 – 7 mm broad at the outset and (4 –) 7 – 12 mm across the middle, directed downwards at an angle, sparsely hairy, variously coloured.

Habitat: open woodland, garrigue, poor grassland, damp meadows; up to 1,200 m; on base-rich (but also lime-free) soils. **Flowers:** March – June. **Photos:** Ga, Dept. Var 11.5.83 (l); Bl, Mallorca 10.3.75 (r); p264.
Distribution: Mediterranean region, eastwards to the central and southern Aegean; in southern and central France also in the temperate zone. • **Floristic element:** mediterranean submediterranean s-atlantic s-subatlantic. **Countries: Eur; SE**   Cr, Ge, Al, Ju, **S**   Me, Si, It, Sa, Co, **SW**   Bl, Hs, Lu, **W**   Ga; **Afr:** Tn, Ag, Ma.

Serapias

Dull Ophrys   *Ophrys fusca* Link

Problem: the species is very variable in form and a thorough reappraisal is required.

Key to the subspecies:

1   Middle lobe about a third the length of the lip, weakly curved, jutting forward; uniformly coloured or, more rarely, with a pale border .... 1. *O. f. subsp. fusca*

1* Middle lobe almost half as long as the lip, bent backwards; pattern with a W-shaped pale border .2. *O. f. subsp. vasconica*

1.   *O. f. subsp. fusca*

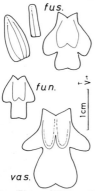

Stem 10 – 40 cm tall; 2 – 9 flowered; lateral petals ²⁄₃ – ⁴⁄₅ as long as the green sepals; lip dark brown to blackish-violet, a longitudinal groove at the base, with a narrow smooth border. **Habitat**: open woodland, garrigue, poor grassland, former cultivated land; to 1,400 m; on calcareous soils. **Flowers**: December – June. **Photos**: AE, Rhodes 11.4.82 (u/l); It, Prov. Grosseto 11.4.81 (c/l); Ju, Hvar 9.4.80 (u/r); Cr, Nomos Rethimnon, 31.3.72 (c/r).

Distribution: Mediterranean region, in France northwards to the Depts. Vendée, Indre. The records for the Levant require confirmation; those for Rumania are seldom correct.

● **Floristic element**: mediterranean sub-mediterranean s-atlantic. **Countries**: Eur: SE   Cr, Gr, Tu, Al, Ju, ?Rm, **S**   Me, Si, It, Sa, Co, **SW**   Bl, Hs, Lu, **W**   Ga, (not Britain); **Asi**: ?LS Cy An AE; **Afr**: Li Tn Ag Ma.

Variation: the subspecies contains several variants differing in flower size (sepals 7.5 – 10/10 – 13.5 mm long, lip 9 – 13 (13 – 17 mm long; small-flowered plants correspond to *O. f. subsp. funerea* (Viv.) E. G. & A. Camus & Bergon), lip colour (pattern grey to brown/lilac to blue; border yellow/brown) and flowering times (up to April/from May onwards). The variants can often be separated quite well when they occur in the same region, but become confused if all the variants over the whole area are considered. With present knowledge it is scarcely possible to separate them into 2 or more types.

2.   *O. f. subsp. vasconica* O. & E. Danesch

Stem 10 – 20 cm tall; 1 – 6 flowered; lip blackish-purple, pattern brown (– purple) sometimes with paler marbling. **Flowers**: April, May.

Distribution: southern France (Dept. Gers) ● **Floristic element**: w-submediterranean. The subspecies has been little noticed; it may have a wider distribution (northern Spain?).

Rainbow Ophrys   *Ophrys iricolor* Desf.

Synonym: *O. fusca subsp. iricolor* (Desf.) K. Richter

Stem 10 – 35 cm tall; 1 – 5 flowered; sepals green 11 – 18 mm long; lateral petals 8 – 12 mm long; lip blackish-violet velvety, underside brownish-red, 15 – 23 mm, slightly arched with basal longitudinal groove, bare border very narrow and dark, pattern in the form of two ovate areas shining blue often with faint blackish or purplse marbling, hardly ever with a pale border.

Habitat: open pine wood and maquis, garrigue; up to 1,100 m; generally on calcareous soils, often on marl. **Flowers**: February – April, some 2 weeks later than *O. fusca*. **Photos**: Cy, Limassol area 26.3.83 (l); An, Vil. Antalya 4.4.80 (r).

Distribution: eastern Mediterranean area; northwards to the Bosphorus, Euboea, Attica and Kefallinia.

● **Floristic element**: e + c-mediterranean (e-submediterranean). **Countries**: Eur: SE   Cr, Gr, Tu; **Asi**: IJ, LS, Cy, An, AE.

large-flowered variant

169

Atlas Ophrys *Ophrys atlantica* Munby

Synonyms: *O. fusca subsp. atlantica* (Munby) E. G. & A. Camus *O. fusca subsp. durieui* (Reichenb. fil.) Soó

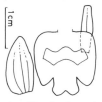

Plant with 2 spherical-ovoid tubers; stem 15–39 cm tall with 1–2 basal scale leaves, 3–5 foliage leaves in a rosette and one leaf sheathing the lower half of the stem, rosette leaves lanceolate 5–7 cm long and 1.3–2.7 cm wide; inflorescence 1–4 flowered; bracts longer than the ovaries; sepals (yellow-) green, ovate 11–15 mm long and 5–8.5 mm wide, the central one bending forwards, the laterals pointing at right angles to the sides; lateral petals greenish-brown tongue-shaped 8.5–13.5 mm long, wavy edges, bent backwards, bare; lip blackish-purple velvety with short hairs 15–20 mm long and (when spread out) 12–16 mm broad, with a 1–3.5 mm long stem-like base, saddle-shaped in the middle, 3-lobed in front which is strongly arched (convex), middle lobe broadly rectangular, crenate in front, scarcely longer than the side lobes, pattern plain grey to bluish-violet. **Habitat:** open broad-leaved and coniferous woodlands, poor grassland with bushes, garrigue; up to 1,500 m; on fairly dry base-rich (but not always calcareous) soils. **Flowers:** March–June. **Photos:** Ag, Prov. Algiers 13.5.73 (l); Hs, Prov. Malaga 2.4.79 (r). **Distribution:** North Africa, southern Spain (Prov. Malaga) ● **Floristic element:** w-mediterranean. **Countries:** Eur: SW Hs; Afr: Tn, Ag, Ma.

Pale Ophrys *Ophrys pallida* Rafin.

Synonyms: *O. fusca subsp. pallida* (Rafin.) E. G. & A. Camus & Bergon, *O. pectus* Mutel

Plant with 2 ellipsoidal-spherical tubers; stem 10–30 cm tall with 1–2 basal scale leaves, 3–6 foliage leaves in a rosette and 1–3 sheathing the stem, rosette leaves lanceolate 2.5–6 cm long and 1–1.7 cm wide; inflorescence 2–6 flowered; bracts somewhat longer than the ovaries, concave; sepals whitish to greenish, rarely reddish, broadly ovate to elliptic 7.5–10 mm long and 4.5–6.5 mm wide, the central one bent strongly forwards, the laterals pointing sideways at right angles and curving forwards; lateral petals greenish-yellow to brownish, tongue-shaped 5–7 mm long, bending forward, edge not wavy, bare; lip brown (–purple), (spread out!) 7.5–11 mm long and 6–9.5 mm broad, a longitudinal furrow and white hairs in the inner third, 3-lobed with dark-haired lobes, bent down at right angles behind the attachment of the side lobes; side lobes turned down; middle lobe transversely elliptic, crenate in front; pattern in the area of the bend, plain, divided by the groove, greyish-brown to violet, front border indistinct.

Habitat: open pine woods, garrigue, former cultivated land; up to 900 m; on calcareous soils. **Flowers:** February–April. **Photos:** Si, Prov. Palermo 4.4.76.

Distribution: western Sicily, North Africa (Tunisia, eastern Algeria). Records for Sardinia and Malta require confirmation.

● **Floristic element:** c + w-mediterranean.
Countries: Eur: S Afr: Tn, Ag.

Ophrys

171

Omega Ophrys *Ophrys omegaifera* H. Fleischm.

Synonym: *O. fusca subsp. omegaifera* (H. Fleischm.) E. Nelson

Plant with 2 ovoid tubers; 3 – 5 ovate – lanceolate basal foliage leaves 3 – 10 cm long and 1.3 – 4 cm wide, 1 – 2 leaves sheathing the stem; sepals green, the central one curving strongly forwards, the laterals pointing sideways at right angles; lateral petals yellow-green, often tinged brown 0.6 – 0.8 × the length of the sepals, with wavy edge; lip flat at the base (without longitudinal groove), 3-lobed, with short to long hairs, middle lobe jutting out 0.3 – 0.45 of the lip length; pattern plain, front border omega-shaped.

Problem: Here *O. omegaifera* is divided into 3 subspecies. Sometimes they are looked upon as separate species but while the two eastern subspecies *omegaifera* and *fleischmannii* are easily distinguished, the western subspecies *dyris* is morphologically intermediate and many of its populations are scarcely different from one or other of the eastern subspecies.

Key to the subspecies:

1　Lip (spread out!) 11 – 15 mm long and 10 – 12.5 mm broad, generally held straight out and the rear half slightly arched; middle lobe mostly curved downwards and, seen from the side, is approximately at right angles to the base; pattern often dotted or marbled with a paler colour .... 2.　*O. o. subsp. fleischmannii*

1*　Lip 13 – 21 mm long and 11 – 19 mm broad often bent sharply down in the rear half; middle lobe often curved back in the shape of a claw so that it is parallel with the base; pattern seldom marbled ... 2

2　Pattern surface mostly brown (without an obvious red component), w-border usually greyish-blue or whitish; lip hairs generally brown, rarely lilac
　　1.　*O. o. subsp. omegaifera*

2*　Pattern surface brownish-red, brownish-lilac, or brown, w-border usually whitish or greyish-lilac; lip hairs often lilac, rarely brown .... 3.　*O. o. subsp. dyris*

1.　*O. o. subsp. omegaifera*
Stem 10 – 25 cm tall, 1 – 4 flowered; sepals 12 – 17 mm long.
Habitat: open pine woods and maquis, garrigue; up to 1,000 m; generally on calcareous soils. **Flowers:** March, April. **Photos:** An, Vil. Mugla 31.3.80 (l/l).
Distribution: southern and eastern Aegean; recorded in Crete, Karpathos, Rhodes, Kos, Chios and on the Anatolian mainland (near Bodrum). Distribution is not sufficiently well known. ● **Floristic element:** e-mediterranean. **Countries: Eur: SE** Cr; **Asi:** An, AE.

2.　*O. o. subsp. fleischmannii* (Hayek) Del Prete
Synonyms: *O. fleischmannii* Hayek, *O. fusca subsp. fleischmannii* (Hayek) Soó
Stem 10 – 25 (– 35) cm tall, 2 – 5 (– 10) flowered; sepals 10 – 13.5 mm long; pattern surface mostly whitish, w-border whitish; lip hairs usually lilac. **Habitat:** similar to subspecies *omegaifera*. **Flowers:** December – April. **Photos:** Cy, Limassol region 17.3.84 (u/l); An, Vil. Hatay 10.4.80 (u/r).
Distribution: eastern Mediterranean region; westwards as far as Crete and Hydra, in the Greek mainland only in Attica. ● **Floristic element:** e-mediterranean. **Countries: Eur: SE** Cr, Gr; **Asi:** IJ, LS, Cy, An, AE.

3.　*O. o. subsp. dyris* (Maire) Del Prete
Synonyms: *O. dyris* Maire. *O. fusca subsp. dyris* (Maire) Soó
Stem 10 – 25 cm tall, 1 – 5 flowered; sepals 11.5 – 17 mm long.
Habitat: open woodland, garrigue, poor grassland; up to 1,800 m. **Flowers:** December – May. **Photos:** Hs, Prov. Barcelona 9.4.71 (c/l, c/r).
Distribution: western Mediterranean region, especially in the meridional zone, northwards as far as submeridional Catalonia.
● **Floristic element:** w-mediterranean w-submediterranean. **Countries: Eur: SW** Bl, Hs, Lu; **Afr:** Ma.

O. o. subsp. omegaifera, above: *O. o. subso, dyris* (2x)

173

Yellow Ophrys *Ophrys lutea* Cav.

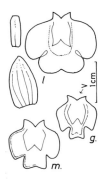

Stem 10–25 (–40) cm tall with 1–2 basal scale leaves, 3–6 foliage leaves in a rosette and 1–2 above, rosette leaves lanceolate 3–9 cm long and 1–2.7 cm wide; lower bracts somewhat longer than the ovaries; sepals (yellow-) green, the central one curving forwards, the laterals sticking out sideways at right angles; lateral petals (greenish-)yellow, naked, often with a wavy edge; lip 3-lobed with longitudinal groove as the base, centre dark brown to blackish-violet with a broad, spread out, or turned-up border, rear edges usually rounded-truncate, rarely broadly wedge-shaped; pattern grey-violet generally dotted or marbled in brown to dark violet, basal area and callosities absent.

Habitat: open woodland, garrigue, poor grassland, former cultivated land; on base-rich, usually calcareous, soils.

Key to the sub-species:

1 The dark colour of the lip centre spreading out into the margins, yellow border very narrow . . . . 3. *O. l. subsp. melena*
1* Lip with a wide yellow border 2
2 Lip 14–18 mm long, bent down at the point where the stem-like base (claw) joins the rounded flat area (limb) . . . . 1. *O. l. subsp. lutea*
2* Lip 8–13.5 mm long, limb held almost straight out, not bent down or only slightly so . . . . 2. *O. l. subsp. galilaea*

1. *O. l. subsp lutea*

Inflorescence 1–4 (–6) flowered; sepals 11–13 mm long; lateral petals 7–8 mm long; lip border shining yellow up to 6 mm wide; naked; dark colouration often not spreading out in the middle lobe.

Flowers: February–May. **Photos:** Bl, Mallorca 8.3.75 (u/l); Lu, Prov. Estremadura 30.3.71 (u/r). **Distribution:** Mediterranean

region especially in the meridional zone (eastwards to western Greece and Crete) spreading further north in western Europe (Catalonia, southern France as far as the Depts. Charente, Cantal); up to 1,800 m. ● **Floristic element:** mediterranean w-sub-mediterranean s-atlantic. **Countries: Eur:** SE Cr, Gr, Al, **S** Me, Si, It, **SW** Bl, Hs, Lu, **W** Ga; **Afr:** Tn, Ag, Ma.

2. *O. l. subsp. galilaea* (H. Fleischm. & Bornm.) Soó

Synonyms: *O. galilaea* H. Fleischm. & Bornm., *O. l. var. minor* (Tod.) Guss., *O. l. subsp. minor* (Tod.) O. & E. Danesch, *O. sicula* Tineo, *O. l. subsp. murbeckii* Soó (not *O. murbeckii* H. Fleischm., *see* following subspecies).

Inflorescence 2–6 (–9) flowered; sepals 7–10 mm long; lateral petals 4.5–7.5 mm long; lip margin shining to greenish-yellow, (1–) 2–3 mm broad, often with light-coloured hairs, the dark colouration in the tip of the middle lobe spreading. **Flowers:** January–June. **Photos:** AE, Rhodes 6.4.82 (c/l); It, Prov. Fóggia 22.4.81 (c/r). **Distribution:** Mediterranean region, appears to have not yet reached the Iberian peninsula and France (whether on the Côte d'Azur?); up to 1,500 m. ● **Floristic element:** mediterranean c + e-submediterranean. **Countries: Eur:** SE Cr, Gr, Tu, Al, Ju, **S** Me, Si, It, Sa, Co; **Asi:** IJ, LS, Cy, An, AE; **Afr:** Tn, Ag, Ma.

3. *O. l. subsp. melena* Renz

On the whole, similar to the subspecies *galilaea*; sepals 7.5–11 mm long; lateral petals 5.5–7 mm long; darker lip margin bare or with dark hairs. **Flowers:** March, April. **Photos:** Gr, Nomos Attica 14.4.72 (l/l); Cy, area round Girne (Kyrenia) 22.3.70 (l/r). **Distribution:** southern Balkan peninsula, northwards to southern Thessaly, Fokis, Kerkira (Corfu) and southern Albania; also on Lesbos (eastern Aegean) and on the Monte Gargano (southern Italy); up to 1,300 m. ● **Floristic element:** e + c-mediterranean (c-submediterranean).

Countries: Eur: SE Gr, Al, **S** It; **Asi:** AE **Relationship:** similar plants, whose status needs clarification, are known from north Africa as *O. l. subfusca* (Reichenb. fil.) Murbeck (= *O. murbeckii* H. Fleischm. subsp.)

O. l. subsp. lutea

Ophrys

O. l. subsp. melena, above: *O. l. subsp. galilea* (2x)

Sawfly Ophrys   *Ophrys tenthredinifera* Willd.

Synonym: *O. t. subsp. praecox* Tyteca

Plant with 2 ovoid-spherical tubers; stem 10 – 30 (– 45) cm tall with 2 basal scale leaves, 3 – 5 foliage leaves in a rosette and 1 – 4 sheathing the lower half of the stem; rosette leaves broadly lanceolate 4 – 12 cm long and 1 – 3.5 cm wide; inflorescence 1 – 10 flowered; sepals red to pink, upright or directed backwards, broadly ovate to elliptic, 11 – 13 mm long and 6.5 – 10 mm wide; lateral petals broadly triangular, 4 – 6 mm long; lip yellow to light brown with a reddish- to blackish-brown centre, trapezoid, 11 – 16 mm long and 12 – 20 mm broad, densely hairy, convex, the side edges generally spread out or occasionally turned down, 2 low basal protruberances and a turned-up appendage at the front; pattern small, surrounding the basal area, grey-lilac to bluish with a whitish border; column blunt.

Habitat: open pine woods and maquis, garrigue, poor grassland; up to 1,800 m; on basic to slightly acid soils. **Flowers:** February – May. **Photos:** Lu, Prov. Estremadura, type population ('praecox') 25.2.84 (l); It, Priv. Grosseto 14.4.81 (r); p266.

Distribution: Mediterranean area, eastwards to southern Turkey (Vil. Hatay); absent from the Levant and Cyprus.

● **Floristic element:** mediterranean w + c + (e)-submediterranean.

Countries: Eur: SE Cr, Gr, Tu, Al, Ju, **S** Me, Si, It, Sa, Co, **SW** Bl, hs, Lu, **W** Ga; **Asi:** An, AE; **Afr:** Li, Tu, Ag, Ma.

Variation: an early-flowering variant has been described from Portugal ('praecox'): stem 1 – 4 flowered; lip appears narrow because the sides are turned down. Similar plants also turn up in other districts.

Relationship: the species is related to the *fuciflora* types, differing particularly in the blunt column.

Schulze's Ophrys   *Ophrys schulzei* Bornm. & H. Fleischm.

Synonym: *O. luristanica* Renz

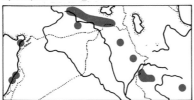

Plant with 2 ovoid-spherical tubers; stem 25 – 65 cm tall with basal scale leaves, 4 – 5 foliage leaves on the lower part, not concentrated in a rosette, and 1 – 2 further up the stem; leaves ovate – lanceolate, 10 – 18 cm long and 2 – 3.5 cm wide; inflorescence extended, lax, 4 – 12 flowered; lower bracts somewhat longer than the ovaries; sepals violet-pink strongly reflexed (the central one often horizontal), ovate 9 – 11 mm long and 4 – 5 mm wide; lateral petals pink, broadly triangular, 1 – 2.5 mm long, smooth or with a few hairs at the base; lip 5 – 7 mm long, deeply 3-lobed; middle lobe chestnut brown, arched into a hemisphere, short hairs in front, a large appendage at the tip turned downwards, 2 – 2.5 mm long ending in a central tooth; pattern extended from the basal area over the middle lobe, branching with a brownish to whitish border; side lobes 4 – 6 mm, strongly arched, hairy, the inside of the arch green to whitish, the outside brown and deeply serrated; column with a 1 – 2 mm long straight extension.

Habitat: open oak-woods and scrubland, poor meadows; 500 – 1,500 m; on fresh calcareous soils. **Flowers:** April, May. **Photos:** An, Vil. Hatay 5.5.78 (l/r); An, Vil. Mardin 15.5.80 (u/r); An, Vil. Diyarbakir 12.5.82 (l).

Distribution: south-eastern Anatolia, westwards to the Amanus mountains (Turkish and Syrian parts) extending into Lebanon; also through Iraqi Kurdestan to western Iran. **Floristic element:** e-mediterranean oriental. **Countries: Asi:** LS, An.

Bee Orchid *Ophrys apifera* Hudson

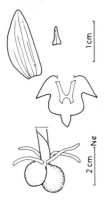

Plant with 2 spherical-ovoid tubers; stem 20 – 50 (– 70) cm tall, with 2 basal scale leaves, 2 – 4 foliage leaves forming a rosette and 4 – 7 further up, the uppermost bract-like; the largest leaves lanceolate 6 – 13 cm long and 1.5 – 2.8 cm wide; inflorescence extended, lax, 3 – 10 (– 17) flowered; bracts shorter to longer than the flowers; sepals pink to red, reflexed, ovate – lanceolate 11 – 17 mm long and 5 – 9 mm wide; lateral petals pink to greenish, triangular 2.5 – 7 mm long, hairy; lip (spread out!) 9 – 14 mm long, deeply 3-lobed, middle lobe chestnut brown, the front part strongly arched with a reflexed tip, hairy round the edge, with a large appendage up to 3 mm long, lanceolate or trapeziform, turned downwards with a central tooth; pattern surrounding the basal area often extending forwards or sideways, brown to whitish border; side lobes turned down, with tubercles at the base, densely hairy; base of lip with 2 yellowish dark-tipped callosities, 2 red staminodal spots; column with 2 – 3 mm long curved extension.

Habitat: open broad-leaved and coniferous woodland, poor grassland, garrigue; up to 1,800 m; on fairly dry or varying dryness, base-rich soils.

Flowers: March – July. **Photos**: Ge, Hessen 16.6.60 (u/l), 12.6.83 (u/r); Ge, Südwürttemberg 14.7.81 (c/l); Al, Prov. Sarandë 23.5.80 (c/r); He, Kt. Neuchâtel 28.6.69 (l/l); Ge, Südbaden 18.6.71 (l/r).

Distribution: In Europe, North Africa and the Near East from the meridional to the temperate zones, penetrates furthest north in oceanic western Europe, absent from the Baltic region and from continental eastern Europe; also in Caucasia.

Floristic element: mediterranean sub-mediterranean pannonic s + m-atlantic s + (n)-subatlantic s-centraleuropean. **Countries**: **Eur**: **SE** Cr, Gr, Tu, Al, Ju, Rm, RK, **S** Me, Si, It, Sa, Co, **SW** Bl, Hs, Lu, **W** Ga, Be, Ho, Br, Hb, **C** He, Au, Hu, Ge, Cz; **Asi**: IJ, LS, Cy, An, AE; **Afr**: Tn, Ag, Ma.

Propagation: the flowers are only rarely cross-pollinated by insects; the usual method is self-pollination (autogamy). To achieve this the pollinial stalks bend down, bringing the pollinia into contact with the stigma; *see* p263.

Variation: the species is variable in flower-form and colour; variants differing from the normal type are not uncommon; they are able to spread because of the autogamic pollination.

1. 'friburgensis' variant (= *O. a. var. friburgensis* Freyhold, *O. botteronii* Chodat, *O. a. subsp. jurana* Ruppert): lateral petals larger than in the normal type – ²/₃ to almost as long as the sepals and of a similar colour, generally glabrous; compared with the norm the lip is generally reduced; middle lobe strongly arched to mostly extended; appendage small, directed downwards or forwards; pattern often reduced, degenerating into irregular yellowish spots; side lobes often smaller with hardly any tubercle (photo l/r).

2. 'trollii' variant (*O. trollii* Hegetschw.); lip stretched out, middle lobe narrow-lanceolate, appendage held straight out or turned up; pattern greatly reduced (to pale spots or patches) or absent, (photo l/l). In Britain most frequent in Avon, Wiltshire and Gloucestershire.

3. Colour variants: these have the same flower structure as the normal type but differ in colouration; they include 'bicolor'; lip yellowish behind, brown in front (photo c/r), 'flavescens' ('chlorantha'): lip yellow, sepals white (photo c/l).

Key to the species of the *Ophrys apifera* group:

1 Lip 9 – 13 mm long; side lobes with 1 – 4 mm-high tubercle, occasionally tubercle absent; beak-like extension of the column bent into an S-shape . . . . *O. apifera*

1* Lip 5 – 7 mm long; side lobes with a 4 – 6 mm high tubercle; column appendage straight . *O. schulzei*, p176

Ophrys

'trollii', above: 'flavescens'   'friburgensis', above: 'bicolor'

Fly Orchid *Ophrys insectifera* L.

Synonyms: *O. muscifera* Hudson, *O. myodes* Jacq.

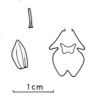

1 cm

Plant with 2 spherical tubers; stem 15 – 40 (– 60) cm tall with 1 – 2 basal scale leaves and 2 – 5 foliage leaves in the lower half (not usually forming a rosette); leaves longish-lanceolate up to 10 cm long and 2.5 cm wide; inflorescence extended, very lax 2 – 10 (– 20) flowered; bracts longer than the ovaries; sepals green, erect or very slightly inclined forwards, concave, the laterals ovate 6 – 9 mm long and 3 – 4 mm wide, the central one shorter and narrower; lateral petals dark-coloured, narrow linear 4.5 – 6.5 mm long, hairy; lip brown, often with red or violet components, papillose, deeply 3-lobed, side lobes spreading or directed forward, mostly longer than broad, rarely as broad as long 9 – 12 × 6 – 10 mm; pattern plain in the centre of the lip, grey-blue; basal area slightly arched, dark with 2 black callosities; column rounded in front; pollen sac (bursicle) red.

Habitat: open pine woods, poor grassland, also fenland; up to 1,700 m; on fairly dry to variably moist calcareous soils. **Flowers:** May – July. **Photos:** Ge, Südwürttemberg 30.5.83 (l); He, Kt. Zürich 23.5.81 (r).

Distribution: in the submeridional and temperate zones of Europe but only occasionally in continental eastern Europe (Upper Volga), isolated also in the meridional zone and in the boreal zone (Scandinavia).

● **Floristic element:** (w + e-mediterranean) w + c-submediterranean pannonic atlantic subatlantic centraleuropean sarmatic scandinavian.

Countries: Eur: SE Gr, Al, Ju, Rm, **S** It, SW, Bl, Hs, **W** Ga, Be, Ho, Br, Hb, **C** He, Au, Hu, Ge, Da, Cz, Po, RB, **N** Su, No, Fe, **E** RW, RC.

Aymonin's Ophrys *Ophrys aymoninii* (Breistr.) Buttler

Synonym: *O. insectifera subsp. aymoninii* Breistr.

1 cm

Distinguished from *O. insectifera* by the different shape and colour of the flower; lip with spreading triangular side lobes so that in outline it appears almost as broad or broader than long 9.5 – 12 × 8.5 – 12 mm, dark brown (without red component), the yellow border of the middle lobe 1.5 – 2 mm wide; pattern grey-blue, generally extending forwards into 2 short points and sometimes surrounding the basal area; pollen sac yellow.

Habitat: open pine woods and beech/pine mixed woods; 700 – 900 m; on fairly dry calcareous soils. **Flowers:** May, June. **Photos:** Ga, Dept. Aveyron 20.5.83.

Distribution: endemic in southern France, discovered in 1959 it is known from the Causses (Causse du Larzac, C. Noir, C. Méjean, C. de Sauveterre). It may be more widely distributed in the central mountains of France; it needs to be checked whether records of the hybrid *O. insectifera × lutea* in the Corbières belong to this species.

● **Floristic element:** w-submediterranean. **Country:** Eur: W Ga.

Relationship: the yellow border on the lip indicates that this species may have arisen from a cross between *O. insectifera* and *O. lutea* or *O. araneola*. However, this hypothesis is not very convincing. The *aymoninii* type appears to have developed without the influence of any other species of the *insectifera* type.

Key to the species of the *insectifera* group:

1 Lip lobes with (violet-) brown border; lateral petals dark brown to purplish-violet
 . . . . *O. insectifera*
1* Lobes with a broad yellow border; lateral petals green to brownish-green . . . .
 . . . . *O. aymoninii*

Mirror Ophrys *Ophrys ciliata* Biv.

Synonyms: *O. speculum* Link, *O. vernixia* in the broad sense

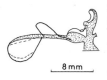

Stem 5–25 cm tall; 2–8 flowered; sepals 7–10 mm long often striped or tinged brownish-red; lateral petals 4–6 mm long, brown (red); lip 12–16 mm long; middle lobe (excluding the wreath of long dark hairs) 0.6–1.1× as long as broad, slightly arched with a 0.5–1.5 mm wide, dark, hairless border; side lobes broadly lanceolate to ovate; pattern dark blue to deep violet surrounded by yellow to orange border.

Habitat: open woodland, garrigue, poor grassland, former cultivated land; up to 1,000 m; on dry to fresh base-rich soils. **Flowers:** February–April. **Photos:** It, Prov. Grosseto 20.4.82 (l); Al, Prov. Fier 9.4.82 (r); *see also* p253.

Distribution: Mediterranean region; large gaps in the c + e-submediterranean and in the e-mediterranean. • **Floristic element:** mediterranean submediterranean. **Countries:** **Eur: SE** Gr, Tu, Al, **S** Me, Si, It, Sa, Co, **SW** Bl, Hs, Lu, **W** Ga; **Asi:** LS, An, AE; **Afr:** Li, Tn, Ag, Ma.

Iberian Ophrys *Ophrys vernixia* Brot.

Synonym: *O. speculum subsp. lusitanica* O. & E. Danesch

Stem 15–50 cm tall; 5–15 flowered; size of flower parts as in *O. ciliata*; sepals unstriped or only faintly striped brownish-red; lateral petals yellow (orange) or light brownish-red; middle lobe (without the wreath of long hairs) 0.8–1.8× as long as broad with a yellow, hairless border, strongly arched both lengthwise and across; side lobes linear-lanceolate, half as long as the middle lobe or longer; pattern dark blue with an orange or olive (brown) border.

Habitat: Garrigue, poor grassland; up to 500 m; its demands appear to be similar to those of *O. ciliata*. **Flowers:** March–May, 2–3 weeks later than *O. ciliata*. **Photos:** Lu, Prov. Estremadura 31.3.71. **Distribution:** the Iberian Peninsula: central Portugal (Estremadura), southern Portugal (Algarve) and southern Spain (Prov. Córdoba, Jaén). • **Floristic element:** w-mediterranean/disjuncted. **Countries: Eur: SW** Hs, Lu.

King Ferdinand's Ophrys *Ophrys regis-ferdinandii* (Renz) Buttler

Synonyms: *O. speculum var. regis-ferdinandii* (Renz) Soó, *O. vernixia subsp. regis-ferdinandii* (Kuzmanov) Renz & Taubenheim

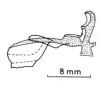

Stem 5–30 cm tall, 2–11 flowered; flowers smaller than those of *O. ciliata*; sepals heavily tinged with brownish-red; lateral petals yellow with a brown base or brown, often narrow; middle lobe (without the wreath of long hairs) 2–4.5× as long as broad with a dark or yellowish hairless border, lengthwise almost straight, but strongly arched across; side lobes linear; pattern violet-blue to dark purple with an orange to yellowish-brown border.

Habitat: similar to that of *O. ciliata*; up to 400 m; on fairly dry, base-rich soils.

Flowers: March, April, 2–3 weeks later than *O. ciliata*, **Photos:** An, Vil. Izmir 3.4.78 (r); An, Vil. Aydin 7.4.70 (l).

Distribution: eastern Aegean in 3 separate parts: Chios and the Çesme Peninsula, in the region of Kusadasi/Söke, Rhodes.

• **Floristic element:** e-mediterranean/disjunct. **Countries: Asi:** An, Ae.

'flavescens'

Ophrys

Bumble Bee Ophrys   *Ophrys bombyliflora* Link

Plant with (2 −) 3 − 5 spherical tubers, the newly formed ones with long runners (vegetative reproduction); stem 5 − 20 (− 30) cm tall with 1 − 2 basal scale leaves, 4 − 8 foliage leaves forming a rosette and 1 − 2 long-sheathing leaves on the lower half; rosette leaves ovate − lanceolate 3 − 10 cm long and 1 − 3 cm wide; inflorescence 1 − 5 flowered; bracts mostly shorter than the ovaries; sepals green, upright or directed backwards slightly, the laterals broadly ovate, blunt, 9 − 12 mm long and 6 − 8 mm wide, the central one somewhat shorter and narrower; lateral petals yellowish-green, hairy, broadly triangular, 3 − 4 mm long; lip dark brown, 8 − 10 mm long and 11 − 13 mm broad, deeply 3-lobed; middle lobe with downward-curving edges, hemispherical, papillose border, a half-hidden reflexed

2 cm
Ne

appendage in front; side lobes curving downwards with a hairy tubercle at the base; pattern not very obvious, brownish to dull violet; column blunt.

Habitat: open woodland, garrigue, poor meadows, little used cultivated land; up to 900 m; on fairly dry to fairly damp base-rich soils. **Flowers:** February − May. **Photos:** It, Grosseto 12.4.81 (l); Bl, Mallorca 3.3.75 (r).

Distribution: Mediterranean region; absent from the eastern part, eastwards only as far as western Anatolia and Rhodes; westwards to the Canaries (Gran Canaria and Tenerife).

● **Floristic element:** mediterranean canarian w + c-submediterranean.

Countries: Eur: SE   Cr, Gr, Al, Ju, **S**   Me, Si, It, Sa, Co, **SW**   Bl, Hs, Lu, **W**   Ga; **Asi:** An, AE; **Afr:** Li, Tn, Ag, Ma, Cl.

Relationship: this species stands isolated in the genus; it is one of the species undergoing little change. The only *Ophrys* in the Canaries.

Cilician Ophrys   *Ophrys cilicica* Schlechter

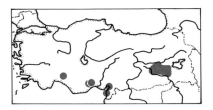

Plant with 2 spherical tubers; stem 15 − 30 (− 60) cm tall, 2 − 5 basal foliage leaves longish-lanceolate up to 13 cm long and 2 cm wide, pointed, above these 1 − 2 leaves sheathing the stem; inflorescence lax, 3 − 12 flowered; bracts longer than the flowers; sepals green, often whitish, tinted red or pink, ovate − lanceolate, 9 − 12 mm long and 3.5 − 4.5 mm wide, the central one bending forward or, occasionally, almost straight upright, the laterals pointing down at an angle; lateral petals greenish-pink, linear-lanceolate, 4.5 − 6 mm long, papillose; lip red- to dark (violet) -brown with a narrow paler edge,

10 − 12 mm long, narrowing to a stalk-like base with 2.5 − 4 mm long basal area, bounded on each side by a low ridge; middle lobe (spread out!) 6 − 9 mm broad, papillose velvety, broadly wedge-shaped in front with a small appendage, the sides turned down making it look narrow; side lobes directed downwards with short hairs, with a 1 − 2 mm high tubercle at the base which has a green strip on its inner side; pattern generally of four longitudinal stripes, each with 1 − 2 cross bands, whitish with a violet border; red staminode spots.

Habitat: open deciduous woodland, scrub, poor meadows; 500 − 1,300 m; on fairly dry to fresh calcareous soils. **Flowers:** April, May. **Photos:** An, Vil. Diyarbakir 17.5.74 (l); An, Vil. Antalya 19.5.83 (r).

Distribution: endemic in southern and south-eastern Anatolia; known from the Vilayet Antalya in the west to the Vilayet Siirt in the east.

● **Floristic element:** e-mediterranean oriental. **Country: Asi:** An.

185

Kotschy's Ophrys *Ophrys kotschyi* H. Fleischm. & Soó

Synonym: *O. cypria* Renz

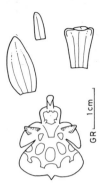

Plant with 2 ovoid-spherical tubers; stem 10 – 35 cm tall with 1 – 2 basal scale leaves, 2 – 7 foliage leaves in a rosette and 1 – 2 leaves higher up; rosette leaves narrow elliptic, 4 – 8 mm long and 1.5 – 2.5 mm wide; inflorescence lax, 3 – 10 flowered; bracts longer than the ovaries; sepals green or pink (-brownish) tinted, 12.5 – 16 mm long and 6 – 8.5 mm wide, the middle one bent forwards, the laterals pointing at right angles to the sides; lateral petals 5.5 – 8 mm long, green with a brownish background, hairy; lip blackish-purple 11.5 – 15 mm long, deeply 3-lobed; middle lobe (spread out!) 14 – 17 mm broad, papillose-velvety, crenate in front with a strong appendage, strongly arched crosswise thus appearing narrow; side lobes more brownish-purple, directed downwards, densely hairy with a 1 – 2 mm high tubercle at the base; pattern spread out in the form of reticulate broad stripes, dull brownish-lilac with a whitish border; basal area 2.4 – 3.2 mm long and broad; basal callosities whitish with darker points; violet staminodal spots present.

Habitat: open coniferous woodland, garrigue, sand dunes, also woodland plantations; up to 1,000 m; on fairly dry to damp calcareous soils. **Flowers:** March, April. **Photos:** Cy, Limassol area 14.3.84 (l); Cy, Troodos area 19.3.70 (r).

Distribution: endemic on Cyprus, more frequent in north. • **Floristic element:** e-mediterranean. **Country: Asi:** Cy.

Relationship: here the species is included in the reinholdii group; its connections with *O. umbilicata* are also open to discussion.

Cretan Ophrys *Ophrys cretica* (Vierh.) E. Nelson

Synonyms: *O. kotschyi subsp. cretica* (Vierh.) Sundermann, *O. c. subsp. naxia* E. Nelson, *O. c. subsp. karpathensis* E. Nelson. Some confusion surrounds the name *O. doerfleri* H. Fleischm. which has recently been used for the species and probably does not belong here.

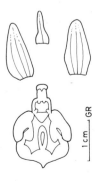

Vegetatively similar to *O. kotschyi*; basal foliage leaves lanceolate, up to 7 cm long and 1.8 cm wide; inflorescence 2 – 8 flowered; bracts scarcely longer than the ovaries; sepals green, often the laterals red tinted, especially in the lower half (or all over), ovate 11 – 15 mm long and 5 – 7.5 mm wide, the centre one directed backwards or upright; lateral petals (greenish-) lilac-pink, narrow, triangular, 6 – 9 mm long hairy; lip blackish-purple, 11 – 14 mm long, deeply 3-lobed; middle lobe (spread out!) 10 – 14 mm broad, fine short hairs near the edge, broadly wedge-shaped in front with a small or strong appendage, strongly arched crosswise; side lobes spreading, densely hairy, with or without tubercles; pattern variable – spread out and reticulate or H-shaped or with parallel stripes, dull brownish-lilac with whitish border or all whitish; basal area and callosities like *O. kotschyi*; red staminode dots generally absent.

Habitat: garrigue, poor grassland, former cultivated land; up to 1,100 m; on base-rich, dry to fresh soils. **Flowers:** March, April. **Photos:** Cr, Nomos Rethimnon 31.3.72 (l); Cr, Nomos Lasithi 5.4.72 (r).

Distribution: centred in the Aegean (known from the islands Aegina, Syros, Naxos, Crete, Karpathos, Rhodes, Samos) also in Attica.

• **Floristic element:** e-mediterranean. **Countries: Eur:** SE, Cr, Gr; **Asi:** AE.

Reinhold's Ophrys   *Ophrys reinholdii* H. Fleischm.

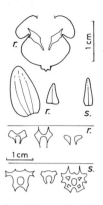

Plant with 2 ellipsoidal-spherical tubers; stem 20–60 cm tall with 1–2 basal scale leaves, 3–6 foliage leaves in a rosette and 1–2 leaves sheathing the stem; rosette leaves longish-lanceolate, 6–12 cm long and 1.5–2.5 cm wide; inflorescence up to 25 cm long, lax, 2–8 flowered; lower bracts longer than the flowers; sepals pink to red, rarely whitish or green, ovate-lanceolate 12–16 mm long and 4–7.5 mm wide, all of them directed more or less backwards, or the central one upright; lateral petals (brownish-)pink to dark red, rarely greenish, 4.5–8 mm long, hairy; lip black to dark brownish-purple, 10–15 mm long, deeply 3-lobed; middle lobe (spread out) 10–14 mm broad, papillose-velvety, broadly wedge-shaped to truncate in front with a small or strong appendage, strongly arched tranversely; side lobes turned down, paler than the middle lobe, dense white hairs, basal tubercle absent or very slight; basal area about as long as broad; basal callosities poorly developed; red staminode spots present.

Problem: the species embraces many forms, several of which have been distinguished as separate subspecies or even species in current literature today. The justification for this needs to be looked into by a new investigation in which the whole distribution of the species is systematically set out. In the meantime, 2 subspecies are described here.

Key to the subspecies:

1   Pattern basically 2 longitudinal marks with extensions to the front and into the recesses in front of the side lobes, separate or with a narrow cross-band, often coloured with a white border; lateral petals broadly triangular, about twice as long as wide ..... *O. r. subsp. reinholdii*

1*   Pattern basically a broad cross-band between the recesses in front of the side lobes with equally wide forward extensions, often completely white lacking the coloured inner-zone; lateral petals usually narrowly triangular to lingulate, about 2.5× as long as wide .. .. *O. r. subsp. straussii*

1.   *O. r. subsp. reinholdii*

Synonym: *O. mimnolea* O. Schwartz

Stem 20–30 (–40) cm tall, 2–6 flowered; lip middle lobe often only slightly arched, which makes it appear quite broad, appendage short up to 1.5 mm long. **Habitat:** open woodland and maquis, garrigue, poor grassland; up to 1,300 m; on fairly dry soils over limestone or sandstone. **Flowers:** March–May. **Photos:** An, Vil. Mugla 10.4.80 (u/l), 8.4.70 (u/r).

Distribution: from southern Albania and Kerkira (Corfu) throughout almost the whole of Greece; the islands in the central and eastern Aegean; south-west Turkey. ● **Floristic element:**   c + e-mediterranean. **Countries:** **Eur: SE**   Gr, Al; **Asi:** An, AE.

2.   *O. r. subsp. straussii* (H. Fleischm. & Bornm.) E. Nelson

Synonym: *O. straussii* H. Fleischm. & Bornm.

Stem 30–60 cm tall, 5–8 flowered; middle lobe often strongly arched giving an elliptical appearance; appendage short or elongated, up to 3 mm. **Habitat:** similar to that of the subspecies *reinholdii*; 200–1500 m. **Flowers:** April–June. **Photos:** An, Vil. Siirt, 13.5.81 (l/l); An, Vil. Hatay 10.5.74 (l/r).

Distribution: southern and south-eastern Anatolia, eastwards to Iraqi and Persian Kurdestan, westwards to Rhodes. **Floristic element:** e-mediterranean oriental.

Countries: **Asi:** An, AE.

Variation: in southern Anatolia there are intermediate forms between the subspecies. *O. r. subsp. leucotaenia* Renz & Taubenheim, which is only known from 2 sites in southern Turkey (Vil. Antalya and Adana), probably belongs to the subspecies *straussii*. It may be a colour variant with almost white side lobes and flower size at the lower limit of size variation. **Photos:** An, Vil. Antalya, type population, end of 5.80 (centre).

Ophrys

O. r. subsp. straussii, above: 'leucotaenia'

Carmel Ophrys *Ophrys umbilicata* Desf.

Synonyms: *O. carmeli* H. Fleischm. & Bornm., *O. u. subsp. carmeli* (H. Fleischm. & Bornm.) J. J. Wood, *O. dinsmorei* Schlechter, *O. carmeli subsp. orientalis* (Renz) Soó, *O. scolopax subsp. orientalis* (Renz) E. Nelson; *O. u. subsp. khuzestanica* Renz & Taubenheim; *O. attica* (Boiss. & Orph.) B. D. Jackson, *O. carmeli subsp. attica* (Boiss. & Orph.) Renz, *O. scolopax subsp. attica* (Boiss. & Orph.) E. Nelson *O. u. subsp. attica* (Boiss. & Orph.) J. J. Wood

Plant with 2 spherical-ovoid tubers; stem 10–45 (–60) cm tall with 0–2 basal scale leaves, 3–8 foliage leaves in a rosette and 1–2 leaves up the stem; rosette leaves ovate–lanceolate, 4–15 cm long and 1.5–3.5 cm wide; inflorescence lax 2–12 flowered, the flowers held at a wide angle (45–90°); bracts longer than the lower flowers; sepals green to greenish- or reddish-white, ovate-elliptic 8.5–13 mm long and 5–7 mm wide, the central one bending forward over the column, the laterals concave, pointing sideways at right angles; lateral petals yellow-green to reddish-white, short or extended, triangular 3.5–6 mm long, hairy; lip reddish- to dark brown, deeply 3-lobed; middle lobe strongly arched and appearing ovoid, widening towards the front from a wedge-shaped base, 9.5–14 mm wide, crenate in front and with a strong up-turned appendage; side lobes turned down, densey hairy, basal tubercle 1–3 mm high; pattern extended, surrounding the basal area, brownish-lilac with a pale border; basal callosities greenish; red staminode spots present.
Habitat: open pine cypress and oak-woods, garrigue, poor grassland; up to 800 m; mainly on calcareous soils, rarely on sandstone.
Flowers: February – May. **Photos:** Cy, Paphos area 8.4.83 (u/l, c/r); Cy, Larnaca area 31.3.70 (u/r); An, Vil. Mardin 19.,4.80 (c/l).
Distribution: the Near East and the southern Balkan Peninsula; northwards to southern Albania, Thessaly and the Bosphorus. Also in Iraqi Kurdestan, western and southern Persia.
Floristic element: e + c-mediterranean oriental e-submediterranean. **Countries: Eur: SE** Gr, Tu, Al; **Asi:** IJ, LS, Cy, An, AE.
Problem: the *O. umbilicata* group with its many forms may be split into as many as 4 species according to one's point of view. For the present, only one will be considered here as an independent species; the others will be treated as variants.
Key to the species:
1 Lip 7–10.5 (–11.5) mm long; edges of middle lobe (apart from the fringe of hairs) 0.5–1.5 mm wide .. 1. *O. umbilicata*
1* Lip 10–14 mm long; edges of middle lobe 2–3 mm wide .. 2. *O. flavomarginata*
1. *O. umbilicata* the characters are described above; the 3 variants are distinguished as follows: 1. ('umbilicata' strict sense, = 'carmeli', 'orientalis'): stem 10–25 (–45) cm tall; sepals greenish- to reddish-white.
2. ('attica'): stem 10–25 (–35) cm tall; inflorescence up to 6 cm wide; sepals green;
3. ('khuzestanica'): stem 25–45 (–60) cm tall; inflorescence up to 4 cm wide; sepals green. Plants with green or whitish to reddish sepals are often found growing together in a population (in varying ratios in different areas) without showing other differences. Also variants 2 and 3 are hardly sufficiently separated to rate their being given subspecies status.
2. *O. flavomarginata* (Renz) H. Baumann & Künkele;
Synonym: *O. attica f. flavomarginata* Renz
All parts of the flowers larger than in *O. umbilicata*; edges of the middle lobe greenish-brown and hairy to yellow and glabrous; sepals green. **Habitat:** as *O. umbilicata*. **Flowers:** somewhat earlier than the other species. **Photos:** Cy, Limassol area 13.3.84 (l/l); Cy, Paphos area 8.4.83 (l/r).
Distribution: Cyprus and the Levant.
● **Floristic element:** e-mediterranean
Countries: Asi: IJ, Cy. The status of this form remains to be confirmed; possibly it will be seen as a subspecies or as a large-flowered variant of *O. umbilicata*.

below: variant 3   *O. umbilicata:* variant 1   below: variant 2

Ophrys

O. flavomarginata

191

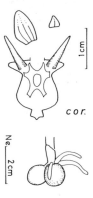

c o r.

Ne.

Plant with 2 ovoid-spherical tubers; stem 10–65 cm tall, with 1–2 basal scale leaves, 3–7 foliage leaves forming a rosette and 1–2 (–4) leaves up the stem; rosette leaves (ovate–) lanceolate, 5–12 cm long and 1.2–2.5 cm wide; inflorescence elongated 2–12 (–20) flowered; sepals pink to red, occasionally whitish-green or green, generally directed backwards and weakly concave, occasionally strongly curving to the front, narrowly elliptic to ovate, 7–15 (–18) mm long and 3–7 (–9) mm wide; lateral petals pink to red 3–7 mm long, hairy; lip chestnut brown, occasionally with a faint violet shade 6–15 mm long, deeply 3-lobed; middle lobe strongly arched, appearing ellipsoid, surrounded by short hairs, with a narrow, yellowish glabrous border, a large turned-up appendage in front; side lobes turned downwards, densely hairy with a tubercle at the base; pattern extended in the front half of the lip, surrounding the basal area, with extensions towards the recesses in front of the side lobes and sometimes also into the front half of the lip, brownish-violet with a pale border; basal callosities blackish; red staminode spots present.

Habitat: open woodland and scrub, garrigue, poor meadows and pasture; up to 2,000 m; on fairly dry to damp base-rich soils. **Flowers**: March–June, often early and late-flowering variants of the same subspecies are present in the same area.

Problem: the *O. scolopax* group is particularly varied in form and is reckoned as one of the most difficult in the genus. Numerous proposals have been made as to how the multiplicity of forms should be arranged and fitted into a taxonomic framework. Depending on the method of evaluation, between 3 and 5 types can be distinguished as species or subspecies by experts who have divergent opinions regarding the significance of particular characters. This situation is confusing and a fundamental re-evaluation is required for the clarification of many open questions. Here 3 types are provisionally considered to be independent and, because of numerous intermediate forms, no sharp lines of demarcation can be drawn according to the present state of knowledge: they are given the status of subspecies. **Hybrid** with O. holoserica, *see* p204.

Key to the subspecies:
1   Lip 13–16 mm long with a 2.5–4.5 mm long appendage . . . .
   . . . . . 3. *O. s. subsp. heldreichii*, p194
1* Lip 7–12 (–15) mm long with a short 1.5–2 (–2.5) mm long appendage . . 2
2   Protuberance on the side lobe (measured on the inner side) (4–) 6–12 mm long .
   . . . . 2. *O. s. subsp. cornuta*, p194
2* Side lobe protuberance up to 4 (6) mm . .
   . . . . 1. *O. s. subsp. scolopax*

1. *O. s. subsp. scolopax*

Synonyms: *O. fuciflora subsp. scolopax* (Cav.) – Variant 2: *O. apiformis* (Desf.) Steudel, *O. s. subsp. apiformis* (Desf.) Maire & Weiller, *O. fuciflora subsp. apiformis* (Desf.) Sundermann – Variant 3: *O. bremifera* Steven, *O. oestrifera subsp. bremifera* (Steven) K. Richter – Variant 4: *O. phrygia* H. Fleischm. & Bornm. The variants are described separately in order to show the variation range and the amount of overlapping: variant 1. ('scolopax'; western half of the area: Hs, Lu, Ga, Co): lateral petals 0.39–0.58 × as long as the sepals, the latter 9–13.5 mm long. – variant 2 ('apiformis'; western half of the area: Si, Tn, Ag, Ma, Hs): lateral petals 0.4–0.51 × as long as the sepals, the latter 7–10 mm long, often pale pink – whitish, rarely green; lip 6–9.5 mm long. – variant 3. ('bremifera'; eastern half of the area: Gr, Cy, An, AE): lateral petals 0.27–0.45 × as long as the sepals, the latter 9–16 mm long; lip 6–12.5 (–15) mm long. – variant 4 ('phrygia'; eastern half of the area: An): lateral petals 0.2–0.29 × as long as the sepals, the latter 12–15 (–18) mm long; lip

Ophrys

O. o. subsp. cornuta

10 – 13.5 (– 15) mm long. **Photos:** variant 1: Hs, Prov. Teruel 12.4.72 (p.193 u/l); Hs, Prov. Cadiz 27.4.79 (p193 c/l). – variant 3; AE, Samos 6.4.77 (p.193 c/r); Gr, Euböea 15.4.84 (p193 u/r). – variant 4: An, Vil. Antalya 14.5.81 (c/l), 29.4.78 (c/r).

Distribution: In Europe, North Africa (with Pantelleria) and the Near East in the meridional and submeridional zones, penetrates into France in the temperate zone; also in Transcaucasia and northern Iran. The subspecies has an obvious distribution gap in the central Mediterranean region where it bypasses Italy, Sardinia and Sicily. This type of distribution is however not unusual; there are several parallel examples. **Floristic element:** mediterranean/disjunct oriental w + (c + e)-submediterreanean s-atlantic s-subatlantic.

Countries: Eur: SE Gr, ?Tu, **S** Si, Co, **SW** Hs, Lu, **W** Ga; **Asi:** Cy, An, AE; **Afr:** Tn, Ag, Ma.

2. *O. s. subsp. cornuta* (Steven) E. G. Camus

Synonyms: *O. cornuta* Steven, *O. fuciflora subsp. cornuta* (Steven) Sundermann, *O. oestrifera* Bieb., *O. s. subsp. oestrifera* (Bieb.) Soó

Lateral petals 0.28 – 0.45 × as long as the sepals, the latter 9 – 14 mm long; lip 8 – 12 mm long. **Photos:** (p193): Gr, Euboea 12.4.84 (l/l); An, Vil. Bolu 19.5.83 (l/r).

Distribution: Balkan peninsula northwards as far as the central mountains of Hungary and the foot of the southern Carpathians; on the western side of the Adriatic to Monte Gargano; Crimea. Also in Caucasia. Whether or not plants with long and short protuberances, which occur near one another in the eastern Mediterranean area (Gr, An, AE), differ in other characteristics enough to merit their being put into different subspecies is still to be tested. **Floristic element:** e + c-mediterranean e + c-submediterranean pannonic danubean.

Countries: Eur: SE Gr, Tu, Al, Ju, Bu, Rm, RK, **S** It, **C** Hu; **Asi:** An, AE.

3. *O. s. subsp. heldreichii* (Schlechter) E. Nelson

Synonyms: *O. heldreichii* Schlechter, *O. oestrifera subsp. heldreichii* (Schlechter) Hayek

Lateral petals 0.31 – 0.48 × as long as the sepals, the latter 12.5 – 15 mm long; protuberance up to 5 mm high; lip appendage often longer than broad, 3 – 5 toothed. **Photos:** Cr, Nomos Lasithi 15.4.80 (u/l), 27.3.68 (u/r).

Distribution: Aegean and southern Balkan peninsula; characteristically distinct on Crete (here without the other subspecies), scattered throughout the Peloponnese, rare towards northern Greece, eastwards to Rhodes, Samos and Lesbos. The relationship between the large-flowered examples of the subspecies *scolopax* (Al, Rm, Gr, An) and the subspecies *heldreichii* needs investigating.

• **Floristic element:** e + c-mediterranean.
Countries: Eur: SE Cr, Gr; **Asi:** AE.

Isaurian Ophrys   *Ophrys isaura* Renz & Taubenheim

O. attica
Rhodes
GR
1cm

Stem up to 50 cm tall, up to 15 flowered; sepals generally green, also reddish or red, 11 – 12 mm long and 4 – 5 mm wide, strongly reflexed; lateral petals whitish (– pink), 3 – 4 mm long: lip 9.5 – 11 mm long, similar to that of *O. scolopax* but the side lobes have a broad attachment – wider than the height of the tubercle (up to 2 mm); basal callosities blackish, united by a pedestal-shaped elevation.

Habitat: pine woods, oak-woods; 800 – 900 m; on marl. **Flowers:** May. **Photos:** An, Vil. Içel 14.5.83 (l); type population 14.5.80 (r). **Distribution:** southern Anatolia; known from a single site near Gülnar in Isauria. • **Floristic element:** e-mediterranean. **Country: Asi:** An **Relationship:** Here the species has provisionally been treated as separate but its position in the *O. scolopax*-group has not been clarified. The same goes for similar plants with green, reflexed sepals on Rhodes which are known as *O. attica* (*see* Nelson 1962, Landwehr 1977 and the drawing on the left). Green sepals are occasionally to be found in *O. scolopax* – variant apiformis'.

Ophrys

195

Argolis Ophrys   *Ophrys argolica* H. Fleischm.

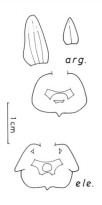

arg.

ele.

Plant with 2 spherical tubers; stem 15 – 30 (– 50) cm tall, with 0 – 2 basal scale leaves, 3 – 6 foliage leaves forming a rosette and 2 – 3 leaves up the stem; rosette leaves lanceolate 3 – 18 cm long and 1 – 2.5 cm wide; inflorescence lax, 2 – 8 flowered; bracts generally longer than the ovaries; sepals red to pink, narrowly ovate, 10.5 – 15.5 mm long and 5 – 8 mm wide, the central one upright or directed slightly backwards, the laterals pointing upwards at an angle; lateral petals pink to red, broad- to narrow-triangular, 5.5 – 9 mm long, hairy; lip dark (reddish-) brown, sometimes with a violet shade round the edge, roundish 9 – 15 × 12 – 16.5, undivided to 3-lobed, more or less arched, dense long white hairs along the back edge, a small or robust appendage in front; pattern in the form of 2 separate or joined spots seldom surrounding the basal area, greyish violet with a paler border; basal callosities blackish; red staminode spot present.

Habitat: open coniferous woodland and maquis, garrigue, poor grassland; up to 1,000 m; on calcareous soils. **Flowers**: March – May. **Photos**: Gr. Nomos Argolis 7.4.66 (u/l); Gr, Nomos Lakonia 19.4.84 (u/r).
Distribution: eastern Mediterranean region; Akarnania, Fokis, Attica, Peloponnese, southern Aegea (Crete, Kasos, Karpathos, Rhodes), eastern Aegean (Lesbos), south-western and southern Anatolia.
● **Floristic element**: e-mediterranean.
Countries: Eur: SE Cr, Gr; **Asi:** An, AE.
Relationship: a close relative is *O. elegans* (Renz) H. Baumann & Künkele (**synonym**: *O. argolica subsp. elegans* (Renz) E. Nelson).
Stem 5 – 15 (– 25) cm tall, 2 – 4 flowered; sepals strongly reflexed; lip mostly 3-lobed; middle lobe often strongly convex and appears triangular; the size of the flower parts lie within the range of those of *O. argolica*.
Habitat: similar to *O. argolica*; up to 1,400 m; on calcareous and marl soils.
Flowers: February – April, **Photos**: Cy, Morphou area 20.3.70 (c/l); Cy, Limassol area 18.3.84 (c/r). **Distribution**: Cyprus. Similar plants have also been found in southern Anatolia (Vil. Icel, Hatay). ● **Floristic element**: e-mediterranean. **Country**: Asi: Cy. Whether or not the differences are sufficient to separate the Cypriot plants from *O. argolica* as a separate species is still to be properly investigated.

Delphis Ophrys   *Ophrys delphinensis* O. & E. Danesch

1cm

Stem 20 – 40 cm tall, 3 – 10 flowered; basal leaves 3 – 6, longish-lanceolate; sepals pinkish-red 12 – 16 mm long and 6 – 9 mm wide; lateral petals dark red 4.5 – 7 mm long, hairy; lip chestnut-brown 10 – 12.5 mm long, 3-lobed; middle lobe (spread out!) 11 – 16 mm broad, short hairs near the edge, convex, a 3-toothed appendage in front; side lobes reflexed, basal tubercle to 2 mm high, covered in dense, long pale hairs; pattern in the shape of 2 separate or joined

spots, with extensions into the recesses in front of the side lobes, and sometimes towards the basal area, lilac with a pale border.
Habitat: coniferous woodland, garrigue, poor grassland, formerly cultivated land; up to 1,100 m. **Flowers**: April, May. **Photos**: Gr, Nomos Fokis 17.4.84. **Distribution**: northern Peloponnes (Achaia, Corinth) and central Greece (Aetolia, Fokis, Boetia, Attica, Fthiotis, Euboea).
● **Floristic element**: e-mediterranean.
Country: Eur: SE Gr.
Relationship: the species probably originated from a cross between *O. argolica* × *oestrifera*.

Ophrys

197

Horseshoe Ophrys   *Ophrys ferrum-equinum* Desf.

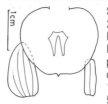

Stem 10 – 30 cm tall, 2 – 8 flowered; basal leaves 4 – 8, broadly lanceolate sepals pinkish-red, occasionally whitish, 12 – 17 mm long and 5 – 8.5 mm wide, generally slightly reflexed; lateral petals dark red, narrowly triangular, 7 – 11 mm long, finely papillose; lip dark brown (– violet), rounded 13 – 16.5 × 14 – 19 mm, slightly arched, occasionally superficially 3-lobed, without tubercles, dense, short dark hairs along the back edge, a small appendage in front; pattern in the centre of the lip, horseshoe-shaped or as separate spots, lilac to greyish-blue, rarely with a pale border; basal callosities blackish; staminode spots absent.
Habitat: open coniferous woodland, garrigue, poor grassland; up to 1,000 m; on base-rich soils. **Flowers:** March – May. **Photos:** Gr, Nomos Attica 13.4.84 (l); An, Vil. Izmir 30.3.80 (r).
Distribution: eastern Mediterranean region; southern Albania; Greek mainland; Aegean (occurring widely but not on Crete); western and southern Anatolia. ● **Floristic element:** e + c-mediterranean.
Countries: Eur: SE Gr, Al; **Asi:** An, AE.

Gottfried's Ophrys   *Ophrys gottfriediana* Renz

Synonym: *O. ferrum-equinum subsp. gottfriediana* (Renz) E. Nelson

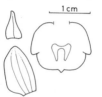

Similar to *O. ferrum-equinum* in appearance, in flower dimensions, in the hairiness of the lip and the pattern shape; sepals green to pale pink, the lateral ones generally more intensely coloured in the lower half, rarely all uniformly pinkish-red; central sepal often bent forwards; lip weakly 3-lobed or undivided, strongly convex in the front half so that it appears triangular and pointed.
Habitat: open woodland, garrigue, poor grassland; up to 600 m. **Flowers:** April. **Photos:** Gr. Kefallonia, 12.4.77 (l); Gr, Zakinthos (Zante) 9.4.80 (r).
Distribution: Greece; concentrated in the Epirus and on the Ionian islands, otherwise scattered in southern Greece and the Aegean (Kythera, Kykladen, Karpathos). ● **Floristic element:** e + c-mediterranean. **Countries: Eur: SE** Cr, Gr.
Problem: the status of this heterogenic species should be researched more exactly.

Lycian Ophrys   *Ophrys lycia* Renz & Taubenheim

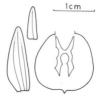

Stem up to 30 cm tall with 3 – 4 longish-lanceolate foliage leaves at ground level and 1 – 2 sheathing the stem; inflorescence fairly dense, 3 – 5 flowered; bracts scarcely longer than the ovaries; sepals purplish-pink, the laterals often with darker spots about 16 mm long and 5 mm wide, the central one upright and S-shaped seen from the side; lateral petals pink 7 – 9 mm long, glabrous or papillose at the base; lip dark brownish-purple, rounded 13 – 15 mm long and broad, slightly arched, light-coloured, short hairs along the back edge, otherwise papillose-velvety, a small appendage in front; pattern H-shaped, sometimes with 2 cross bars, greyish-lilac with a lighter border. **Habitat:** poor meadows; up 500 m; on calcareous soil. **Flowers:** March, April. **Photos:** An, Vil. Antalya, type population 3.4.80. **Distribution:** south-western Anatolia; one site between Finike and Kas in Lycia.
● **Floristic element:** e-mediterranean.
Country: Asi: An. **Relationship:** the species shows connections with the sphegodes group.

199

Spectacle Ophrys   *Ophrys biscutella* O. & E. Danesch

Synonyms: *O. fuciflora subsp. pollinensis* E. Nelson, *O. holoserica subsp. pollinensis* O. & E. Danesch, *O. exaltata subsp. sundermannii* Soó

Similar to *O. crabronifera* in general appearance and in the range of variation of the different measurements. Stem 10 – 50 cm tall, 2 – 10 flowered; sepals 13 – 18 mm long and 6 – 9 mm wide; lateral petals 6.5 – 9 mm long; lip 12.5 – 15 mm long and 15.5 – 20 mm broad, basal area hardly any lighter colour than the rest, some tubercles absent; pattern on average larger, generally as spots joined with a cross-band, often broadly surrounding the basal area occasionally isolated spots; red staminode spots usually present. **Habitat:** open woodland, poor grassland with bushes, garrigue; up to 1,300 m on fresh soils mostly over limestone, occasionally on slate. **Flowers:** April, May. **Photos:** It, Prov. Foggia 24.4.76 (l), 11.4.83 (r). **Distribution:** southern Italy from the Prov. Cosenza (Monte Pollino area) northwards as far as the Prov. Salerno (Monti Alburni) and Foggia (Monte Gargano); Dalmatia, island of Korcula. • **Floristic element:** c-mediterranean c-submediterranean. **Countries:** Eur: SE Ju, S It.

Key for the species of the *Ophrys crabronifera* group:

1   Lip appears broadly elliptic, widest in the centre; stigma head 4 – 6 mm wide at the base getting narrower upwards (seen from the front!) . . . . *O. crabronifera*

1*   Lip trapeziform, widest in the front ⅓; stigma head 3 – 4 mm wide at the base, getting wider upwards . . . . *O. biscutella*

Tall Ophrys   *Ophrys crabronifera* Mauri

Synonyms: *O. exaltata* autorum (not Ten. strict sense, *see* p212) *O. fuciflora subsp. exaltata* autorum

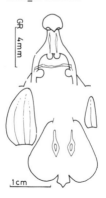

Plant with 2 ovoid-spherical tubers; stem 20 – 60 cm tall with 1 – 2 basal scale leaves, 4 – 6 foliage leaves forming a rosette and 1 – 2 leaves sheathing the stem; rosette leaves lanceolate up to 18 cm long and 2 cm wide; inflorescence extended 3 – 7 (– 12) flowered; lower bracts often much longer than the flowers; sepals whitish to pink, occasionally yellowish-green, ovate – lanceolate, 12.5 – 17 mm long and 6.5 – 8.5 mm wide, reflexed; lateral petals pink to red, occasionally greenish, broadly triangular 4.5 – 10 mm long, hairy; lip dark (reddish-) brown, with a lighter-coloured and more yellowish basal area, 11 – 15 mm long and 13 – 19 mm broad, convex, with weak tubercles, the whole of the edge zone densely covered in long hairs, usually a strong 3-toothed appendage in front, or, more rarely, a small triangular appendage; pattern in the form of 2 spots which may be separate or joined, sometimes extending backwards around the basal area, greyish-brown; basal callosities brownish to blackish; staminode spots often absent. **Habitat:** open pine woods, garrigue, poor grassland; up to 600 m, predominantly near the coast; on fairly dry to damp base-rich soils. **Flowers:** March, April. **Photos:** It, Prov. Grosseto 14.4.67 (l) 11.4.82 (r). **Distribution:** central Mediterranean area; in Italy along the west coast from the Prov. Livorno to Salerno, on Corsica around Bastia and Bonifacio. • **Floristic element:** (c-mediterranean) c-submediterranean. **Countries:** Eur: S It, Co.

Late Spider Ophrys *Ophrys holoserica* (Burm. fil.) W. Greuter

Synonyms: *O. fuciflora* (F. W. Schmidt) Moench, *O. arachnites* (L.) Reichard – Variant 2: *O. h. subsp. maxima* (H. Fleischm. W. Greuter, *O. episcopalis* Poiret – Variant 3: *O. h. subsp. chestermanii* J. J. Wood – Variant 4: *O. h. subsp. gracilis* (Büel, O. & E. Danesch – Variant 5: *O. h. subsp. elatior* (Gumprecht) Gumprecht – Variant 6: *O. h. subsp. heterochila* Renz & Taubenheim
Problem: The *O. holoserica* group with its many forms is difficult to classify. From the numerous types which have been described, 3 are dealt with here as subspecies and 5 as variants.
Hybrids with *O. scolopax, see* p204
Key to the subspecies:
1   Lateral petals (0.4 –) 0.45 – 0.6 times as long as the sepals; lip 13.5 – 17 mm long, transversely and often lengthwise strongly convex, the sides of the front half turned up . . *O. h. subsp. apulica*, p204
1* Lateral petals 0.25 – 0.45 × as long as the sepals; lip with other character combinations, often shorter 2
2   Sepals whitish-pink to red; hairs at the back edge of the lip usually short and velvety . . . . *O. h. subsp. holoserica*
2* Sepals green (the odd plant pink); hairs on the back edge of the lip long and shaggy . . . . . *O. h. subsp. parvimaculata*, p204

O. h. subsp. holoserica (variant 1)

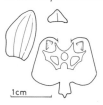

Stem 10 – 30 (– 40) cm tall, 2 – 10 flowered; basal foliage leaves 4 – 7, lanceolate, 4 – 10 cm long and 0.5 – 2.5 cm wide; sepals coloured, very rarely green, 10 – 14 mm long and 5.5 – 8.5 mm wide, upright to slightly reflexed; lateral petals pink to red, 3 – 6 mm long, hairy; lip dark brown, trapeziform, slightly convex, 8 – 12 mm long and (spread out!) 12 – 18 mm broad, tubercles up to 3 mm high, crenate in front with a large upright appendage; pattern variable, complicated to H-shaped, grey-violet (-brownish) with a whitish border; red staminode spots present.

1cm

Habitat: open woodland, scrubland edges, garrigue, poor grassland; up to 1,400 m; on fairly dry to damp, mostly calcareous, soils.
Flowers: March – July (but *see* variant 5).
Photos: variant 1: Ge, Southern Baden 29.5.83 (u/r); Ge, Southern Würtemberg 19.6.65 (c/r) – Cr, Nomos Iraklion 30.3.72 (l/l) – Variant 3: Sa, Prov. Cagliari, type population ('chestermanii') 21.4.80 (l/r) – variant 5: Ge, Southern Baden 22.8.81 (u/l) – *see also* p260. **Distribution:** Mediterranean region; western and central Europe. Rare in UK: restricted to Kent. ● **Floristic element:** (w) + c + e-mediterranean oriental w + c + (e)-submediterranean pannonic s + m-atlantic s-subatlantic s-centraleuropean. **Countries: Eur: SE** Cr, Gr, Tu, Ju, Rm **S** It, Sa, ?Co, **SW** Bl, Fa, **W** Ga, Be, Br, **C** He, Au, Hu, Ge; **Asi:** IJ, LS, An, AE; **Afr:** Li.
Variants: the following variants show slight differences from variant 1. Flower size is classified according to lip length: the terms small/medium/large refer to lip lengths 7 – 9/9 – 12/12 – 18 mm.   –   Variant 2 ('maxima') is distinguished from variant 1 in having large flowers; it occurs here and there within the range of the subspecies, especially in the eastern Mediterranean. – Variant 3 ('chestermanii'): stem 10 – 30 cm tall, 2 – 5 flowered; flowers large; petals narrowly triangular; pattern H-shaped, not branching to the sides. Central mountains around Iglésias (Sa); otherwise variant 1 on the island. – Variant 4 ('gracilis'): stem 25 – 50 cm tall, 4 – 7 (– 10) flowered; flowers small; lateral petals only about a quarter the length of the sepals; flowers 2 weeks later than variant 1; damp,shady habitats, Prov. Salerno, Cosenza, Potenza (It); – Variant 5 ('elatior'): stem 15 – 90 cm tall, (2 –) 6 – 18 flowers; flowers small; in flower from July – September. Rhine plain from Basel to Strasburg (Ge, Ga), near Geneva (He). – Variant 6 ('heterochila'): stem up to 25 cm tall, 3 – 6 flowered; lip small, undivided or slightly 3-lobed, strongly arched; lateral petals only about a quarter the length of the sepals, the latter 10 – 12 mm long. From 3 sites in the Vil. Mugla and Antalya (An). The status and position of the type require scrutiny.

'elatior'

typical variant, also below

Ophrys

'maxima'

chestermanii

Small-Patterned Ophrys *Ophrys holoserica* (Burm. fil.) W. Greuter *subsp. parvimaculata* (O. & E. Danesch) O. & E. Danesch

Synonym: *O. fuciflora subsp. parvimaculata* O. & E. Danesch

Stem 10−35 cm tall, 2−7 flowered; sepals 12.5−15.5 mm long and 6.5−8.5 mm wide, the central one usually strongly reflexed; lateral petals the same colour as the sepals (yellow-) green, sometimes pale pink, 4−7 mm long, hairy; lip dark brown, (spread out) broader than long 11−14×15−18.5 mm, slightly convex, appears trapeziform to rounded, tubercles greenish on their inner sides, a small 3-toothed appendage in front, long hairs round the edge; pattern simple, often H-shaped or with extensions to the base of each of the tubercles. **Habitat:** Downy oak-woods and scrub, poor grassland, occasionally pine woods; to 600 m. **Flowers:** April, May. **Photos:** It, Prov. Foggia 9.4.74. **Distribution:** southern Italy; Apulia (Prov. Foggia to Lecce) and Basilicata (Prov. Matera). ● **Floristic element:** c-mediterranean c-submediterranean. **Country: Eur: S** It.

Apulian Ophrys *Ophrys holoserica* (Burm. fil.) W. Greuter *subsp. apulica* (O. & E. Danesch) Buttler

Synonyms: *O. fuciflora subsp. apulica* O. & E. Danesch, *O. apulica* (O. & E. Danesch) O. & E. Danesch

Stem 15−30 (−55) cm tall, 3−8 (−14) flowered; sepals (greenish-) pink to red, 14−18.5 mm long; lateral petals 6.5−8.5 mm long; lip strongly arched (*see* in key), (spread out!) 17−21.5 mm broad, tubercles 2−4 mm high, short hairs on the rear edge; pattern extensive with several branches, brownish-violet with a pale border. **Habitat:** open oak- and pine woods and scrub, garrigue, poor grassland; up to 900 m; on base-rich soils. **Flowers:** April, May. **Photos:** It, Prov. Taranto 13.4.74 (l); It, Prov. Foggia 13.4.82 (r). **Distribution:** southern Italy (from Molise and Monte Gargano southwards) and Sicily (rare). Similar plants are known from Toscana, Umbria and Kos (Aegean); their classification is unsolved. ● **Floristic element:** c-mediterranean c-submediterranean. **Countries: Eur: S** Si, It.

Hybrids *Ophrys holoserica X scolopax*

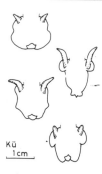

Kü
1 cm

The two species form manifestly fertile hybrids which have developed several independent extensive populations. Some of them are growing outside the present-day distribution of *O. scolopax*. They show great variability; most of the plants are intermediate between the parents, but individuals appear which hardly differ from *O. holoserica* (lip undivided, only slightly convex, with small tubercles) or from *O. scolopax* (lip 3-lobed, strongly convex, with large protuberances). The drawings on the left show in outline the different lip shapes. The different subspecies and variants of the parents all participate in the hybridization. **Distribution:** northern Carpathians (Mähren, Slovakia − designated as *O. fuciflora subsp. holubyana* (Andrasovsky) Jav.). Istria, Dalmatia, southern Italy, northern France, Aegean and certainly in other places. **Photos:** Cz, Mähren 3.6.74.

Ophrys

Bornmueller's Ophrys *Ophrys bornmuelleri* M. Schulze

Relationship: the *O. bornmuelleri* group contains 2 species which have only recently been separated. Several questions still need answers. **Key to the species**:

1 Lip inclined forward at an angle or horizontally (the edge as seen from the side!), 6 – 10 mm long and 8 – 12.5 mm broad; column 4 – 5 mm high . . . .
. . . . 1. *O. bornmuelleri*

1* Lip directed vertically downwards or backwards, 9 – 12.5 mm long and 11.5 – 17 mm broad; column 5 – 6 mm high . . . . 2. *O. levantina*

1. *Ophrys bornmuelleri*

Synonyms: *O. fuciflora subsp. bornmuelleri* (M. Schulze) B. & E. Willing, *O. holoserica subsp. bornmuelleri* (M. Schulze) autorum, *O. b. subsp. carduchorum* Renz & Taubenheim

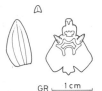

Stem 15 – 50 cm tall, 4 – 15 flowered; sepals green to whitish or reddish, 10 – 13 mm long and 5 – 7 mm wide; lateral petals 1.5 – 2.2 mm long; lip appears trapeziform or square, hairy round the edge, with strong tubercles and a large appendage in front; pattern generally H-shaped with side branches.

Habitat: open woodland, garrigue, poor grassland; up to 1,000 m; on base-rich soils. **Flowers**: March – May. **Photos**: Cy, Limassol area 12.4.83 (u/r); An, Vil. Siirt, type population ('carduchorum') 18.4.80 (c/r). **Distribution**: Near East; Cyprus, Levant, south-eastern Anatolia. Also in Iraqi Kurdestan. **Floristic element**: e-mediterranean. **Countries**: Asi: IJ, LS, Cy, An.

2. *Ophrys levantina* Gölz & Reinhard

Synonyms: *O. bornmuelleri subsp. grandiflora* (H. Fleischm. & Soó) Renz & Taubenheim, *O. fuciflora subsp. bornmuelleri var. grandiflora* (H. Fleischm. & Soó) B. & E. Willing

Stem 10 – 30 cm tall, 2 – 8 flowered; sepals greenish-white, occasionally reddish, 11 – 14.5 mm long and 5.5 – 9 mm wide; lateral petals 2 – 3.2 mm long; lip shape similar to that of the other species; pattern H-shaped or reduced. **Habitat**: similar to the other species; up to 1,400 m; sometimes on damp soils. **Flowers**: February – April. **Photos**: An, Vil. Siirt 23.4.80 (u/l); Cy, Limassol area 12.3.84 (c/ll). **Distribution**: Near East; south-eastern and southern Anatolia, Levant, Cyprus, Rhodes. • **Floristic element**: e-mediterranean. **Countries**: Asi: IJ, LS, Cy, An, AE.

Bianca's Ophrys *Ophrys discors Bianca*

Synonym: *Ophrys biancae* (Tod.) Macchiati, *O. anapei* O. & E. Danesch

Stem 10 – 25 cm tall, 4 – 10 flowered; basal foliage leaves 4 – 6, lanceolate; sepals whitish to pink, sometimes greenish, 10 – 14 mm long and 5 – 7 mm wide, the central one upright or inclined slightly forwards; lateral petals pink to red, broadly triangular, 2 – 3 mm long, at most only a quarter the length of the sepals; lip trapeziform (spread out!), 8 – 10.5 mm long and 10 – 14 mm broad in front, brownish-red centre or occasionally dark brown, yellow near the edge, hairy round the perimeter, tubercles at the base, in the front half with a longitudinal ridge in the centre, sides turned down; appendage up to 4 mm long, upright; pattern H-shaped, brownish-violet with a narrow whitish border. **Habitat**: garrigue, open pine woods, former cultivated land; to 700 m. **Flowers**: March, April; 2 – 3 weeks earlier than *O. oxyrrhynchos*. **Photos**: Si, Prov. Siracuse 11.4.76. **Distribution**: endemic in south-eastern Sicily (Prov. Siracuse, Ragusa, Catánia). • **Floristic element**: c-mediterranean. **Country**: Eur: S Si.

O. levantina *O. bornmuelleri*, below: 'carduchorum'

Ophrys

Lacaita's Ophrys *Ophrys lacaitae* Lojac.

Synonyms: *O. fuciflora var. lacaitae* (Lojac.) E. G. Camus, *O. f. subsp. lacaitae* (Lojac.) Sundermann

In general appearance similar to *O. oxyrrhynchos*; sepals green 11.5 – 14 mm long and 5 – 6.5 mm wide; lateral petals 2 – 3 mm long, at most only quarter the length of the sepals; lip (spread out!) 11.5 – 14 mm wide and in front 14.5 – 18.5 mm broad with a small very convex central area and a broad yellow border, long hairs only along the rear edge, otherwise glabrous, front part with a strong central ridge and turned up, often toothed, sides, very large appendage, upright; pattern H-shaped, brownish-violet with a white border. **Habitat:** open scrubland, poor grassland with bushes; up to 1,200 m; on fairly acid soils. **Flowers:** March – June; 2 – 3 weeks later than *O. oxyrrhynchos*. **Photos:** It, Prov. Isérna 19.6.78 (l); It, Prov. Salerno 23.5.70 (r). **Distribution:** Sicily, southern Italy (Prov. Potenza, Salerno, Isérnia, Latina). ● **Floristic element:** c-mediterranean. **Countries:** Eur: S Si, It.

Beaked Ophrys *Ophrys oxyrrhynchos* Tod.

Synonyms: *O. fuciflora subsp. oxyrrhynchos* (Tod.) Soó, *O. holoserica subsp. celiensis* (O. & E. Danesch) O. & E. Danesch

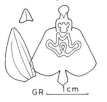

Stem 10 – 25 cm tall, 3 – 9 flowered; basal foliage leaves 5 – 6, lanceolate; sepals mostly green, occasionally brownish-red, 11.5 – 15 mm long and 5.5 – 8 mm wide, the central one reflexed; lateral petals triangular 2.5 – 5 mm long, hairy; lip (spread out!) 9.5 – 12 mm long and 14 – 18 mm broad in front, rear half brownish-red, small tubercles, densely hairy, front half red to yellowish-brown, occasionally yellow, almost glabrous with a ridge along the centre and turned up edges; appendage up to 4 mm long, upright; pattern usually extended, violet with a white border. **Habitat:** open oak-woods, garrigue, former cultivated land; up to 600 m. **Flowers:** March – May. **Photos:** Si, Prov. Caltanisetta 15.4.76 (l); Si, Prov. Palermo 5.4.76 (r). **Distribution:** Sicily, Basilicata, Apulia (whether also in Calabria?). ● **Floristic element:** c-mediterranean. **Countries:** Eur: S Si, It.

Kandia's Ophrys *Ophrys candica* W. Greuter? Matthäs & Risse

Synonyms: *O. fuciflora subsp. candica* E. Nelson, *O. f. var. candica* Sundermann, *O. holoserica subsp. candica* Renz & Taubenheim

Stem 15 – 40 cm tall, 2 – 7 flowered; sepals whitish to pink, 11.5 – 15 mm long and 4.5 – 7 mm wide, reflexed; lateral petals 3 – 4.5 mm long, hairy; lip brown (spread out!) 9.5 – 12 mm long and 12 – 16 mm broad, hairy periphery, small tubercles; large appendage, upright; pattern shield-shaped with a broad white border, surrounding the tiny basal area, brownish-violet, often with pale marbling, occasionally with distinct paler lines. **Habitat:** pine woods, garrigue, poor grassland; up to 900 m. **Flowers:** April, May; later than *O. holoserica* and *O. oxyrrhynchos*. **Photos:** An, Vil. Mugla 14.5.76 (l); Cr. Nomos Chania 11.4.72 (r). **Distribution:** eastern and central Mediterranean areas; south-western Anatolia, Samos, Rhodes, Crete, southern Peloponnes, southern Apulia, southern Sicily. ● **Floristic element:** e + c-mediterranean/disjunct. **Countries:** Eur: SE Cr, Gr, S Si, It; Asi: An, AE.

Crescent Ophrys   *Ophrys lunulata* Parl.

Synonym: *O. sphegodes subsp. lunulata* Sundermann

pattern variation

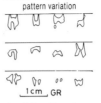

1cm, GR

Plant with 2 spherical-ovoid tubers; stem 10−40 cm tall with 0−2 basal scale leaves, 3−6 foliage leaves in a rosette and 1−3 leaves sheathing the stem; rosette leaves narrow-lanceolate 5−12 cm long and 1−2 cm wide; inflorescence lax, (4−) 6−10 flowered; lower bracts longer than the flowers; sepals pink to red, the central one curving forwards, the laterals pointing downwards at an angle, ovate-elliptic (11−) 12.5−16 mm long and (4.5−) 5.5−7 mm wide; lateral petals pink, linear-lanceolate, 8.5−11 mm long glabrous or with hairs along the edge; lip reddish- to dark brown with a bare yellowish to pale brown margin, deeply 3-lobed, the sides turned down so that it appears as a narrow rectangle 10.5−14 mm long and (spread out!) 13.5−18 mm broad; middle lobe hairy along the sides, with a tooth-like appendage in front; side lobes turned backwards, densely hairy, with small tubercles at the base; pattern generally half-moon shaped, sometimes with extensions towards the basal area, bluish to brownish; lip base with 2 blackish callosities; red staminode spots poorly developed (?absent).

Habitat: poor grassland, garrigue, former cultivated land, open woodland; up to 800 m; on fairly dry to moist, base-rich (but also weakly acid) soils. **Flowers:** March, April. **Photos:** Si, Prov. Palermo 5.4.70 (l); Si, Prov. Siracuse 11.4.76 (r).

Distribution: Sicily and the Aeolian Islands; as far as present knowledge goes the species is endemic in this area. Records for other regions (Maltese islands, Calabria: Monte Pollino, Sardinia, Elba) are questionable and require confirmation. ● **Floristic element:** c-mediterranean. **Country:** Eur: S Si.

Spruner's Ophrys   *Ophrys spruneri* Nyman

Synonyms: *O. sphegodes subsp. spruneri* (Nyman) E. Nelson, *O. sphaciotica* H. Fleischm., *O. sphegodes subsp. parnassica* (Vierh.) J. J. Wood

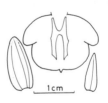

1cm

Plant with 2 spherical-ovoid tubers; stem 15−40 (−50) cm tall with 1−2 basal scale leaves, 3−6 ovate−lanceolate foliage leaves forming a rosette and 1−2 leaves on the stem; inflorescence lax, 2−8 flowered; sepals ovate, 10−16.5 mm long and 5−6.5 mm wide, ground colour whitish-green, in the laterals the lower half is tinged red (occasionally the whole sepal), pointing downwards at an angle, the central sepal upright, uniformly coloured; lateral petals 7−10.5 mm long, greenish-pink to red, glabrous or with short hairs, often wavy; lip blackish-violet, 11−15 mm long, deeply to slightly 3-lobed; middle lobe convex, papillose near the edge, with a small appendage; side lobes turned down, tubercles small or absent, covered in short hairs; pattern H-shaped, surrounding the basal area, sometimes with 2 cross-bars or none, violet-blue with a pale border; basal callosities blackish; red staminode spots usually present.

Habitat: open broad-leaved or coniferous woodland, garrigue, poor grassland; up to 900 m; on base-rich soils. **Flowers:** March − May.

Photos: Cr, Nomos Rethimnon 7.4.80 (l); Gr, Nomos Lakonia 19.4.84 (r). **Distribution:** southern Balkans and the Aegean; on the Greek mainland northwards as far as Epirus and southern Macedonia, on the Ionian islands Zakinthos and Kephallinia, on the Aegean islands eastwards to Ikaria and Chios (? also on the Cyclades). ● **Floristic element:** e + c-mediterranean **Countries:** Eur: SE Cr, Gr; **Asi:** AE. **Relationship:** it is agreed that plants from southern Turkey which are sometimes put with *O. spruneri* belong to *O. transhyrcana* (see p220)

Early Spider Ophrys *Ophrys sphegodes* Miller

Synonyms: *O. aranifera* Hudson, *O. arachnitiformis* Gren. & Philippe

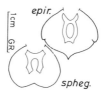

Sepals green or whitish to pink ('arachnitiformis'); lateral petals yellowish-green to brownish-red, glabrous, often wavy; lip (reddish-) brown, undivided or slightly – rarely deeply – 3-lobed, tubercles usually present, short hairs at the back; pattern greyish-blue or blue with pale border. The range of variation of some characters is subdivided into grades (*see* the subspecies): stem short/medium/tall = 10 – 25/25 – 40/40 – 55 cm; inflorescence few-/many-flowered = 2 – 8/5 – 15 flowers; sepals short/long = 12 – 14/12 – 16 mm; lateral petals short/long = 0.55 – 0.75/0.7 – 0.85 × as long as the sepals; lip small/large = 9 – 13 × 11 – 16.5/12 – 15 × 14.5 – 19 mm length × breadth.

Habitat: open woodland, maquis, garrigue, poor grassland; up to 1,300 m; on fresh to fairly dry, base-rich soils.

Problem: the *O. sphegodes* group shows a rich variety of forms and is difficult to classify; two subspecies are distinguished here:

2. *O. s. subsp. epirotica* (Renz) Gölz & Reinhard
Similar to the other subspecies, but differing in the shape and degree of curvature of the lip; lateral sepals often brownish-red in the lower half; pattern H-shaped. **Flowers:** May. **Photos:** Gr, Nomos Thesprotia 17.5.79 (l/l); Al, Prov. Sarandë 21.5.80 (l/r).

Distribution: central Greece, western Macedonia, Epirus, southern Albania.
• **Floristic element:** e + c-mediterranean e-submediterranean. **Countries: Eur:** SE Gr Al.
Problem: *see* under *O. hebes,* p214.

1. *O. s. subsp. sphegodes*
Synonyms: Variant 2: *O. exaltata* Ten., *O. trinacrica* Del Prete, *O. s. subsp. panormitana* (Tod.) E. Nelson, *O. spruneri subsp. panormitana* (Tod.) Soó, *O. s. subsp. sicula* E. Nelson. – Variant 3: *O. s. subsp. cephalonica* B. & H. Baumann. – Variant

4: *O. s. subsp. praecox* Corrias. – Variant 5: *O. s. subsp. provincialis* E. Nelson. – Variant 6: *Ophrys sphegodes subsp. gortyna* H. Baumann & Künkele. – Variant 7: *Ophrys sphegodes subsp. cretensis* H. Baumann & Künkele. – Variant 8: *Ophrys sphegodes subsp. montenegrina* H. Baumann & Künkele. Many variants (V1 – V8) V1 ('sphegodes'): stem short/medium, few-flowered; sepals and lateral petals short; lip small. – V2: stem medium/tall, many-flowered; sepals long; lateral petals short, lip small (large), undivided ('sicula') or deeply 3-lobed ('panormitana'). – stem short/medium, few-/many-flowered; sepals and lateral petals long; lip large. – V4: like variant 3, but sepals short. – V5: pattern with side branches extending to the inner side of the tubercles (in the other variants, unbranched H-shape), otherwise like V1, but the lateral petals sometimes long. V6 and V7 are large- and small-lipped plants from Crete, respectively; in the former, the lip has an extended oval shape and the basal tubercles are not obvious. The latter has a characteristic yellow edging to the lip and distinct tubercles. V8 is similar to variant 'provincialis'.

Flowers: January – June. **Photos:** V1: Ge, Oberbayern 4.6.79 (u/l); Ga, Dept. Gers 17.5.73 (u/r). – V2: Si, Prov. Palermo 6.4.76 (p.214 u/l); Si, Prov. Siracuse 12.4.76 (p214 u/r, p215 u/l). – V3: Gr, Kefallonia 2.4.83 (p215 u/r). – V4: Sa, Prov. Sassari 11.3.76 (c/r) – V5: Ga, Dept. Var 14.4.71 (c/l).

Distribution: Mediterranean region; western and central Europe, eastwards to northern Anatolia; doubtful in northern Persia. V1: throughout almost the whole area of distribution (absent from Si, Sa); V2: Sicily and southern Italy (Prov. Réggio, Cosenza, Salerno); V3: Ionian islands (Kefallonia, Ithaca); V4: northern Sardinia (Prov. Sassari), southern tip of Corsica; V5: Provence; V6: Crete – V7: Crete – V8: Yugoslavia (Montenegro). • **Floristic element:** mediterranean submediterranean pannonic s + m-atlantic s-subatlantic s-centraleuropean. In Britain, restricted to the southern coast and a few inland sites in Kent.

below: 'provincialis'   *O. s. subsp. sphegodes*   below: 'praecox'

Ophrys

O. s. subsp. epirotica

'sicula'   'panormitana'

Small Spider Orchid   *Ophrys araneola* Reichenb.

Synonyms: *O. tommasinii* Vis., *O. sphegodes subsp. tommasinii* (Vis.) Soó *O. litigiosa* E. G. Camus, *O. sphegodes subsp. litigiosa* (E. G. Camus) Becherer

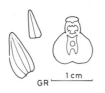

GR |—— 1 cm ——|

Stem 20 – 45 cm tall, 2 – 12 flowered; sepals green, 8 – 12 mm long and 4 – 6 mm wide; lateral petals 5 – 8 mm long, glabrous; lip reddish- to blackish-brown with a yellow glabrous edge, 6.5 – 9 mm long and 7.5 – 11.5 mm broad, weakly convex, rarely with tubercles, long pale hairs especially near the base, crenate in front and often without appendage; pattern H-shaped, grey-violet or -brown.

Habitat: similar to that of *O. sphegodes*; up to 1,100 m. **Flowers:** February – May – earlier than *O. sphegodes*. **Photos:** Ju, Istria 10.5.79 (r); Ge, Südwürttemberg 14.5.83 (l); p260.

Distribution: from France to Catalonia, central Italy, Dalmatia and central Germany.
● **Floristic element:** c + w-submediterranean s-atlantic s-subatlantic.

Countries: Eur: SE Ju, **S** It, **SW** Hs, **W** Ga, C, He, Ge.

Hebes Ophrys   *Ophrys hebes* (Kalopissis) E. & B. Willing

Synonym: *O. sphegodes subsp. hebes* Kalopissis

GR |—— 1 cm ——|

Stem 10 – 30 cm tall, 2 – 10 flowered; sepals green, the lateral ones often red-tinged in the lower half, 11 – 14 mm long and 5 – 6.5 mm wide; lateral petals 7 – 10 mm long, glabrous; lip dark reddish-brown with a yellow or brown glabrous edge, 8 – 12 mm long and 10 – 15 mm broad, undivided to weakly 3-lobed, convex, sometimes with small tubercles, short velvety hairs, truncate in front with a small appendage; pattern generally extensive (longitudinal stripes with 2 – 3 cross-bars and branching sideways) rarely approaching the H-shape, brown with a pale edge. **Habitat:** open woods and scrubland, poor grassland; up to 1,400 m; on fresh, base-rich soils. **Flowers:** March – June. **Photos:** Al, Prov. Shkodër 18.4.82. **Distribution:** Greece and northern Albania, expected in southern Yugoslavia, ● **Floristic element:** e + c-mediterranean e + c-submediterranean.

Countries: Eur: SE Gr, Al.

214

'panormitana'

'cephalonica'

Ophrys

215

Gargano Ophrys   *Ophrys garganica* O. & E. Danesch

Synonym: *O. sphegodes subsp. garganica* E. Nelson; neither the species nor the subspecies are validly published according to the rules of nomenclature.

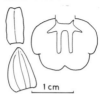

Stem 25–35 cm tall, 4–8 flowered; 6–9 basal foliage leaves ovate – lanceolate; sepals green 10.5–13.5 mm long and 4–7 mm wide; lateral petals strikingly large – ⅔ as long as the sepals, 0.4–0.55 × as wide as long (wider than *O. sphegodes*) olive-green to brown with a wavy, often darker, edge, glabrous; lip dark- to blackish-brown, undivided or weakly 3-lobed, slightly convex, the sides turned down slightly at an angle or spread out (similar to *O. sphegodes subsp. epirotica*), tubercles absent or small, short hairs along the back edge, often an appendage in front; pattern H-shaped with side branches at the rear (similar to *O. sphegodes* variant 'provincialis') grey-blue or violet.

Habitat: garrigue, poor grassland, open pine-woods and oakwoods; up to 500 m; **Flowers:** April, May. **Photos:** It, Prov. Fóggia 8.4.82.

Distribution: Apennine peninsula; Sicily, Apulia, Calabria, Basilikata, Tuscany.

• **Floristic element:** c-mediterranean c-submediterranean. **Countries: Eur:** S Si, It.

Problem: *O. garganica* belongs to a section of the *O. sphegodes* group which still throws up many open questions. Its status requires further more investigation particularly as to whether or not its classification as a separate species can be defended. Further work is also required to decide whether plants growing in Catalonia which have been assigned to *O. garganica* correspond to the Italian specimens. For example, for all their similarity, the former lack the strikingly wide lateral petals. Also in southern France similar plants are occasionally found which are the variant 'provincialis' of *O. sphegodes*.

Aesculapius Ophrys   *Ophrys aesculapii* Renz

Synonyms: *O. sphegodes subsp. aesculapii* (Renz) Soó, *O. ae. subsp. pseudoaranifera* Renz

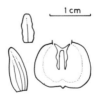

Stem 15–40 cm tall; 5–7 lanceolate to longish-ovate foliage leaves at ground level with 1–2 up the stem; inflorescence lax, 3–10 flowered; bracts longer than the ovaries; sepals (yellowish-) green, the laterals occasionally with brownish-red spots on the lower halves, 9–13 mm long and 3.5–5.5 mm wide, the central one upright, concave; lateral petals yellowish-green to yellow, 5–8.5 mm long with a wavy edge, glabrous; lip dark brown to reddish-brown, velvety-papillose with a 2–3 mm wide pale to orange-yellow glabrous border, sometimes weakly 3-lobed, tubercles very small or absent, a small appendage in front; pattern H-shaped, sometimes with side branches or with 2 cross-bands in front, surrounding the basal area, greyish-brown or greyish-violet with a pale violet border; basal callosities greenish, with darker tips; red staminode spots absent.

Habitat: open pine woods, garrigue, poor grassland; up to 1,000 m; on base-rich, fairly dry soils. **Flowers:** March – May. **Photos:** Gr, Eubœa 11.4.84 (l); Gr, Nomos Argolis, 'pseudoaranifera' 5.4.80 (r).

Distribution: endemic in southern Greece, but absent from the western part; Peloponnese (eastern half), Fokis, Buetia, Attica, Fthiotis, Magnissia, Euboea. • **Floristic element:** e-mediterranean. **Country: Eur:** S Gr.

Variation: sometimes plants appear with smaller lips (8–9 × 9–10 mm) which have a narrow yellow border: 'pseudoaranifera'. Their status requires investigation.

217

Helene Ophrys   *Ophrys helenae* Renz

Synonym: *O. sphegodes subsp. helenae* (Renz) Soó & D. Moresby Moore

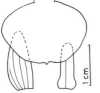

Stem 15 – 40 cm tall, 2 – 8 flowered; perianth segments green, often suffused with red; sepals ovate, 11 – 15.5 mm long and 5.5 – 8 mm wide, the central one reflexed; lateral petals 7 – 12 mm long, glabrous; lip wine-red to dark, brownish-red, velvety, 11.5 – 17.5 mm long (spread out!) and 15 – 23 mm broad, convex, tubercles absent or very small, small appendage in front; pattern absent or very indistinct (visible in light coming from behind) basal callosities indistinct.

Habitat: poor pastures and meadows, garrigue, open woodland; up to 1,000 m; on dry to damp, base-rich soils. **Flowers:** April – June. **Photos:** Gr, Nomos Ioannina 17.5.79 (l), 1.6.77 (r). **Distribution:** centred in northern Greece (Epirus, Thessaly, western Macedonia), isolated as far as southern Albania, central Greece, and the Peloponnese (Ilia). ● **Floristic element:** e + c-mediterranean e-submediterranean. **Countries: Eur: SE** Gr, Al.

Dark Ophrys   *Ophrys incubacea* Bianca

Synonyms: *O. atrata* Lindley, *O. sphegodes subsp. atrata* (Lindley) E. Mayer

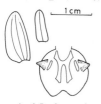

Stem 20 – 40 (– 60) cm tall, 3 – 8 flowered; sepals green, occasionally pink, 10.5 – 15.5 mm long and 4 – 7.5 mm wide; lateral petals green or tinged with red, 6.5 – 9 mm long with a wavy edge, glabrous; lip dark reddish-brown to blackish-brown (– violet) 10 – 14 mm long and broad, tubercles up to 3.5 mm high, lip crenate in front, often with a small appendage, long, dark, shaggy hairs round the edge; pattern H-shaped with side branches from the base to the inner sides of the tubercles, greyish-blue with a light border; stigmatic head strongly waisted at the base.

Habitat: Open wood and scrubland, garrigue, poor grassland; up to 1,000 m. **Flowers:** March – May, later than *O. sphegodes*. **Photos:** Bl Mallorca 14.3.75 (l); It, Prov. Fóggia 10.4.82 (r). **Distribution:** western and central Mediterranean region; south-eastwards to Corfu. ● **Floristic element:** c + w-mediterranean c + w-submediterranean. **Countries: Eur: SE** Gr, Al, Ju, **S** Me, Si, It, Sa, Co, **SW** Bl, Hs, Lu, **W** Ga.

Taranto Ophrys   *Ophrys tarentina* Gölz & Reinhard

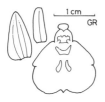

Stem 10 – 30 cm tall, 3 – 8 flowered; sepals green, 10 – 14.5 mm long and 4.5 – 7 mm wide; lateral petals yellowish-green, sometimes reddish, 8 – 10 mm long, glabrous with a wavy edge; lip blackish- to reddish-brown, 10.5 – 14 mm long and (spread out) 13 – 17 mm broad, undivided or slightly 3-lobed, convex, tubercles absent or small, surrounded by a fringe of long shaggy hairs with a narrow yellowish glabrous edge, a small appendage in front; pattern variable, H-shaped and surrounding the basal area, or reduced to a horseshoe, or to 2 separate longitudinal spots, greyish-violet; basal callosities blackish; staminode spots absent.

Habitat: garrigue, poor grassland, occasionally open woodland; up to 600 m; on fairly dry, stony and base-rich soils. **Flowers:** March, April. **Photos:** It, Prov. Táranto 13.4.74 (l); It, Prov. Cosenza 24.4.73 (r). **Distribution:** southern Italy: Prov. Cosenza, Matera, Táranto, Bríndisi. ● **Floristic element:** c-mediterranean. **Country: Eur: S** It.

Ophrys

Mammose Ophrys *Ophrys mammosa* Desf.

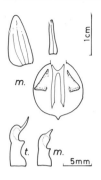

Stem 20–60 cm tall with 1–2 basal scale leaves, 3–6 (–9) foliage leaves in a (lax) rosette and 1–2 leaves on the stem; leaves lanceolate up to 20 cm long and 4 cm wide; inflorescence 2–10 (–18) flowered; bracts longer than the ovaries; sepals green, the lower half of the laterals and sometimes the central one coloured purple to varying degrees of intensity, upright to reflexed, ovate–lanceolate 10–19 mm long and 4–8.5 mm wide; lateral petals yellowish-green to purple 7–12 mm long, glabrous; lip reddish-brown, brownish-violet or blackish-purple 10–17 mm long (spread out!) and 10–19 mm broad, convex, generally with large cone-shaped tubercles, short hairs on the back edge, papillose to glabrous in front, appendage absent or small; pattern in the shape of an H or 2 stripes, greyish-blue to lilac; stigmatic cavity half as high as wide; basal callosities blackish; staminodal spots absent.

Habitat: open coniferous and broad-leaved woodland, maquis, garrigue, poor grassland; up to 1,400 m; on fairly dry to fairly damp, often base-rich soils. **Flowers:** February – May.

Key to the subspecies:

1   Beak-like extension of the column (connective) 0.5–1.5 (–2) mm long; lip with large tubercles (up to 7.5 mm high), usually undivided; pattern not branching to the sides 1. *O. m. subsp. mammosa*

1* Connective extension 1.5–3.5 mm long; lip with small tubercles (up to 3 mm high), often slightly 3-lobed; pattern sometimes branched at the sides . . . .
. . . . 2. *O. m. subsp. transhyrcana*

1. *O. m. subsp. mammosa*

Synonyms: *O. sphegodes subsp. mammosa* (Desf.) E. Nelson, *O. taurica* (Aggeenko) Nevski, *O. m. subsp. grammica* B. & E. Willing, *O. m. subsp. serotina* B. & E. Willing

Photos: An, Vil. Izmir 21.3.78 (l/l); Cy, Paphos area 10.4.83 (l/r).

Distribution: Balkan peninsula, Asia Minor, Crimea; northwards to Bulgaria, southern Yugoslavia and central Albania, eastwards as far as Vil. Trabzon in northern and Adana in southern Anatolia. ● **Floristic element:** e + c-mediterranean e + (c)-submediterranean.

Countries: Eur: SE Cr, Gr, Tu, Al, Ju, Bu, RK; **Asi:** Cy, An, AE.

2. *O. m. subsp. transhyrcana* (Czerniakovksa) Buttler

Synonyms: *O. transhyrcana* Czerniakovska, *O. sphegodes subsp. transhyrcana* (Czerniakovska) Soó, *O. sintenisii* H. Fleischm. & Bornm., *O. sph. subsp. sintenisii* (H. Fleischm. & Bornm.) E. Nelson

Photos: IJ, Galilee 19.4.81 (u/l); An, Vil. Icel 23.4.78 (u/r); Cy, Limassol 19.3.84 (c/l).

Distribution: Near East; westwards into southern Anatolia (Vil. Antalia); also in Iraqi Kurdestan, southern, western and northern Persia and Turkomania. **Floristic element:** e-mediterranean oriental. **Countries: Asi:** IJ, LS, Cy, An.

Problem: Both subspecies are very variable regarding flower size, lip curvature and colour and tubercle size; in addition, early and late flowering variants are found growing together on the same sites. Morphologically the separation is indistinct. Where the distribution areas overlap (southern Anatolia and Cyprus) intermediate forms abound and even further to the west or east, plants can be found which come close to resembling the other subspecies.

The status of plants in southern Anatolia (Mersin to Iskenderun) requires clarification. They are known as *O. transhyrcana subsp. amanensis* Renz & Taubenheim (= *O. sphegodes subsp. amanensis* E. Nelson) but sometimes assigned to *O. spruneri*. Characteristics: sepals whitish-green to strong pink; lip blackish-violet, undivided or 3-lobed; connective extension long as in *O. m. subsp. transhyrcana*. **Photo:** An, Vil. Hatay 20.5.71 (c/r).

Ophrys

O. m. subsp. mammosa   above: 'amanensis'

221

Moris's Ophrys *Ophrys morisii* (U. Martelli) Ciferri & Giacomini

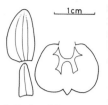

Stem 15 – 40 cm tall, 3 – 10 flowered; sepals whitish to lilac-pink, less often green, 10.5 – 15 mm long and 5.5 – 8.5 mm wide, slightly reflexed; lateral petals orange- to dark brownish-red, 6.5 – 10 mm long, hairy, with wavy edge; lip dark brown (– lilac) 10 – 13.5 and (spread out!) 13 – 18.5 mm broad, occasionally weakly 3-lobed, convex, short hairs along the back edge, usually without tubercles, with a fairly strong triangular or 3-toothed appendage; pattern variable, large and much branched, also shield- or H-shaped, brownish-violet with a paler border; basal callosities blackish-purple; staminode spots may be present or absent.
Habitat: open maquis, garrigue, poor meadows; up to 900 m; on basic to slightly acid soils. **Flowers:** March, April. **Photos:** Sa, Prov. Cagliari 3.4.71 (r); Sa, Prov. Nuoro 6.4.71 (l).

Distribution: Sardinia; recent records for Corsica require confirmation. ● **Floristic element:** c-mediterranean ?c-submediterranean. **Countries:** Eur: S Sa ?Co.

Nowadays, it is customary to designate as arachnitiform plants of the *O. sphegodes* group which have coloured sepals – whitish to lilac-pink instead of the usual green. However, plants with this character do not form a systematic unit, but are found in several of the species, for example: *O. sphegodes, O. araneola* and *O. incubacea.* The arachnitiform variants differ from the normal types only in the sepal colouration. The appearance of the coloured sepals is certainly striking but is a normal variation arising from the genetic background and this causes confusion.

In the central and western Mediterranean regions there are also arachnitiform types which have probably arisen from a cross between plants of the sphegodes group (sepals predominantly green) and those of the fuciflora or the ferrum-equinum groups (sepals predominantly coloured). In these stabilized hybrid populations, plants with coloured sepals outnumber the ones with green, but in addition possess features which are absent from the sphegodes group, such as hairy lateral petals and large lip appendages. The best researched types are described on pages 222 – 225. Others are known from Castilia, Dalmatia and Apulia.

Tyrrhenian Ophrys *Ophrys tyrrhena* Gölz & Reinhard

Synonym: *O. exaltata* sensu Del Prete (not Ten., *see* p212)

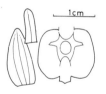

Stem 15 – 35 cm tall, 2 – 8 flowered; sepals usually whitish to lilac-pink rarely green, ovate 11 – 17 mm long and 5 – 8 mm wide, upright; lateral petals white, lilac-pink or brown, sometimes with a darker edge, 7 – 10 mm long, often hairy; lip dark brown, 10 – 14 mm long and (spread out!) 11 – 17 mm broad, undivided or weakly 3-lobed, convex, tubercles small or absent, short hairs around the edge, usually truncate in front with a fairly strong triangular or 3-toothed appendage; pattern variable, generally branched, sometimes H-shaped, (grey-) brown to dark violet with a pale border; basal callosities blackish; red staminode spots often present.

Habitat: open woodland, poor grassland with bushes; up to 500 m; on dry to fresh, base-rich soils. **Flowers:** March, April. **Photos:** It, Prov. Genoa 17.4.70 (r); It, Prov. Grosseto 7.4.79 (l). **Distribution:** endemic along the west coast of Italy; known from the Prov. Genoa, Livorno, Siena, Grosseto, Latina, Frosinone. ● **Floristic element:** c-submediterranean. **Country:** Eur: S It. **Relationship:** the species shows close connections with *O. morisii.* One school of thought amalgamates them under the name *O. arachnitiformis* Gren. & Philippe in accordance with original descriptions.

Splendid Ophrys   *Ophrys splendida* Gölz & Reinhard

Synonym: *O. arachnitiformis* sensu Del Prete (not Gren. & Philippe, *see* p212)

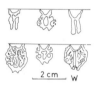

Stem 10 – 25 cm tall, 2 – 8 flowered; sepals whitish to lilac-pink, 10.5 – 14.5 mm long and 5.5 – 8 mm wide, upright; lateral petals strikingly 2-coloured, white to pink with a yellowish-green or (orange-) red edge, often wavy, glabrous; lip dark brown with a narrow yellow edge, 8 – 12 mm long and (spread out!) 10 – 14 mm wide, convex, often without tubercles, short hairs along the back edge, the front crenate, appendage small or absent; pattern H-shaped, often the lines merge into a shield shape, greyish-blue to dark violet with a white border; staminode spots absent.

Habitat: open woodland, garrigue, poor grassland; up to 400 m; on dry to fairly fresh, base-rich soils. **Flowers:** April, May. **Photos:** Ga, Dept. Bouches-du-Rhône 16.4.79 (l), 14.5.73 (r). **Distribution:** southern France; from the Rhône (Arles) to the vicinity of Cannes. ● **Floristic element** w-submediterranean. **Country: Eur:** W Ga.

Aveyron Ophrys   *Ophrys aveyronensis* (J. J. Wood) Delforge

Synonym: *O. sphegodes subsp. aveyronensis* J. J. Wood

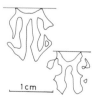

Stem 10 – 40 cm tall, 3 – 8 (– 12) flowered; sepals lilac-pink, sometimes cream, 12 – 16 mm long and 6 – 8 mm wide, erect; lateral petals pink with a more intense (orange-) red edge, 7 – 10 mm long, papillose; lip brown or brownish-lilac, 9 – 15 mm long and (spread out!) 12 – 16 mm broad, undivided or weakly 3-lobed, short hairs around the edge, mostly lacking tubercles, a small appendage in front; pattern variable, usually large and much branched, rarely H-shaped or strips, greyish-lilac with pale border; basal callosities blackish-olive; staminode spots absent.

Habitat: poor meadows with a few bushes; 600 – 700 m; on fairly dry, calcareous soils. **Flowers:** May, June. **Photos:** Ga, Dept. Aveyron 6.6.82. **Distribution:** southern France (Dept. Aveyron, Hérault); only a few locations around Causse du Larzac. ● **Floristic element:** w-submediterranean. **Country: Eur:** W Ga.

Siponto Ophrys   *Ophrys sipontensis* O. & E. Danesch

Synonyms: *O. sphegodes subsp. sipontensis* Gumprecht, *O. garganica subsp. sipontensis* Del Prete. Neither name is valid according to the rules of nomenclature.

The species is similar to *O. incubacea* (*see* p218), especially in the fringe of long hairs round the lip, the dark lip colour and the constriction at the base of the column. Significant differences are the somewhat larger average flower size; sepals whitish to lilac-pink; lateral petals pink to brownish-red; tubercles absent or small; pattern sometimes more strongly branched, with branches at the front as well as at the base.

Habitat: poor pastures and meadows; up to 600 m; on fairly dry calcareous soils. **Flowers:** April. **Photos:** It, Prov. Fóggia 11.4.74 (l), 9.4.82 (r). **Distribution:** endemic in Italy on the southern slopes and foot of Monte Gargano (Manfredonia and the hinterland). ● **Floristic element:** c-submediterranean. **Country: Eur:** S It.

Problem: the connections between this plant and *O. incubacea* (which likewise occasionally has red sepals) need investigating.

Bertoloni's Ophrys *Ophrys bertolonii* Moretti

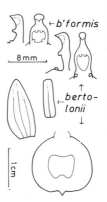

Stem 10 – 35 cm tall, 2 – 8 flowered; sepals mostly pink, also green, 13 – 18.5 mm long and 6 – 8 mm wide, erect; lateral petals pink to red, fairly narrow (2.5 – 4.5 × as long as wide), with fine hairs, tips bend forwards; lip blackish-purple, undivided or rarely 3-lobed, 12.5 – 18.5 mm long, (spread out!) as broad as long, but because of the turned-down sides appears narrow, short hairs round the edge, tubercles absent, crenate in front with an erect yellowish appendage; pattern shield-shaped in the front half of the lip, shining blue, without border; staminode spots absent.

Habitat: open wood- and scrubland, garrigue, poor grassland; up to 1,200 m; on fresh to dry base-rich soils. **Flowers**: March – June. **Photos**: It, Prov. Fóggia 9.4.82 (u/l); Si, Prov. Siracuse 11.4.76 (u/r). **Distribution**: Apennine peninsula from Liguria southwards; the Balkan peninsula from Istria to Montenegro, also Corfu. • **Floristic element**: c-mediterranean c-submediterranean. **Countries**: Eur: SE Gr, Ju, S ?Me, Si, It, ?Co.

Relationship: stabilized hybrid types have arisen from crosses between *O. bertolonii* and species of the sphegodes group. They grow in the central and western Mediterranean regions, often in large populations, ½ partly outside the range of *O. bertolonii*. Since there is such a great variability in the hybrid types which extends throughout all the range, they are all brought together under the name *O. bertoloniformis* O. & E. Danesch (= *O. b. subsp. bertoloniformis* (O. & E. Danesch) Sundermann and *O. pseudobertolonii subsp. bertoloniformis* (O. & E. Danesch) H. Baumann & Künkele) (= *O. b. subsp. bertoliniformis* (O. & E. Danesch) Sundermann). Some of them are introduced briefly; characters in addition to

those given in the key are: lateral petals often glabrous, wavy and reflexed; lip often with tubercles, with a small turned-down appendage and sometimes only slightly convex.
1. Sepals predominantly green: *O. bertoliniformis* Monte Gargano; Photos: It, Prov. Fóggia 26.4.73 (l/l), 10.4.74 (l/r). – *O. promontorii* O. & E. Danesch, similar to the previous, lateral petals strikingly large, tubercules prominent, Prov. Fóggia, Frosinone, Latina; Photo: It, Prov. Fóggia 14.4.81 (p228 c/l) – 2. Sepals predominantly whitish to pink;
2.1. Lips small, 10 – 14 mm long: *O. catalaunica* O. & E. Danesch, *O. catalaunica* O. & E. Danesch (*O. pseudobertolonii subsp. catalaunica* [O. & E. Danesch] H. Baumann & Künkele) Catalonia. Photos (p228): Hs, Prov. Barcelona 30.4.75 (u/l), 28.4.77 (u/r). – similar types in southern France; Sicily; Dalmatia (? *O. dalmatica* (Murr) Soó). Photos (p229): Ju, Croatia 16.4.80 (l/l), 1.4.83 (l/r). – 2.2. Lips large, 12 – 16 mm long: *O. benacensis* (Reisigl) O. & E. Danesch, *O. benacensis* (Reisigl.) O. & E. Danesch (*O. pseudobertolonii subsp. pseudobertolonii* Murr) lip undivided or weakly 3-lobed, southern edge of the Alps (Como to Treviso); Photos (p229): It, Prov. Brescia 20.4.73 (u/l); It, Prov. Triente 28.4.82 (u/r). – Similar types in south-eastern France. **Photos**: Ga, Dept. Var 15.4.71 (p228 l/l, l/r); central Italy – '*O. b. f. triloba* Renz' similar to the previous, but the lip often deeply 3-lobed, Balearics. Photo: Bl, Mallorca 19.3.75 (p228 c/r).

Key to species of *O. bertolonii* group:
1   Middle of the lip arched to almost a right angle (saddle-shaped); stigma cavity 1.3 – 1.8 × as high as wide; black basal callosities sitting on a swelling of the stem-like narrowing of the lip base, 1.5 – 2 mm in front of the base of the column; column 7.5 – 9 mm high, slender, getting narrower towards the foot (seen from the side) . . . .
. . . . *O. bertolonii*
1* Lip bent slightly upwards or straight; stigma cavity up to 1.2 × as high as wide, often wider than high; basal callosities sitting at the base of the column; column 4.5 – 7.5 mm high with a broad base . . . .
. . . . *O. bertoloniformis*

Ophrys

'bertoloniiformis'

below: 'promontorii' 'catalaunica' below: 'triloba'

type Var

228

'benacensis'

Ophrys

type Dalmatia

229

Calypso   *Calypso bulbosa* (L.) Oakes

Synonyms: *C. borealis* (Schwartz) Salisb., *C. americana* R. Br., *C. occidentalis* (Holz.) A. A. Heller, *Cypripedium bulbosum* L.

Plant with an ovate tuber; a single foliage leaf grows out of the sheaths of dead previous leaves; leaf 7 cm long, stalked, the blade ovate up to 6 cm long and 5 cm wide. Stem 10 – 20 cm tall with a few sheathing scale leaves on the lower part; a single large flower growing from the axil of a pink-coloured bract, on a short stalk, nodding; sepals and lateral petals similar, purplish-pink, lanceolate, 12 – 22 mm long and 2.5 – 4 mm wide, erect to spreading; lip 15 – 23 mm long, hollowed into a shoe-shape, the rear part terminating in a broad bifid spur, lip interior with strong purple spots and stripes, front part flattened, whitish with a basal tuft of yellow hairs.

Habitat: shady, damp, coniferous woods.
Flowers: May, June.
Photos: Su, Västernorrland 16.6.76.
Distribution: in the northern European coniferous belt, southwards to 57°N. The species occupies a circumpolar area in the temperate and boreal zones; in North America reaches further south in the mountains; in Asia there are large gaps in the distribution, e.g. in western Siberia and eastern Yakut.
Floristic element: scandinavian n-russian n-siberian. **Countries: Eur:** C   RB, **N**   Su, Fe, Rn, **E**   RE.
Variation: the colouration of the lip and the tuft of hairs varies insignificantly. The North American types which differ somewhat from the Euroasiatic plants however scarcely deserve a higher status than varieties (c.f. Luer 1975).
Relationship: the lip is similar to the Lady's Slipper in appearance (c.f. the nomenclature by Linnaeus; the two genera are not, however, closely related.

Coral Root   *Corallorhiza trifida* Châtel

Synonyms: *C. intacta* Cham., *C. innata* R. Br.

Plant with a coral-like branched rhizome without roots or foliage leaves; stem 7 – 30 cm tall, the lower part surrounded by a few sheathing scale leaves, yellowish-green; inflorescence lax, 2 – 12 flowered; flowers with short stalks, standing out; bracts up to 2 mm long; sepals greenish, often spotted or tinted (brownish-) red, 5 – 6 mm long and 1 – 1.5 mm wide, the two laterals extending into a short spur-like process under the lip insertion; lateral petals of a similar colour, somewhat shorter, forming a lax hood with the central sepal; lip white, often with red spots, tongue-shaped 5 – 6 mm long, with 2 inconspicuous tooth-like side lobes at the base and 2 longitudinal ridges. **Habitat:** shady damp woods, also tundra and damp dune hollows; up to 2,000 m; prefers nutrient-starved, weakly acid soils. **Flowers:** May – August. **Photos:** Ge, Southern Baden 1.6.66 (l), 21.6.62 (c); Ge, Southern Würtemberg 17.6.71 (r). **Distribution:** widely in Europe and Asia from the arctic to the submeridional zones, very rare in the meridional zone; infrequent in the w-submediterranean and s + m-atlantic floristic regions. Species with a circumpolar distribution; concentrated in the temperate and boreal zones becoming isolated further north and in the mountains to the south. In Britain as far south as Yorkshire. **Floristic element:** (meridional/montane) submeridional/montane temperate boreal (arctic). **Countries: Eur: SE**   Gr, Al, Ju, Bu, Rm, RK, **S**   It, **SW**   Hs, **W**   Ga, Be, + Ho, Br, **C**   He, Au, Hu, Ge, Da, Cz, Po, RB, **N**   Su, No, Fe, RN, Is, **E**   RW, RC; **Asi:** An.

Fen Orchid *Liparis loeselii* (L.) L. C. M. Richard

ovata

Plant with a horizontal rhizome from the end of which the new flowering stem arises near to that of the previous year; stem 5 – 25 cm tall with a pseudobulb at the base surrounded by the leaf sheaths, above sharplyangled, 3 – 5 corners; 2 (3) foliage leaves, lanceolate to elliptic, 2 – 11 cm long and 0.7 – 2 cm wide, erect; inflorescence lax 2 – 10 cm long, 3 – 18 flowered; bracts short, scale-like; flowers yellowish-green with short stalks; sepals 4.5 – 5.5 mm long and 1.4 – 1.8 mm wide, longer than the linear (about 0.5 mm wide) lateral petals and the lip; lip sickle-shaped and folded lengthwise, divided into a wide ovate front section and a short narrow hind section, with a wavy notched edge. **Habitat**: fens and intermediate mires, also wet dune hollows; up to about 900 m; on wet calcareous soils. **Flowers**: May – July. **Photos**: Ge Allgäu 20.6.67 (l), 25.6.83 (r).
Distribution: in the temperate zone in Europe, sporadic in the submeridional zone; uncommon because of its special demands. Also eastwards in the temperate zone to central Siberia; a second area of distribution in the temperate and boreal northern America except Alaska. In Britain: East Anglia (fens of Cambridgeshire, Norfolk and Suffolk); south Wales (coastal dune slacks). **Floristic element**: temperate (submeridional). **Countries**: Eur: SE Ju, ? + Bu, Rm, S It, SW Hs, W Ga, Be, Ho, Br, C He, Au, Hu, Ge, Da, Cz, Po, RB, N Su, No, Fe, E RW, RE, RC. **Variation**: a species showing little variation; in the dunes of South Wales variants appear with ovate-elliptic leaves; these have been described as the variety 'ovata'.

Single-Leaved Bog Orchid *Malaxis monophyllos* (L.) Swartz

Synonyms: *M. m. var. brachypoda* (A. Gray) Morris & Ames, *M. m. var. diphyllos* (Cham.) Luer, *Microstylis monophyllos* (L.) Lindley

Plant with a vertical rhizome; stem 10 – 30 (– 50) cm tall; a basal pseudobulb covered with leaf sheaths (close above that of the previous year), upper part of the stem angular, 1 scale leaf and 1, rarely 2, foliage leaves, latter elliptic-ovate 3 – 10 cm long and 1.5 – 5 cm wide; inflorescence 3 – 15 (– 25) cm long, fairly dense and many-flowered; bracts short, scale-like; flowers yellowish-green on 1 – 1.5 mm long stalks which are twisted through 360° (or 180°); sepals 2 – 2.7 mm long ovate – lanceolate; lateral petals 1.7 – 2.4 mm long, linear; lip 1.7 – 2.4 mm long, rounded with a triangular point and two small side lobes, dished, directed upwards (or downwards).

Habitat: damp woods, especially in river valleys, damp meadows, wet mossy rocks; to 1,600 m; on base-rich soils, prefers growing in half-shade. **Flowers**: June, July. **Photos**: Ge, Allgäu 15.7.71
Distribution: in Europe in the temperate and boreal zones, absent from western Europe; southwards as far as the Alps and Carpathians. Species with a circumpolar areal in the temperate and boreal zones; in the mountains of eastern Asia and northern America as far as the meridional zone.
Floristic element: alpine carpathian (s) + n-subatlantic centraleuropean sarmatic c-siberian scandinavian (n-russian). **Countries**: Eur: SE Ju, Rm, S It, C He, Au, Ge, Cz, Po, RB, N Su, No, Fe, RN, E RW, RC. **Variation**: almost all the North American plants have flowers which are twisted through 180°, in which the lip points downwards ('brachypoda') otherwise they resemble the Eurasian variant which reaches Alaska.

Liparis

Malaxis

Borg Orchid *Hammarbya paludosa* (L.) O. Kuntze

Synonym: *Malaxis paludosa* (L.) Swartz
Plant with a vertical rhizome; stem 5–25 cm tall with one of the leaf-sheath enveloped pseudobulbs at the base (1–2 cm above that of the previous year), 3–5 cornered, with 1–2 scale leaves and 2–3 foliage leaves on the lower part, the uppermost foliage leaf is the largest, lanceolate, 8–30 mm long and 5–11 mm wide; inflorescence 2–15 cm long, lax, many-flowered; bracts short, scale-like; flowers yellowish-green, on 1.5–2 mm-long stalks twisted through 360°; sepals 2.4–3 mm long, ovate, the laterals shorter than the central one; lateral petals 1.5–2 mm long, ovate, with bent back tips; lip 1.5–2 mm long ovate, pointed, concave. **Reproduction:** bulbils are formed on the front edges of the leaves; they fall off and grow into new plants. **Habitat:** raised bog hollows, intermediate mires, wet dune hollows; up to 1,100 m; on impoverished acid soils. **Flowers:** July, August. **Photos:** Ge, Oberbayern 31.7.65 (l); Ge, Allgäu 8.8.78 (c), 1.8.77 (r). **Distribution:** in Europe in the temperate and boreal zones, sometimes in the submeridional zone; a species with a circumpolar distribution (Eurasia and North America). Scattered sites in southern England, west and north Wales with the main area of distribution in Scotland. **Floristic element:** temperate boreal (pannonic) (pontic). **Countries: Eur: SE** Ju, Rm, **S** It, **W** Ga, Be, Ho, Br, Hb, Fa, **C** He, Au, Ge, Da, Cz, Po, RB, **N** Su, No, Fe, RN, **E** RW, RE, RC. **Relationship:** The genus *Hammarbya* is monotypic, but very closely related to the genus *Malaxis* and has also been united with it.

—— ADDENDUM ——

Widder's Vanilla Orchid *Nigritella widderi* Teppner & E. Klein

Inflorescence spherical to ovoid; flowers pink, the buds more intensely coloured than the open flowers; lip on the lower flowers 6–9 mm long, constricted into a saddle shape 2.4–3.2 mm from the base, hind section widened, ventricose; size of upper flowers somewhat smaller; lateral sepals somewhat wider than the central one and clearly wider than the lateral petals; spur 1–1.4 mm long; asexual reproduction.
Habitat: Alpine calcareous poor grassland; above 1,500 m; basic, fairly dry soils. **Flowers:** July. **Photos:** Au, Steiermark 18.7.85 (l, u/r), 23.7.85 (l/r); scale 1 cm.
Distribution: north-eastern limestone Alps; the species, described in 1985, is known from the Veitschalpe, Hochschwab, Totem Gebirge and Loferer Alpen, it is probably more widespread and may be also present in Bavaria.
Floristic element: alpine. **Countries: Eur: C** Au, ?Ge.
Relationship: *N. widderi*, along with *N. rubra*, *N. stiriaca* and *N. archiducis-joannis*, forms a group of species which reproduce asexually. The other *Nigritella* species, except for the Scandinavian population of *N. nigra*, reproduce sexually, which is the usual method amongst orchids. In the asexual method (apomixis) no female gametes are produced which, after fertilization, would have grown into embryos. Instead, the embryos grow from the nucellus of the seed without fertilization. This makes pollination superfluous. Apomixis offers similar advantages as autogamy (*see* p263): the species is independent of the pollinating insect which enables it to invade new habitats such as places high up in the mountains.

235

IDENTIFICATION KEYS

Summary

1. Key to the genera, p8
2. Key to the species groups and species

In the case of the large genera *Orchis* and *Ophrys* partial keys to some of the groups have been inserted in the species descriptions.

Using the Identification Keys

Keys are helpful in the identification of unknown plants. Here they are constructed on a binary system; at each stage a choice between two possibilities has to be made. They have the same number (1/1*, 2/2* etc.). Starting at alternatives 1, both possibilities must be considered and the one which gives the best fit should be chosen. This leads to a number indicating the next pair of alternatives to be considered and the process is repeated until it leads to the name of the species or subspecies. The choice is then confirmed by means of the species' descriptions and photographs. The numbers in brackets make it easier to work backwards.

However, when dealing with orchids, this procedure, although simple in concept, leads to several problems. Other species are very similar and it is difficult to find characters which can be used as suitable alternatives, since they need to be easily recognizable from a short description. The less conspicuous the differences between the species, the finer must be the detail used in the key, and the more exact the observations needed. In many cases the use of a lens with 10x magnification will be required and it may not be possible to complete identification without the use of a millimetre scale. Ideally, it should be possible to identify every individual plant using the key. This goal, however desirable, is not realistic and should not be expected using the keys in this or any other book. Plants are always turning up, however infrequently, which differ markedly from the usual appearance of the species (a colour or structural variant, for instance, which has arisen either through mutation or environmental influences). A key which set out to cover every eventuality would become indistinct, over long and therefore useless. Similar problems arise when the species are very variable, especially in the case of *Dactylorhiza* (*see* remarks on p239 at the start of the key) and, to a lesser extent, also with *Ophrys* and some *Orchis* groups. A useful ploy is not to try and identify the first individual plant found, but begin by looking in leisurely fashion at the whole population growing in a particular place. In this way an overview can be gained of the amount of variation and then the chance of a mistake being made is reduced. Experience has shown that the longer the key, the greater the chance of it being unreliable! For this reason, in this book the process of identification is divided into separate steps, from the recognition of the plant as an orchid to the confirmation of it belonging to a particular species. The first key on pp8 – 11 leads to the genus, and subsequent keys to the species and subspecies. Where necessary, especially in the large genera *Ophrys* and *Orchis*, intermediate steps have been interpolated. The process of identification follows the scheme:

family → genus → group* → subgroup* → species → subspecies*

The units marked * are only used as steps where required. This subdivision has advantages for the person who is already knowledgeable. It is not necessary to start at the beginning every time, but entry is possible at the point with which he or she is already familiar. In the construction of the keys, their use as a practical aid to identification is the first consideration. For this reason, easily distinguishable characters are chosen whenever possible. Less attention is paid to relationships. Species which are near together in the key are not necessarily closely related. The opposite case occurs when, during the construction of a key, indications of a relationship arise where, unexpectedly, two species appear in the same alternative.

Each identification key has its own 'inner life' – and its weak points. If the person using the key finally discovers these, he has usually made such progress in species recognition that he no longer needs the key! This discovery will at least compensate for all the hard work involved in many unsuccessful attempts at identification.

Epipactis

1   Rear part of lip (hypochile) with a lobe on each side; rear and front part (epichile) connected by a movable joint 2

1* Hypochile without side lobes; hypo- and epichile do not move in relation to each other 3

2   Hypochile boat-shaped with upright, narrowly triangular side lobes; epichile narrow triangular, with glabrous edge, pointed . . . . *E. veratrifolia*, p14

2* Hypochile saucer-shaped, side lobes broadly triangular spreading at an angle; epichile rounded, with wavy edge, truncate . . . . *E. palustris*, p14

3   (1) Inflorescence stalk glabrous or slightly hairy 4

3* Inflorescence stalk densely hairy, downy or felt-like 5

4   Flowers hanging or at least strongly nodding when fully out; leaves pale green . . . . *E. phyllanthes*, p28

4* Flowers standing out horizontally or scarcely inclined; leaves dark green, sometimes purple . . . . *E. troodi group*, p30

5   (3) Epichile with 3 wrinkled-warty outgrowths: 2 roundish lateral tubercles and 1 longitudinal central 'crest' . . . . *E. microphylla group*, p22

5* Epichile flat or with 2 (rarely 3) outgrowths which are smooth or with a slight longitudinal furrow 6

6   Cross-pollinated: in the fully open flower a cone-shaped sticky gland is present (the rostellum gland), pollinia lie intact in the

pollen sacs (or have already been removed together with the sticky gland) 7

6* Self-pollinating: no rostellum gland present; this was either absent or was present in the bud and dried out as the flower opened, pollinia disintegrate in the bud or after opening 9

7 Plant dark grey-green (the inflorescence stalk often pale green), leaves and the whole stem a uniformly violet shade; leaves lanceolate to narrowly ovate; flowers shining like silk *E. purpurata*, p16

7* Plant green, violet shading absent or concentrated on the stem; leaves ovate to rounded, rarely lanceolate; flowers not shining 8

8 Sepals green, lateral petals whitish and often with a pink lustre, hypochile blackish-violet inside; stem always green
. . . . *E. condensata*, p16

8* All perianth segments including the lip tinged with red, if green then the hypochile is not blackish-violet but lighter; stem often tinged violet . . . .
. . . . *E. helleborine*, p18

9 (6) Epichile sometimes slightly, but generally clearly, longer than broad, pointed; sepals (10 –) 11 – 15 mm long, often (but not always) tapered . . . .
. . . . *E. leptochila*, p28

9* Epichile broader than long or as broad as long, truncate; sepals 6 – 11 (– 12) mm long, not obviously tapering 10

10 Leaves stiff, folded lengthwise and grooved, bent into a sickle-shape, with a wavy edge, at a wide angle to the stem – (plant 25 – 90 cm tall; leaves lanceolate, yellowish-grey-green; sepals 7 – 10 (– 12) mm long) . . . . . *E. muelleri*, p24

10* Leaves soft, usually flat, erect to overhanging 11

11 Flower stalks 5 – 10 mm long – (plant 20 – 60 cm tall; leaves lanceolate dark green, shaded violet; sepals 9 – 12 mm long) . . . . *E. greuteri*, p24

11* Flower stalks up to 4 mm long 12

12 One pointed tubercle on each side at the base of the stigma – (plant 30 – 60 cm tall; leaves lanceolate, yellowish-green; sepals 8 – 11 mm long) . . . .
. . . . *E. youngiana*, p24

12* Stigma without pointed tubercles 13

13 Column with pollen dish, stigmatic surface at an angle to the long axis of the ovary (*see* drawing p24) 14

13* Pollen dish absent, stigmatic surface at right angles to the long axis of the ovary 15

14 Stem green; epichile usually with upturned edges and extended point, without red colouration (plant 10 – 30 (– 45) cm tall; leaves lanceolate, pale green; sepals 6 – 9.5 mm long) . . . .
. . . . *E. albensis*, p24

14* Stem violet below; epichile with flat edges and turned-back tip, usually tinged reddish – (plant 20 – 60 cm tall; leaves ovate-lanceolate, yellowish-green; sepals 6 – 8 mm long) . . . . . . *E. dunensis*, p24

15 (13) Leaves broadly ovate, with smooth edge; bracts shorter than, to as long as, the flowers; sepals (8 –) 9 – 11 mm long autogamic '*neerlandica*' – race, p18

15* Leaves ovate-lanceolate, with wavy edge; lower bracts much longer than the flowers; sepals 6 – 8 mm long 16

16 Hypochile pale olive to brownish inside; epichile greenish-white, sometimes with a pink sheen; leaves concentrated in the middle of the stem (apart from the scale leaves) – (plant 15 – 35 cm tall; leaves light green) . . . .*E. pontica*, p24

16* Hypochile (dark) red inside; epichile white, generally tinged reddish; leaves fairly evenly distributed along the stem (*see* alternative 14*) . .*E. dunensis*, p24

Cephalanthera

1 Flower lip with a short spur; foliage leaves often rolled into a cone . . . .

. . . . *C. epipactoides* group
1*   Lip without a spur; leaves flat 2
2   Flowers purplish-red; inflorescence stalk, together with the ovaries, densely covered in glandular hairs *C. rubra*, p34
2*   Flowers (yellowish-) white; stalk and ovaries sparsely hairy 3
3   Leaves lanceolate, 4 – 6 times as long as wide; bracts (except for the lowest one or two) much shorter than the ovaries . . . .
. . . . *C. longifolia*, p34
3*   Leaves ovate, 2 – 3 times as long as wide; bracts get smaller towards the top, lower one longer, upper shorter than the ovaries
. . . . *C. damasonium* group, p32

Platanthera

1   Spur longer than 13 mm (*Platanthera*, strict sense.) 2
1*   Spur shorter than 90 mm 4
2   The 2 pollen sacs parallel, about 1 mm apart . . . . *P. bifolia*, p54
2*   Pollen sacs at an angle to each other, 2 – 4 mm apart at the base 0.5 – 2 mm between them at the top 3
3   Flowers (at least the lateral sepals) white or yellowish-white . . *P. chlorantha*, p54
3*   Flowers green or yellowish-green . . . . .
. . . . *P. algeriensis* group, p52
4   (1) Plant with only 1 basal foliage leaf (*Lysiella*) . . . . *P. obtusata*, p58
4*   Plant with several leaves arranged along the stem (*Limnorchis*) 5
5   Lip turned up at the tip; spur 7 – 9 mm long . . . . *P. azorica*, p56
5*   Lip straight or turned down; spur 2 – 5 (– 7) mm long 6
6   Lateral sepals ovate, scarcely twisted, their surface oriented in the same direction as the lip; spur 2 – 3 mm long .
. . . . *P. micrantha*, p56
6*   Lateral sepals lanceolate, twisted in relation to the lip; spur 3.5 – 5 (– 7) mm long . . . . *P. hyperborea*, p56

The species in this area fall into 3 distinct sections which are sometimes regarded as separate genera. They are named in the key.

Dactylorhiza

sub-divisions of the genus:

1.   Sambucina group
        D. romana sub-group: *D. romana*, *D. markusii*, *D. flavescens*, *D. insularis*, *D. sambucina*.
2.   Iberica group
        D. iberica
3.   Maculata group
     a) *D. umbrosa*, *D. osmanica*; *D. urvilleana* sub-group: *D. urvilleana*, *D. nieschalkiorum*
     b) *D. foliosa*, *D. saccifera*, *D. maculata*
     c) *D. majalis* sub-group: *D. euxina*, *D. majalis*, *D. cordigera*; *D. purpurella* sub-group: *D. purpurella*, *D. kerryensis*
     d) *D. baltica*
     e) *D. lapponica*, *D. cruenta*, *D. traunsteineri*, *D. baumanniana*
     f) *D. kalopissii*, *D. praetermissa* sub-group: *D. praetermissa*, *D. sphagnicola*
     g) *D. elata*
     h) *D. incarnata* sub-group: *D. incarnata*, *D. ochroleuca*

Of the European orchid genera, *Dactylorhiza* is the most difficult in which to distinguish and identify the members. The problems arise from the genetic make up of the genus and can be expressed in three ways as far as the taxonomics and floristics are concerned: 1. The members differ only slightly from one another, their morphological variation is very slight. 2. There is an unusually large variation within the types and populations – plants being frequently found which differ widely from the mean. 3. Where different types are growing together, hybrids arise in which the morphological boundaries are extinguished. To add to these purely biological criteria there is the added difficulty of a lack of information about distribution.

The identification key tries to take these problems into account: in general it applies to populations rather than to individual plants. In every case several plants have been examined and a consensus of each particular character is used. In order to minimize the chances of a wrong identification, several of the species are built into the key in more than one place. At the same time, relatively extreme forms are rarely indicated since the names of alternative species are given, and the observation of a character at the edge of its variability range could have led to them anyway. In spite of all this, a sound appreciation of the species can only be achieved after a lot of experience in the field.

1   Spur turned upwards 2
1* Spur horizontal or pointing downwards 3
2   Spur straight; lateral sepals spreading out horizontally or upwards at a slight angle; leaves usually spread out along the stem
    . . . . *D. insularis*, p72
2* Spur bent; lateral sepals held vertically upright; lower leaves form a rosette . . . .
    . . . . *D. romana* group, p70
3   (1) Flowers yellow 4
3* Flowers red, pink, sometimes white . . 6
4   Spur straight, cylindrical, 1.5 – 2 mm thick . . . . *D. insularis*, p72
4* Spur bent, cone-shaped, generally clearly more than 2 mm thick at its base 5
5   Lip (spread out!) 11 – 17 mm broad; spur 10 – 15 mm long . . . *D. sambucina*, p74
5* Lip 5 – 9 mm broad; spur 6.5 – 10 mm long . . . . *D. incarnata* group, p90
6   (3) Spur narrow, cylindrical 1 – 1.5 mm thick 7
6* Spur wide, cylindrical or cone-shaped; thicker than 2 mm 9
7   Lateral sepals twisted towards the outside, held up vertically or at an angle,

or pointing forwards with the upper side facing downwards . . *D. maculata*, p100
7* All the perianth segments pointing forwards at an angle, at times coming together to form a hood, not twisted and with the upper side facing inwards . . . 8
8   Foliage leaves longish-lanceolate, 3 – 4 times as long as wide; lip broader than long . . . . *D. foliosa*, p98
8* Foliage leaves linear-lanceolate, more than 7 times as long as wide; lip often longer than broad . . . . . *D. iberica*, p74
9   (6) Largest leaves linear-lanceolate, more than (6) 7 times as long as wide 10
9* Largest leaves lanceolate to ovate, at most 6 (7) times as long as wide 15
10 Lip with small dots over the whole surface, sometimes also with short lines and a suggestion of a horse-shoe pattern; flowers pink . . . . . *D. sphagnicola*, p86
    . . . . see also *D. praetermissa*, p86
    . . . . see also *D. incarnata*, p90
10* Lip with a horseshoe pattern of lines and large dots, sometimes small dots; flowers often purplish-red, also pink 11
11 Lip entire or shallowly 3-lobed with protruding middle lobe and obtuse angled recesses (sinuses), leaves often stiffly erect, held close to the stem, with cowl-shaped tip . . . . *D. incarnata*, p90
    . . . . see also *D. traunsteineri*, p94
11* Lip 3-lobed with deep acute-angled sinuses between the middle and side lobes; leaves at an angle or standing out widely from the stem, usually flat at the tip
    12
12 Strong plants, more than 25 (30) cm tall, with (4 –) 5 – 10 leaves, largest leaves more than (10) 15 cm long 13
12* Delicate plants, up to 30 (40) cm tall, with 2 – 6 leaves, largest leaf up to 12 (16) cm long 14
13 Spur 6 – 9 mm long; lip 6.5 – 9 mm long; leaves usually with small spots, rarely unspotted . . . . *D. baltica*, p88

13* Spur 9 – 16 mm long; lip 9 – 15 mm long; leaves often unspotted, sometimes spotted . . . . *D. elata*, p88

14 (12) Spur cone-shaped with a wide base and tapering regularly towards the tip (seen from above) *D. traunsteineri*, p94
. . . . *see also D. lapponica*, p92
. . . . *see also D. maculata*, p100

14* Spur cylindrical with a narrow base, often somewhat swollen in the middle (seen from above) . . . . *D. baumanniana*, p96
see also D. majalis subsp. brevifolia/ turfosa, p96

15 (9) Lip yellowish around the spur entrance, flowers vermillion or carmine (warm red) . . . . *D. sambucina*, p74

15* Lip without yellow, flowers purplish-red (cold red), sometimes carmine (in which case the spur is shorter than 10 mm) 16

16 Lip with only dots or fine dashes in loops and many (small) dots 17

16* Lip with dashes and lines mostly in loops, often also (large) spots 20

17 Tall plants, stem more than 20 cm, mostly over 30 cm; largest leaves longer than 8 cm, mostly over 12 cm; flowers generally pale colours (pink) 18

17* Short plants, stem up to 30 (40) cm tall; largest leaves up to 12 (16) cm long; flowers usually dark purplish-red . . . 19

18 Spur 5 – 9.5 mm long, usually less than 8.5 mm; leaf spots if present usually large, often ring-shaped, covering the whole leaf surface . . . .
. . . . *D. praetermissa*, p86

18* Spur 8 – 12.5 mm long, usually more than 8.5 mm; leaf spots if present usually small dots confined to the front half of the leaf
. . . . *D. kalopissii*, p80
. . . . *see also D. elata*, p88

19 (17) Lip edge with irregular large teeth .
. . . . *D. euxina*, p80

19* Lip edge not toothed (sometimes the side lobes have a large notch . . . .
. . . . *D. purpurella* group, p84

. . . . *see also D. baumanniana*, p96

20 (16) Spur ²/₃ to ¾ as long as the lip . . .
. . . . *D. osmanica*, p76

20* Spur almost as long (⁹/₁₀) or longer than the lip 21

21 Lip with markings over the whole surface, either fan-shaped or horse-shoe pattern, and copiously also at the sides 22

21* Lip with horse-shoe pattern but very few or no markings down the (sometimes narrow) sides 26

22 Spur 5 – 10 (– 11) mm long; lower bracts often shorter than the flowers 23

22* Spur 9 – 17 mm long, lower bracts longer than the flowers 24

23 Stem (usually) filled with pith, with 2 – 4 (– 6) small, not sheathing, leaves, the uppermost one not usually reaching the inflorescence . . . .
. . . . *D. maculata (fuchsii)*, p100
. . . . *see also D. saccifera*, p98

23* Stem hollow, without or with 1 – 3 non-sheathing leaves, the uppermost one reaching the inflorescence . . . .
. . . . *D. purpurella* group, p84
. . . . *see also D. majalis*, p82
. . . . *see also D. cruenta*, p92
. . . . *see also D. praetermissa*, p86

24 (22) Middle lobe large, its area (⅓) ½ as large, to as large, as that of one of the side lobes; stem often full of pith . . . .
. . . . *D. saccifera*, p98

24* Middle lobe small less than a ¼ (⅓) the area of one side lobe; stem hollow . . 25

25 Lateral sepals inclined forwards or held up at an angle; spur straight, cylindrical
. . . . *D. urvilleana* group, p78
see also D. majalis and *D. kalopissii*, p80

25* Lateral sepals held vertically upright; spur often bent, cylindrical to conical . . . .
. . . . *D. elata*, p88

26 (21) Spur shorter than, or only slightly longer than, the lip, sometimes strongly bent 27

26* Spur more than 1.2 × as long as the lip,

straight or slightly bent 28

27 Lip broader than long, broadly wedge-shaped/rounded at the base; lateral sepals held up vertically . . *D. elata*, p88

27* Lip usually longer than broad, narrowly wedge-shaped at the base; lateral sepals held up at an angle . . *D. umbrosa*, p76

28 (26) Leaves ovate-lanceolate, 2 – 3.5 (– 4.5) times as long as wide 29

28* Leaves lanceolate, (3 –) 4 – 6 times as long as wide 30

29 Lip mostly less than 7 mm long and 8.5 mm broad; leaves up to 2.5 cm wide, often spotted on both sides . . . .
. . . . *D. cruenta*, p92

29* Lip usually more than 7 mm long and 8.5 mm broad; leaves wider than 2 cm, often spotted on one side . . . .
. . . . *D. majalis* group, p82
. . . . . see also *D. purpurella* group, p84

30 Spur conical with a broad base (as viewed from above) 31

30* Spur cylindrical with narrow base (seen from above) 32

31 Leaves heavily spotted on the upper surface; the uppermost leaf not usually reaching the inflorescence, the latter lax, 5 – 20 flowered . . . .
. . . . *D. lapponica*, p92

31* Leaves spotted on both sides, or unspotted, the uppermost leaf generally reaching the dense, 10 – 30 flowered inflorescence . . . . *D. cruenta*, p92

32 (30) Lip clearly (up to 1.8 ×) broader than long; side lobes and sometimes the middle lobe toothed; inflorescence dense, broadly cylindrical . . . . *D. majalis*, p82

32* Lip only a little broader (to 1.3 ×) than long, side and middle lobes with entire edges; inflorescence somewhat lax, narrowly cylindrical . . . .
. . . . *D. baumanniana*, p96

Orchis

sub-divisions of the genus:

1. Coriophora group
    O. coriophora, O. sancta

2. Laxiflora group
    O. laxiflora, O. palustris

3. Mascula group
    O. mascula, O. olbiensis subsp. olbiensis, O. o. subsp. ichnusae, O. signifera, O. scopulorum;
    O. pinetorum sub-group: *O. pinetorum, O. langei, O. pallens, O. provincialis;*
    O. pauciflora sub-group: *O. pauciflora, O. laeta; O. anatolica*

4. Collina group
    O. collina, O. spitzelii, O. canariensis; O. patens sub-group: *O. patens, O. prisca*

5. Papilionacea group
    O. papilionacea

6. Quadripunctata group
    O. quadripunctata, O. brancifortii

7. Boryi group
    O. boryi, O. israelitica

8. Morio group
    O. morio subsp. morio, O. morio subsp. syriaca, O. m. subsp. albanica, O. longicornu sub-group: *O. longicornu, O. champagneuxii*

9. Militaris group
    O. punctulata, O. galilaea; O. tridentata sub-group: *O. tridentata, O. conica, O. lactea; O. purpurea;*
    O. militaris sub-group: *O. militaris, O. stevenii;*
    O. italica, O. simia, O. ustulata

The first part of the key leads to several groups as well as direct to a few species. The species in the different groups can be identified in the later parts of the key. *See also* the special key for those species in which the normal sequence of flower opening is reversed, p245

1 Lip undivided 2

Orchis: Mascula group

surface can be seen from the front, rarely directed upwards at an angle and slightly twisted 8

6 Stem (10 −) 20 − 60 cm tall; inflorescence (5 −) 8 − 20 cm long, with more than (10) 15 flowers, these purplish-red (a cold-red shade) . . . . *O. mascula*, p114

6* Stem 1 − 25 (− 35) cm tall; inflorescence 3 − 8 (− 12) cm long with 6 − 15 (− 25) flowers, these whitish, pale or deep pink (often a warm red shade): *O. olbiensis*

7 Spur 13 − 19 mm long, 1⅓ − 2 × as long as the lip, curving upwards . . . . *O. o. subsp. olbiensis*, p114

7* Spur 9 − 14 mm long, 1 − 1¼ × as long as the lip, straight, directed slightly upwards . . . . *O. o subsp. ichnusae*, p114

8 (5) Sepals pointed, with a short or elongated point . . . . *O. signifera*, p114

8* Sepals blunt, rounded 9

9 Spur 6 − 8 mm long . . . . *O. scopulorum*, p116

9* Spur 10 − 15 mm long . . . . *O. pinetorum* group, p118

Orchis: Collina group

1 Lip undivided . . . . *O. collina*, p124

1* Lip 3-lobed 2

2 Lip with a pale ground colour (whitish to pale violet); ridges on each side of the spur entrance straight when viewed from the side; sepals without dots on the inner surface . . . . *O. canariensis*, p126

2* Lip with a deep ground colour (purplish-pink to red); ridges on each side of the spur entrance stepped when viewed from the side; sepals usually with purple dots on the inner side 3

3 Sepals a uniform colour on the inner surface (apart from the dots), olive green, sometimes with a reddish shade, especially towards the edge . . . . *O. spitzelii*, p126

3* Sepals bicoloured on the inner surface, with a green central area and a wide coloured border . *O. patens* group, p128

Orchis: Morio group

1 Lip side lobes usually turned down at right angles to the middle, sometimes the front edges are touching; whitish middle of the lip sharply divided from the more intensely coloured side-lobes . . . . *O. longicornu* group, p138

1* Side lobes almost flat or hanging down at a slight angle; if the side lobes are turned down at right angles then the pale colour of the lip middle continues over into the side lobes with a gradual transition of colour . . . . *O. morio* sub-group, p136

Orchis: Militaris group

1 Flower bracts about as long as the ovaries 2

1* Bracts at most half the length of the ovaries 3

2 Sepals 3.5 − 4.5 mm long, red to blackish-brown on the outer side . . . . *O. ustulata*, p150

2* Sepals longer than 5 mm, green, whitish or pink . . . . . . *O. tridentata* group, p142

3 (1) Flowers yellow, sometimes marked with red 4

3* Flowers red 5

4 Flowers open from below upwards on the inflorescence; the 2 tongues of the middle lobe rounded to narrowly rhombic, up to 2.5 × as long as the central tooth . . . . *O. punctata*, p140

4* Flowers open in the reverse sequence (from the top downwards on the inflorescence); the tongues of the middle lobe linear, much longer than the central tooth . . . . *O. galilaea*, p140

5 (3) Side lobes and tongues of the middle lobe with long points; leaves wavy along the edges . . . . *O. italica*, p148

5*   Side lobes and middle lobe tongues blunt; leaves with smooth edges 6

6   Side lobes and middle lobe tongues linear, about 10 × as long as wide, irregularly twisted . . . . *O. simia*, p148

6*   Side lobes and middle lobe tongues longish to broadly ovate, at most 5 × as long as wide, usually flat 7

7   Inflorescence comes into flower from the top downwards: *see* alternative 4* (*O. galilaea*) . . . .

7*   Inflorescence starts flowering from the bottom 8

8   Outer side of the sepals pink to pale violet . . . . *O. militaris* group, p146

8*   Outer side of sepals shaded or spotted brownish-red, rarely pale brownish-pink . . . . *O. purpurea*, p144

Special key to the species with an inverse flowering sequence:

In a few species the flowers open from the top of the inflorescence downwards. In normal types the flowers at the bottom of the inflorescence open first, the top ones last.

1   Sepals not curving to form a hood; spur longer than 9.5 mm . . . . Boryi group, p134

1*   Sepals form a closed hood; spur up to 6 mm long 2

2   Lip 14 – 20 mm long, whitish with purple tongues, dotted red . . . . *O. simia*, p148

2*   Lip 10 – 12 mm long, white, pink or pale yellow, spotted red . . *O. galilaea*, p140

Himantoglossum

A difficult genus, the systematics of which have not yet been completely elucidated. The amount of variation within all the species has to be taken into account. This means that the characters must be assessed over several plants in the population. It is often difficult or even impossible to identify individual plants.

1   Lip middle lobe divided at the tip to a depth of up to 3.5 (7) mm; inflorescence

dense, flowers in the centre about 2 – 4 (– 5) mm apart . . . . *H. hircinum*, p154

1*   Middle lobe cut in to a depth of 5 – 50 mm; inflorescence lax, flowers in the centre 5 – 10 (– 15) mm apart 2

2   Lip with no markings, other than perhaps tiny dots, on a whitish background; side lobes 3 – 6 mm long; middle lobe horizontal or hanging slightly downwards . . . . *H. affine*, p156

2*   Lip with strong spots on a whitish ground (rarely unmarked); side lobes 5 – 25 mm long; middle lobe directed down at an angle 3

3   Spur 2.5 – 3.5 (– 5) mm long; sepals hood small, lateral sepals 8.5 – 11.5 mm long . . . . *H. adriaticum*, p154

3*   Spur (5 –) 6.5 – 13 mm long; sepal hood large, lateral sepals 13 – 18.5 mm long . . . . *H. caprinum*, p156

Serapias

Some of the species look very similar and can only be identified with certainty if exact measurements can be made of the flowers. To do this, it may sometimes be necessary to spread out the lip – which can be done with the tip of a finger without damaging the flower. The lip is jointed, consisting of an anterior part (epichile) and a posterior section (hypochile).

1   Base of lip with 1 undivided (but sometimes lobed) callosity which can be seen by looking into the flower . . . . *S. lingua*, p166

1*   Base of lip with 2 longish small callosities (ridges) which can only be seen when the flower is pulled apart 2

2   Lip 14 – 19 mm long, epichile 7 – 11.5 mm long . . . . *S. parviflora*, p166

2*   Lip longer than 20 mm, epichile longer than 12 mm 3

3   Epichile ovate – lanceolate, its greatest breadth at least 1.7 × its breadth at the base, ⅔ to about as broad as the (spread out!) hypochile 4

3* Epichile lanceolate, its greatest breadth at most 1.6× its breadth at the base, ⅓ – ⅔ as broad as the hypochile ... 5

4 Stem and leaves speckled purple at the base, lip callosities spreading outwards .... *S. cordigera*, p160

4* Stem and leaves not speckled; lip callosities parallel ....
.... *S. neglecta* group, p158

5 (3) Lip 32 – 42 mm long; epichile 18 – 28 mm long; sepals 23 – 33 mm long
.... *S. vomeracea* group, p162

5* Lip 23 – 31 mm long; epichile 12 – 18.5 mm long; sepals 18 – 26 mm long 6

6 Stem with 2 – 4 (– 5) flowers; epichile densely hairy right to the tip; plants growing in groups, each plant producing 2 new tubers each year ....
.... *S. olbia*, p160

6* Stem with 4 – 12 flowers; epichile somewhat hairy, but only at the base; plants growing singly producing only 1 new tuber each year 7

7 Epichile a uniform colour; hypochile (spread out!) 11.5 – 14.5 mm broad; side lobes usually a darker colour than the middle lobe ....
.. *S. bergonii (S. v. subsp. laxiflora)*, p164

7* Epichile bicoloured (brownish-red with a pale border); hypochile 15 – 18 mm broad, side lobes a light colour ....
.... *S. nurrica*, p164

Ophrys
sub-divisions of the genus:

1. Lutea group
   O. fusca subsp. fusca, O. f. subsp. vasconica, O. iricolor, O. atlantica, O. pallida, O. omegaifera, O. o. subsp. fleischmannii, O. o. subsp. dyris, O. lutea subsp. lutea, O. l. subsp. galilaea, O. l. subsp. melena

2. Insectifera group
   O. insectifera, O. aymoninii

3. Speculum group
   O. ciliata, O. vernixia, O. regis-ferdinandii

4. Bombyliflora group
   O. bombyliflora

5. Reinholdii group
   O. cilicica, O. kotschyi, O. cretica, O. reinholdii subsp. reinholdii, O. r. subsp. straussii

6. Scolopax group
   O. umbilicata sub-group: O. umbilicata, O. flavomarginata; O. scolopax subsp. scolopax, O. s. subsp. cornuta, O. s. subsp. heldreichii, O. isaura
   Should perhaps be included here:
   O. apifera sub-group: O. apifera, O. schulzei

7. Ferrum-equinum group
   O. argolica, O. elegans, O. delphinensis, O. lycia, O. ferrum-equinum, O. gottfriediana; O. crabronifera sub-group: O. crabronifera, O. biscutella
   Should perhaps be included here:
   O. lunulata
   O. bertolonii sub-group: O. bertolonii, O. bertoloniformis

8. Fuciflora group
   O. holoserica subsp. holoserica, O. h. subsp. apulica, O. h. subsp. parvimaculata;
   O. bornmuelleri sub-group: O. bornmuelleri, O. levantina; O. oxyrrhynchos sub-group: O. oxyrrhynchos, O. lacaitae; O. discors, O. candica, O. tardans
   Should perhaps be included here:
   O. tenthredinifera

9. Sphegodes group
   O. sphegodes subsp. sphegodes, O. s. subsp. epirotica, O. araneola, O. hebes, O. garganica, O. aesculapii, O. tarentina, O. helenae, O. incubacea, O. mammosa subsp.

mammosa, O. mammosa subsp.
transhyrcana
Arachnitiform types:
O. morisii, O. tyrrhena, O.
sipontensis, O. splendida, O.
aveyronensis
Should perhaps be included here:
O. spruneri, O. caucasica, O.
turcomanica

The first part of the key leads to several groups and sub-groups as well as direct to a few species. The species in the groups and sub-groups can be identified in the later parts of the key.

While the majority of species can be recognized through well defined combinations of characters, a few of them occupy intermediate morphological positions. It is not possible to place them clearly in any of the main groups and a probable explanation is that they are stabilized populations of hybrid origin. In the construction of a key, they cause as many difficulties as some particularly variable species.

The key attempts to cope with the problem cases. Some of the species are built into it in several places so that fewer variants are included. Also, relatively rare extreme forms are allowed, since the type is mentioned under those alternatives to which one may occasionally be led ('*see also* . . .'). Again what is always true here is the fact that identification is easier and more certain if the range of variation of the whole population is considered, and not just the characteristics of one individual.

1 End of column (= connective) blunt and rounded 2
1* End of column tapering or extended into a beak, pointed 6
2 Sepals pink to purplish-red; lip with a large turned up appendage . . . .
. . . . *O. tenthredinifera*, p176
2* Sepals green, occasionally with a

brownish, reddish or purple tinge; lip appendage absent or small and turned back 3
3 Lip with a wreath of longer hairs near the edge and surrounding all 3 lobes . . . . . .
. . . . Speculum group, p249
3* Lip without such a wreath of hairs round the edge 4
4 Middle lobe of lip with strongly reflexed edges, thus becoming hemispherical, papillose; side lobes also strongly arched, with shaggy hairs . . . .
. . . . *O. bombyliflora*, p184
4* All lip lobes flat or arched, but not hemispherical, only papillose (not shaggy) hairs 5
5 Lip with 2 black basal callosities; lateral petals linear, at least 5 × as long as wide, appearing even narrower because of the rolled edges . . . .
. . . . Insectifera group, p180
5* Lip without basal callosities; lateral petals longish rectangular, up to 4 × as long as wide . . . . Lutea group, p249
6 (1) Lip undivided, sometimes slightly notched with an indication of 3 lobes (sides and middle equally curved in the same plane) 7
6* Lip deeply 3-lobed, side lobes reduced to the rear half, turned down and not in the same plane as the middle lobe 17
7 Lip saddle-shaped: bent up longways in the middle, the sides turned down . . . . . .
. . . . *O. bertolonii* group, p226
7* Lip not saddle-shaped 8
8 Lip with a large (usually) 3-toothed appendage at the tip; lateral petals always hairy; pattern surrounding the basal area of the lip (except occasionally in *O. levantina*) . . . . . . Fuciflora group, p250
see also O. crabronifera group, p200
8* Lip appendage small, triangular or absent; lateral petals glabrous or hairy; pattern may surround the basal area or be remote from it (should the lip have a large

appendage, then the pattern is isolated) 9

9　Sepals green, sometimes the laterals tinged red in the lower half 10

9*　Sepals whitish, pink or red 13

10　Pattern surrounding the basal area of the lip, usually H-shaped, sometimes as 2 separate stripes or even more branched (absent in *O. helenae*!) . . . .

. . . . Sphegodes group, p251

10*　Pattern remote from lip basal area or even concentrated in the middle of the lip (spots) and with interrupted extensions to the lip base 11

11　Lip edge with longer hairs behind, shorter hairs to almost glabrous, in front; because of down-turned sides the lip often appears acutely triangular from above . . . .

. . . . *O. gottfriediana*, p198

11*　The whole of the lip edge with long hairs and turned down evenly; front of lip rounded (seen from above) 12

12　Lip with a yellow edge; hairs yellow-brown to brown or light red . . . .

. . . . *O. tarentina*, p218

12*　Lip with a red-brown edge; hairs dark (red-) brown . . . .

. . . . *O. bertoloniiformis*, p226

see also the *Ferrum-equinum* group, p250

13　(9) Pattern surrounding the basal area of the lip, H-shaped or with several limbs, occasionally shield-shaped 14

13*　Pattern remote from basal area in the form of spots which may be isolated or joined across the lip 15

14　Central sepal more or less curving forwards right to the tip . . . .

. . . . Sphegodes group, p251

. . *see also* the *Ferrum-equinum* group, p250

14*　The tip area of the central sepal suddenly turning backwards . . . . . *O. lycia*, p198

15　(13) Lip with a large 3-toothed appendage at the tip . . . .

. . . . *O. crabronifera* group, p200

. . . . *see also O. levantina*, p206

15*　Lip appendage small, triangular or absent 16

16　Lip slightly arched, with flat or slightly turned-down edges, longer and denser hairs in the rear half than in front; if equally hairy all round, then brown . . . . .

. . . . Ferrum-equinum group, p250

16*　Lip strongly arched with turned-down edges, long hairs all round, blackish-purple . . . .

. . . . *O. bertoloniiformis*, p226

17　(6) Lip with a large, often 3-toothed appendage at the tip 18

17*　Lip appendage small, triangular or absent 21

18　Tip of middle lobe bent backwards so that the appendage is turned under the lip . .

. . . . *O. apifera* group, p178

18*　Tip of middle lobe extended or curving down, appendage directed forwards 19

19　Lip ground colour dark, blackish- or brownish-purple Reinholdii group, p249

19*　Lip ground colour lighter, (red-)brown, without a purple component (although sometimes pattern purple) 20

20　Tubercles on the side lobes elongated, pointed, horn-shaped; pattern surrounding the basal lip area . . . .

. . . . Scolopax group, p250

20*　Tubercles on the side lobes short and blunt; pattern mostly not close to the basal area, rarely surrounding it . . . .

. . . . *O. delphinensis*, p196

21　(17) Pattern remote from lip basal area, in the form of spots which may be separate or joined across the lip 22

21*　Pattern surrounding the lip basal area, usually H-shaped but may be in the form of 2 stripes 25

22　Pattern white or with a wide white border . . . . Reinholdii group, p249

22*　Pattern without any white or with a very narrow white edge 23

23　Sepals green, sometimes the lower half of

the lateral sepals is tinged with red . . . .
. . . . *O. gottfriediana*, p198

23* Sepals pink or red 24

24 Lip red- or dark brown with a yellowish or pale brown edge, seen from above narrowly rectangular (side lobes and edges of middle lobe turned down) . . . . .
. . . . *O. lunulata*, p210

24* Lip blackish-purple with reddish-brown edge, from above broadly elliptic (side and middle lobes somewhat arched) . . .
. . . . *O. bertoliniiformis*, p226
. . . . see also *O. elegans*, p196

25 (21) Pattern white . . . .
. . . . Reinholdii group, p249

25* Pattern coloured, though sometimes with a narrow white border 26

26 Lip ground colour blackish-violet . . . . . .
. . . . *O. spruneri*, p210

26* Lip ground colour red- to dark brown 27

27 Pattern H-shaped or with more complicated branching, made up of wide stripes . . . . Sphegodes group, p251

27* Pattern in the form of a double spot joined to the basal area by fine strokes . . . . . .
. . . . *O. lunulata*, p210

Ophrys: Lutea group

1 Edge of lip spreading out flat or turned up
. . . . *O. lutea*, p174

1* Edge of lip (side lobes) turned down . . 2

2 Lip without a longitudinal groove at the base, a flat surface leading to the stigma 3

2* Lip with a longitudinal groove in the centre towards the base, flanked by 2 lateral swellings 4

3 Lip saddle-shaped, bending upwards from the middle; pattern without an obvious border . . . . *O. atlantica*, p170

3* Lip curving downwards; pattern with a W-shaped pale border . . . .
. . . . *O. omegaifera*, p172

4* Lip straight or evenly curved, at most the middle lobe turned down 5

5 Pattern shining blue; lip 15 – 23 mm long, underside brownish-red, middle lobe without a yellow edge . . . .
. . . . *O. iricolor*, p168

5* Pattern grey, brown or lilac; if blue, then the underside of the lip olive, often smaller or with a yellow-edged middle lobe . . . . *O. fusca*, p168

Ophrys: Speculum group

1 Lip lobes flat or slightly arched, side lobes broadly lanceolate, pointing diagonally upwards; basal field flanked on each side by 2 ridges of almost equal length . . . . .
. . . . *O. ciliata*, p182

1* Lip lobes strongly arching with turned down edges; side lobes linear-lanceolate, horizontal or only slightly raised; basal area with 2 or 3 obviously unequal ridges on each side 2

2 Lip hairs light-coloured: orange to brownish-yellow, occasionally reddish-brown; middle lobe with a hairless edge 1.5 – 2.5 mm wide; basal area with 2 longitudinal ridges on each side . . . .
. . . . *O. vernixia*, p182

2* Lip hairs dark: brownish-(red) to dark violet; middle lobe with a hairless edge 0.5 – 1 (– 1.5) mm wide; basal area with at most 3 longitudinal ridges on each side
. . . . *O. regis-ferdinandii*, p182

Ophrys: Reinholdii group

1 Lip basal area longer than broad, bounded by 2 low ridges; side lobes clearly originating at a distance from the stigma . . . . *O. cilicica*, p184

1* Lip basal area as long as broad, without lateral ridges; side lobes originating from the base of the lip 2

2 Pattern surrounding the basal area . . 3

2* Pattern remote from the basal area or sometimes joined to it by 2 fine lines . 4

3 Central sepal bent forwards; side lobes directed downwards, from above, only the

tubercles visible; red staminode dots present . . . . *O. kotschyi*, p186

3* Central sepal directed backwards or vertically upright; side lobes spreading diagonally, visible from above; staminode dots often absent . . . . *O. cretica*, p186

4 (2) Side lobes directed downwards; red staminode dots present; sepals usually pink or red, sometimes white or green . . . . *O. reinholdii*, p188

4* Side lobes spreading diagonally; staminode dots often absent; sepals often green, also red-tinged . . . . *O. cretica*, p186

Ophrys: Scolopax group

1 Central sepal bending forwards strongly over the column; middle lobe at its widest in the front third . . . . *O. umbilicata* group, p190

1* Central sepal upright or directed backwards, if it is strongly concave it is not inclined over the column; middle lobe at its broadest in the centre or towards the base 2

2 Attachment of side lobes narrower than the height of the tubercles; basal callosities parted, separated by the basal area . . . . *O. scolopax*, p192

2* Attachment of side lobes broader than the height of the tubercles; basal callosities brought together, joined by a pedestal-shaped elevation . . . . . . *O. isaura*, p194

Ophrys: Ferrum-equinum group

1 Lip surrounded by fairly uniformly long hairs. . . . . *O. crabronifera* group, p200

1* Lip hair surround not uniform, the hairs in the rear half are clearly longer than those at the front 2

2 Lip deeply 3-lobed, side lobes turned down at right angles to the middle lobe . . . . *O. delphinensis*, p196

2* Lip undivided or 3-lobed, if lobed, then the side lobes are on the same plane as the middle lobe and not turned sharply down 3

3 Hairs round the edge of the lip long and shaggy on the rear half of the lip, white at the base turning to pale brown or pale purple towards the middle . . . . *O. argolica*, p196

3* Hairs round the lip short and velvety on the rear half, uniformly darker 4

4 Pattern H-shaped, surrounding the basal area; central sepal bent back towards the end . . . . *O. lycia*, p198

4* Pattern generally separated from the basal area, horseshoe shape or 2 separate spots; central sepal straight or bent forwards towards the end . . . . *O. ferrum-equinum*, p198 . . . . see also *O. gottfriediana*, p198

Ophrys: Fuciflora group

1 Pattern shield-shaped (almost rectangular) with a wide white border, unmarked or faint markings within, occasionally with more distinct lines . . . . *O. candica*, p208 . . . . see also *O. tardans*, p208

1* Pattern a basic H-form often with side branches, with sharp white boundaries 2

2 Lateral petals more than $0.3 \times$ as long as the sepals 3

2* Lateral petals $0.14 - 0.25 \, (-0.3) \times$ as long as the sepals 4

3 A smooth lengthwise ridge in the front half of the lip between the pattern and the appendage, ridge as wide as the appendage . . . . *O. oxyrrhynchos*, p208

3* The middle of the front half of the lip with short hairs, but no ridge . . . . *O. holoserica*, p202

4 (2) Lip fan-shaped, maximum breadth at least twice that at the base, front part (almost) glabrous (*O. oxyrrhynchos* group). 5

4* Lip trapeziform, greatest breadth about

1.5 × the breadth at the base, front part
densely hairy 6

5   Front edge of lip reddish- to yellowish-
     brown, sometimes yellow; pattern covers
     $^2/_5 - ^1/_2$ of the lip area . . . .
     . . . . O. oxyrrhynchos, p208

5*   Lip edge broad, yellow; pattern covers
     about ¼ of the lip area . . . .
     . . . . O. lacaitae, p208

6   (4) Rear of lip velvety, with short hairs, front
     of lip papillose . . . . O. holoserica, p202

6*   Lip surrounded by long hairs, or with long
     hairs at the rear and short hairs in
     front 7

7   A lengthwise ridge, the width of the
     appendage, in the middle of the lip
     between the pattern and the tip, brownish-
     red with an orange to lemon-yellow border
     . . . . O. discors, p206

7*   Lip rarely with a central ridge, brown with
     greenish-yellow edge or without the
     yellow, all without red shades . . . .
     . . . . O. bornmuelleri group, p206

Ophrys: Sphegodes group

This group is one of the most difficult in the
genus. The slight differences between the
types, the large variability in the characters
and, not least, a number of unsolved questions
give rise to problems. This is especially true for
the arachnitiformis-complex (see p222). A
decision is often only possible with a
population, while individual plants steadfastly
resist all attempts at classification.

1   Sepals   green   or   yellowish-green,
     occasionally the laterals are tinged
     brownish-red in the lower half 2

1*   Sepals whitish to pink (arachnitiform
     types) 12

2   Lip without pattern or with an indistinct
     hairy pattern . . . . O. helenae, p218

2*   Lip with a clear smooth pattern 3

3   Lip surrounded by long shaggy hairs . 4

3*   Lip either not surrounded by hairs or the
     hairs are short and velvety 5

4   Lip with strong tubercles, without yellow
     edge, always undivided; hairs reddish-
     brown to blackish-violet . . . .
     . . . . O. incubacea, p218

4*   Lip with small tubercles or without any,
     with a broad yellow edge, often weakly
     3-lobed; hairs yellowish-brown to brown
     or pale reddish . . . . O. tarentina, p218

5   (3) Petals more than $^4/_5$ as long as the
     sepals, remarkably wide (more than $^1/_3$ to
     over ½ as wide as long), often completely
     or round the edge coloured reddish-
     brown; lip dark (red-) brown to blackish .
     . . . . O. garganica, p216

5*   Petals $^2/_3 - ^3/_4$ as long as the sepals;
     where they are longer than $^4/_5$ then the
     other characters do not apply 6

6   Pattern complicated; from the two cross-
     connected lengthwise stripes, it branches
     into the outer parts of the lip, sometimes
     forming a network 7

6*   Pattern simple: 2 lengthwise stripes,
     separate, or with 1 – 2 cross-connections
     8

7   Lip with an up to 2.5 mm wide (greenish-)
     yellow, or more rarely, pale brown edge,
     often   3-lobed,   with   a   triangular
     appendage . . . . O. hebes, p214

7*   Lip without, or with, a very narrow pale
     edge; if a wide border then not also
     3-lobed and with an appendage . . . . .
     . . . . O. sphegodes, p212
     see also O. tyrrhena and O. morisii, p222

8   (6) Lip 6.5 – 9 mm long and 7.5 – 11.5 mm
     broad . . . . O. araneola p214

8*   Lip longer than 9 mm and broader than
     11 mm 9

9   Lip flat or evenly slightly domed over the
     whole breadth, with a wide yellow border
     10

9*   Lip with a slightly domed middle part and
     strongly down-turned sides 11

10   Lip mainly undivided; smooth edge of lip
     flat or slightly up-turned . . . .
     . . . . O. aesculapii, p216

10* Lip mainly weakly 3-lobed; smooth lip edge turned down at an angle .... *O. sphegodes*, p212

11 (9) Sepals green; lip very hairy, shaggy to short hairs round the whole edge, especially on the outer sides of the tubercles .... *O. sphegodes*, p212

11* lateral sepals tinted brownish-red in the lower halves, occasionally green or tinted over the whole surface; lip weakly hairy, only papillose or with short hairs at the rear edge, on the front edge papillose to smooth .... *O. mammosa*, p220

12 (1) Lip with long shaggy hairs all round the edge 13

12* Lip with short velvety hairs round the edge or with none 14

13 Lip with small tubercles or none; lateral petals pink to brownish-red .... *O. sipontensis*, p222 .... see also *O. aveyronensis*, p224

13* Lip with large tubercles; lateral petals dirty (olive-) green to brownish-violet; a rare variant of .... *O. incubacea*, p218

14 (12) Lip deeply 3-lobed .... *O. sphegodes*; 'panormitana'-variant, ... p212

14* Lip not 3-lobed or only weakly so ... 15

15 Lip 6.5 – 9 mm long and 7.5 – 11.5 mm broad; rare variant of .... *O. araneola*, p214 .... see also *O. splendida*, p224

15* Lip longer than 9 mm and broader than 11 mm ....·........ 16

16 Lip with a fairly strong triangular or 3-toothed appendage; lateral petals usually hairy; red staminode dots often present........................... ...... *O. tyrrhena* and *O. morisii* p222 The characters of these two types have an almost identical range; on average the lips of *O. morisii* are somewhat shorter and broader than those of *O. tyrrhena*.

16* Lip with a small tooth-like appendage or none; lateral petals bare or papillose; staminode dots absent 17

17 Pattern mostly large, much branched and appearing almost like a net, occasionally in the form of an H, stripes, marbling or a shield; lateral petals mostly papillose .. .. *O. aveyronensis*, p224

17* Pattern less branching, H- or shield-shaped; lateral petals bare 18

18 Lip usually with a yellow edge and pale hairs; pattern with a shining white border, greyish-blue to dark violet, often the branches merge to form a shield-shaped surface; lateral petals mostly conspicuously 2-coloured .... *O. splendida*, p224

18* Lip usually with a (greenish-) brown edge and dark hairs; pattern does not usually have a striking border, often brownish or reddish and not shield-shaped; lateral petals rarely conspicuously 2-coloured .... *O. sphegodes*, p212

Male wasp *Campsoscolia ciliata* on a flower of *Ophrys ciliata*. The orchid flowers attract the insects by sexual deception. *See* text p265.

Description of orchids

The following brief description provides information for the identification of orchids in general. It includes the more important morphological characteristics and considers the three main groups as well as the tropical and extra-tropical species. In connection with this, there follow detailed descriptions of the parts of the plant to which repeated reference is made in the species descriptions and the identification keys. The various specialist terms are explained.

Short description

Plants perennial, herbs, rooting in the soil − terrestrial (all the European species) − or epiphytic on trees (most of the tropical species).

Roots strong, unbranched, often swollen into tubers.

Stem frequently takes the form of a horizontal rhizome or a vertical stock. The annual aerial stems upright, unbranched; the lower sections (internodes) sometimes swollen to form pseudobulbs (often in tropical but rarely in European species).

Food storage for surviving unfavourable seasons, in rhizomes, root tubers or pseudobulbs.

Leaves entire, arranged spirally or in two rows, sessile (no stalk visible) or occasionally petiolate (short stalk); basal leaves generally sheathing the stem, often reduced to scales on the rhizome, the base and tip of the aerial stem.

Flowers short-stalked or sessile, with inferior ovary, zygomorphic, the flower stalk or the ovary often twisted through 180° (so that the lip is on the lower side) rarely not twisted, or through 360° (with the lip uppermost). Perianth of two whorls, each with 3 segments (tepals), generally differing in appearance. Outer whorl of 3 sepals, inner of 3 petals of which the central one forms the lip or labellum; stamens and pistil fused into a column (gynostemium). Number of stamens 3, 2 or 1 (*see* the three main groups on p257).

Stamens sessile or with a short stalk, anthers with 4 or 2 pollen sacs. Pollen grains separate (Apostasiaceae) or cohering in packets (Cypripediaceae, Orchidaceae). In the Orchidaceae the pollen masses are joined to form stalked pollinia (4 or 2 according to the pollen sacs); pistil with 3-lobed stigma. In the Orchidaceae the central lobe (rostellum) is often extended into a beak-shape, the tip forming a sticky body (the viscidium) which is removed along with the pollinium. Ovary 3-celled (Apostasiaceae and many of the Cypripediaceae) or 1-celled (Orchidaceae), ripens into a capsule opening by 3 or 6 longitudinal slits. Seeds are minute, numerous, with an undifferentiated embryo and no endosperm.

Explanation of specialist terms

The survey particularly concentrates on expressions used in connection with orchids. A few terms in general use in the morphological descriptions are included − where these are not explained at the time in the identification keys or the species descriptions.

1. Vegetative Parts of the Plant

a. Leaves

The following leaf types can be distinguished:

Scale leaves − scale-like leaves at the base of the aerial stems, without leaf blade, brown and lacking chlorophyll

Foliage leaves − flat green leaves

Upper scale leaves − small, green, scale-like leaves on the upper part of the stem

Bracts − leaf-like growths in the inflorescence each bearing a flower in the axil

Basal or rosette leaves + foliage leaves growing together in a rosette at the base of the annual aerial stem

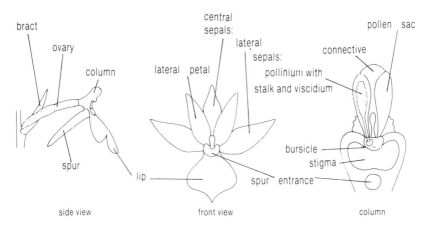

bract
ovary
column
lateral petal
central sepals:
lateral sepals:
pollinium with stalk and viscidium
pollen sac
connective
bursicle
stigma
spur
lip
spur entrance
side view
front view
column

b. Hairs

Orchids have unbranched hairs, many species have vegetative parts which are generally without hairs. A distinction can be made between long and short hairs in the absence of actual dimensions (what is meant in each case can be gathered from the illustrations). Very short cellular outgrowths are described as papillae and the difference between these and short hairs is not always clear.

2.   Generative Parts of the Plant (Flowers)

2.1.   The sterile flower perianth

a. The perianth segments

The perianth consists of 3 outer (sepals) and 3 inner segments (petals) alternating with each other. The central petal differs in form from the others and is known as the lip or labellum. In the text, the 3 sepals and the 2 lateral petals are combined as the perianth segments because of their positions, but this is not strictly correct, since the lip also belongs to the perianth.

b. The position of the perianth segments

An important criterion in many genera is the position of the sepals and lateral petals; they may be directed forwards, at right angles, or backwards. In the last two positions, the lateral sepals are often twisted outwards through 90°. If the perianth segments curve forward and are touching (curved) to form a closed chamber, this is called a hood or helmet (galea)

c. The form of the lip or labellum

If the lip is in 3 parts these are known as lobes. When the lobes are subdivided these are called points. In a lip divided across into two, the hind part nearest the base is called the hypochile, the front part the epichile.

Spur – an outgrowth at the base of the lip, often with nectar

Pattern or mark (in *Ophrys*) – a more glabrous (smooth) area of a different colour in the centre of the lip.

2.2   Generative Organs of the Flower

Stamens and pistils in orchids are greatly modified and in appearance differ from those usually seen in seed plants. The rear part of the 3 carpels is developed as an inferior ovary. Above these, the style and stigma have grown

255

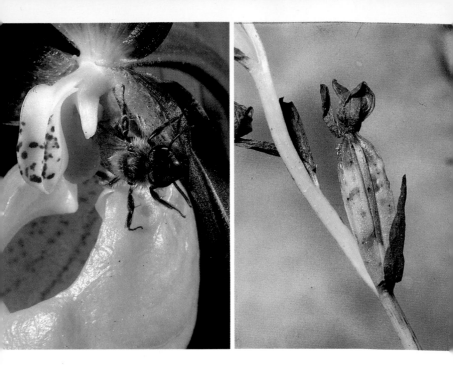

Sand bee of the genus *Andrena* on *Cyptipedium calceolus*. The lip acts as a temporary trap.

Young fruit (capsule) of an *Ophrys* species with shrivelled perianth.

together with the stamens to form a column (the gymnostemium). The structure of the column differs in the Cypripediaceae from that in the Orchidaceae (strict sense.)

Cypripediaceae – the two stamens are borne laterally on the column behind the stigma; above this in the centre, there is a shield-shaped sterile stamen (staminode) which affords some protection.

Orchidaceae (strict sense) – the single stamen is in the centre of the column above the stigma and in the European species generally contains two pollen sacs. The sterile part between the pollen sacs is the connective; occasionally, it is prolonged at the tip into a beak. In each pollen sac the pollen grains stick

together to form a pollinium which is extended into a stalk-like caudicle.

The stigma is basically 3-lobed but develops a single surface. The middle-upper stigma lobe is called the rostellum; its front part, consisting of sterile tissue, is often extended into a beak with an outgrowth on the end of which are one or two sticky glands (viscidia); the pollinia stalks terminate in the viscidia which are often protected by a pocket-shaped cover, the bursicle. The viscidia may be two separate discs or may coalesce into a single one, or may be ball-shaped. The surface behind the rostellum is the pollen dish (clinandrium or androclinium). In it lie the ripe pollinia, when these are freed from the pollen sacs above the stigma.

On the systematics and taxonomy of the orchids

Groups

The orchids comprise three main groups which have been developing along separate evolutionary lines for a very long time. Amongst other features they are clearly separable by the number of stamens in the flower. While experts are agreed on this difference, their opinions vary as far as the taxonomic classification of these main groups is concerned. They can be viewed either as sub-familes of one overall family or as three independent families.

Only two of the three main groups are represented in Europe: the Cypripediaceae with the genus *Cypripedium* and three species, and the Orchidaceae, strict sense with 35 genera and some 250 species and subspecies. The Apostasiaceae are confined to the tropics of south-east Asia and northern Australia. Orchids are almost world-wide in their distribution, with the main concentration in the tropics and sub-tropics; they are absent from desert regions.

In this book, large genera are subdivided into type-groups. They correspond to sections in the conventional terminology. The use of these formal grades can be dispensed with because the type-groups, to some extent, are based on different criteria from those used in the recognized orchid systematics. Closely related and similar species are combined into groups corresponding to the 'aggregates' of many floras.

The Systematics of the Orchids

Arrangement of the genera described in this book into sub-families (-oideae) and tribes (-eae); generic names are in *italics*.

1. Cypripediaceae
   Cypripedium
2. Orchideaceae (strict sense)
   A. Neottioideae
      Epipactis, Cephalanthera,
      Limodorum, Neottia, Listera,
      Spiranthes, Goodyera
   B. Orchidoideae
      a. Orchideae
         Habenaria group: *Herminium,*
         Gennaria, Habenaria
         Platanthera group: *Platanthera*
         Gymnadenia group: *Dactylorhiza,*
         Coeloglossum, Gymnadenia,
         Leucorchis, Nigritella,
         Neottianthe, Chamorchis
         Orchis group: *Orchis, Steveniella,*
         Comperia, Neotinea, Aceras,
         Traunsteinera, Anacamptis,
         Barlia, Himantoglossum,
         Serapias, Ophrys
   C. Epidendroideae
      a. Malaxideae
         Liparis, Malaxis, Hammarbya
      b. Epipogieae
         Epipogium
      c. Calypsoeae
         Calypso
   D. Vandoideae
      a. Maxillarieae
         Corallorhiza

No of stamens	Classification of the main groups		genera/ species
	a)	b)	
	Orchidaceae (widest sense)		
3	Apostasioidea	Apostasiaceae	2/15
2	Cypripedioideae	Cypripediaceae	4/100
1	Orchidoideae	Orchidaceae (strict sense)	730/20,000 +

-aceae ending for family

-oideae ending for sub-family

Variability

It is generally agreed that the Orchidaceae share a common ancestor with the Liliaceae and have become separated from them by specialization of the flower structure. The Orchidaceae are considered to be a relatively recently developed group.

Probably the oldest fossil which can be positively identified as an orchid comes from the Miocene and is about 15 million years old: it would be pure speculation to decide from this the actual age of the family. Nevertheless, its relative youth becomes apparent when you consider that the majority of families of present-day seed plants have fossil records traceable to the Tertiary and Cretaceous, some 60 to 100 million years ago.

The relatively recent emergence of orchids can possibly be associated with one obvious characteristic: their unusually wide variability. This is expressed, above all, in the Orchidaceae (strict sense) by the large number of species which have been achieved within the confines of the basic flower structure. The species themselves are also very variable. The orchids give the strong impression that they are still in an active phase of evolution. Characteristics and relationships frequently show a good deal of fluidity.

First of all, the scientist must tackle the problem of variability in a critical manner. On the other hand, there is the person who tries to identify orchids and wants an unambiguous way of giving a name to a plant. Faced with a variable population, it can be quite a problem assigning a plant to a particular species. Identification can be especially critical in the *Dactylorhiza, Serapias, Epipactis* and some groups of *Ophrys* and *Orchis*. In these cases, the variability is such that the morphological boundaries between the types become blurred and they can often by separated more readily by other criteria (distribution, method of reproduction, flowering times, etc.). In general, populations can be identified by

Euorchis miocaenica Mehl, the oldest known fossil orchid. Found at Öhningen-Wangen near the Bodensee in the fresh-

taking average characteristics, but not from an individual which deviates far from the mean. Colour and structural anomalies can also be considered to be within the usual range of variability. Such variants are known in many species and could turn up in any.

Colour variants are more likely to be discovered than any other. They are not easily overlooked amongst the 'normal' plants. In these, the pigment synthesis disturbed or is non-functional leading to pale or white-flowered specimens (albinos). Excessive colour may also occur. Sometimes, the green colour (chlorophyll) is affected, in which case the plant appears pale yellowish or, if other pigments are present, of a pale colour as is

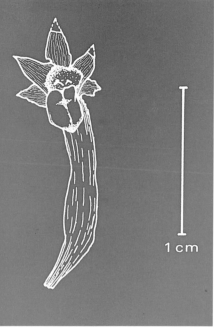

1 cm

water limestone beds of the Upper Miocene. It consists of an orchid flower with ovary and perianth.

over-pigmented).

Structural variants are less common and thus often appear bizarre. Flower structure is most often affected when irregularities occur in the development of the organs. Single organs may be multiplied or distorted; or organs are replaced by others, some sepals are changed with petals, or petals with lips (peloric flowers). In rare cases – as in the bee orchis (*Ophrys apifera*) – self-pollination (autogamy) leads to an increase in such aberrant types (*see* p178), but in general you

A variant of *Epipactis purpurata* without chlorophyll (above). A red/white colour 'chimera' of *Gymnadenia conopsea* (below).

259

Colour variant of *Ophrys araneola*; only the green and yellow colours have developed.

A double lip structural variant of *Ophrys holoserica*

will only meet occasional individuals.

Biological variability should not be forced into the rigid framework of botanical nomenclature: it is superfluous. There seems to be a temptation to devise a name for each and every variant. This has no practical value and such proliferation can only serve to increase the present enormous confusion over orchid names.

Hybrids

No other family of flowering plants can match the orchids in their tendency to hybridize. There are scarcely any barriers to crossing within a genus, or even between genera belonging to the same tribe. This is particularly true of the tribe Orchideae to which most of the European orchids belong.

The reasons for the lack of genetic isolation are not obvious. Sometimes it is suggested that the comparatively short period of development of the orchids is responsible – insufficient time having elapsed for the formation of barriers to cross-fertilization. But, such a connection does not have to exist, since genetic isolation is not necessary if isolation can be ensured by other means. The very specialized pollination mechanisms, evolved in the orchids can be seen to play a central role in this connection, (*see* the section headed 'Reproduction').

Wherever species of the same genus or

Hybrids within a genus: *Ophrys berto-loniiformis x ciliata* (above left); *Ophrys insectifera x scolopax* (above right). Hybrids between genera: *Orchis laxiflora x Serapias vomeracea subsp. orientalis* (below)

tribe are growing together and are not isolated by different flowering times, then you can expect to find hybrids. It is only a matter of time before all possible natural combinations are discovered. Published details in journals show that the pastime of completing the list of hybrids is being vigorously pursued. In this connection, several questions of general interest deserve looking into. For example, it is not clear in most cases whether hybrids are fertile and how the pollinator reacts to the hybrid plants.

Hybrid between different genera:
Anacamptis pyramidalis × *Orchis morio.*

Hybrids occur mostly as single plants and can generally be easily recognized. It is important not to rush to the conclusion that every plant not clearly identified is necessarily a hybrid. It could be a strongly deviant variant, and this possibility should always be tested — especially with *Ophrys*, where hybrids are not as common as might be imagined because of the 'faithfulness' of their insect pollinators.

Hybrid populations which arise through repeated crossing and back-crossing with the parients have only been verified in *Dactylorhiza*, *Ophrys*, and *Orchis*.

With few exceptions, hybrids have not been considered in this book. The combinations which are already known can be found in Sundermann (1980), Baumann and Künkele (1982) or Davies, Davies and Huxley (1983). A list of hybrids would take up a lot of space and would be out of date in a short time. Information concerning the countless hybrid names (binomial) is also dispensed with. These were certainly allowed under the nomenclature regulations, but are scientifically superfluous.

Systematics
Anyone who goes beyond the level of floristics and taxonomy and turns to the question of systematics finds an equally broad and fascinating sphere of activity. Orchids are famous above all for their special adaptation for insect pollination. However, it also pays to look more closely into other aspects of the biology of this fascinating group of plants. Some of these are dealt with below.

The well-known peculiarities of the family, such as the wind dissemination of tiny seeds, the nutrition in symbiosis with mycorrhizal fungi, the pollination using pollen 'packets' carried by insects, and the special flower form appear at first sight to have little connection. However, they are links in a special orchid evolution strategy as evident in the following chain of reasoning:

The tiny seeds require the presence of a suitable fungus, so the chance of any seed germinating is small. To ensure the propagation of the species, it is necessary to produce the largest possible number of seeds; the more seeds there are in the ovary, the smaller they must be (hence absence of endosperm and reduction of embryo). The fertilization of the countless ovules is only ensured if all the pollen grains reach the stigma — hence the uniting of pollen grains into pollinia. Because each plant has only a few pollinia, the transfer must be secure — hence pollination by insects and often in association with particular insect genera or species. To attract the insects, the flowers must have a particular structure. These different features have developed into a many-faceted dependence. The intermediate stages may still be observed, to some extent, in living orchids.

Vegetative reproduction in *Dactylorhiza iberica*: young runners (left). Self-pollination in *Ophrys apifera* (right).

Biology

Reproduction

An increase in population by vegetative reproduction, apart from a few exceptions, is only possible in those European orchid species possessing rhizomes. The number of buds and annual flowering stems can be increased by the branching of the rhizomes themselves. The tuber-forming species cannot readily make use of this method because only one new tuber (very rarely more) with its overwintering bud is formed next to the old one. An increase in numbers is therefore only possible with seeds. As always with orchids, there are exceptions. *Orchis champagneuxii, Ophrys bombylifera* and *Serapias lingua*. These species and a few others form two or more new tubers, mostly on long roots at some distance from the mother plants. *Dactylorhiza iberica* employs another method; in this case, in addition to the new tuber, subterranean runners (stolous) are formed which produce shoots with scale leaves. In each case, groups of plants are produced which form a clone.

Pollination and Propagation

Cross-pollination and subsequent cross-ferilization (allogamy) is the most widespread form of sexual reproduction in orchids. Only rarely does self-fertilization (autogamy) take place, following self-pollination. Intermediate stages show a development from allogamy occur via occasionally (facultative) to constant (obligatory) autogamy. Among the European orchids, there are examples of both types of autogamy. *Ophrys apifera* is a facultative autogam; if pollination by insects has been unsuccessful, the pollinium stalk bends down, bringing the pollinium directly onto the stigma of the same flower. The species appears to be successfully cross-pollinated in the

Mediterranean region, whereas in Central Europe self-fertilization is the norm, possibly because the pollinating insect is rare or absent from the area.

In *Epipactis* obligatory autogamy occurs, with several species reproducing in this way. Changes in the structure of the column, such as reduced viscidia and stigmata, (*see* diagram p24) as well as easily fragmenting pollinia, just about exclude the possibility of cross-pollination. The final stage is achieved in *E. phyllanthes* and *E. leptochila*, in which the flowers do not open and pollination takes place within the bud (cleistogamy): the lip is also reduced since insects no longer need to be attracted.

Autogamy frees a species from dependence on the pollinator and can then, as may be the case with *Ophrys apifera*, permit an extension of the area of distribution. Another consequence of autogamy is the reduction of inherited material (inbreeding) since the recombination brought about by allogamy is forestalled. Any small genetic changes are continually being transmitted, as a consequence of which autogamic species tend towards sub-divisions − showing small differences, but constant local variants.

Reproduction through allogamy is highly developed in orchids. No other family in the plant kingdom shows such a range of specialized adaptations for insect pollination. A few orchids are even pollinated by birds. The special flower formation fulfils the requirements for insect pollination through a combination of features in the zygomorphic structure: the central petal is enlarged into a lip which would normally be uppermost in the flower, but in many species this is brought round to the bottom by a twisting of the flower through 180° − thus making an ideal landing place for insects.

The other prerequisites are the pollinia, the name given to the parcels of adhering pollen grains from one pollen sac. Wagenitz has aptly

A bee on *Orchis tridentata*; many *Orchis* and *Dactylorhiza* species deceive insects into looking for nectar which is not there.

compared them with 'insured parcels' which are entrusted to selected insects for transportation to the stigma. Since the pollinia are a scarce commodity, their transport must be secure. Compare with this the 'direct mail' of other seed plants with their copious production of pollen, much of which can be lost without disastrous consequences as far as reproduction is concerned.

Orchids attract their pollinators by an extraordinary array of methods. Structure, colour and scent of the flowers all play a part. The incentive of food is often used to ensure repeated visits — nectar (possibly in the lip spur), also oils and a pollen-like substance (pseudopollen) in tropical species, but never pollen itself. The protected position of the pollinia usually prevents their loss through being eaten. On visiting a flower, the insect *unintentionally* lifts out the pollinia on its body by means of the sticky disc; adhesion is strong and it is hardly possible to get rid of them except on the sticky stigma. The *Serapias* species' flowers can offer a protective resting cavity, which is something of an advantage to their potential pollinators.

The relationship between orchids and insects has developed even further; mutual advantage now gives way to a system in which only the plant benefits. Many orchids attract their visitor by deception, exploiting certain instinctive behaviour of the insect without offering any service in return. The insect 'falls for it' and pollination is ensured. They could justifiably be called 'deception flowers'. They include flowers with spurs, but without nectar, or ones which resemble the food-providing flowers of other plants. Amongst tropical orchids several cases of this are known and have been investigated. The deception differs in each species, but is always successful in its own particular way.

One of the most amazing adaptations is to be found in the Mediterranean genus *Ophrys*. The phenomenon is described as sexual deception. These flowers produce scents which resemble the sexually attractive pheromones of certain female hymenopterans — bees and wasps. This attracts the males and, because of the appearance, structure and hairiness of the lip, they attempt to copulate with it. During the movement, the pollinia become attached to the insect. The scent, appearance and movement stimulations are so effective that the same male is deceived several times.

The evolutionary path followed by the orchids leads inevitably to an increased specialization in the relationship between flower and pollinator. The more exactly the plant corresponds to the behaviour of the animal, the more certain is the transfer of pollen and subsequent reproduction. The genus *Ophrys* clearly shows this tendency. Within it, all conceivable cases are to be found: one species with several pollinators, sometimes in different parts of the distribution area, sometimes in the same region with early- and late-flowering variants; one species with only one pollinator; even one pollinator for several species, but in this case in areas which do not overlap. The certainty of pollination is indicated by a reduction in the number of flowers in *Ophrys* species where, to some extent, reproduction is accomplished at the least possible cost; an example is the lutea-group where members regularly bear only 1 – 4 flowers.

Burrowing wasp of the genus *Gorytes* on *Serapias lingua*; the cavern-like flower offers a resting place for the insects.

Overleaf:
Longhorn bee on *Ophrys tenthredinifera*.

Isolation of the Species

Since there are no barriers to cross-pollination within a genus and often between genera (see section on hybrids), there remains the question of how isolation of orchid species is achieved.

Without doubt, the adaptation to a particular pollinator is an important factor. However, the present state of knowledge leads to an important question as to whether this isolation mechanism plays the same role in all genera. There are species where separation in space, or indeed time, is more significant – *Ophrys mammosa* and *O. incubacea* (= *O. atrata*) both make use of the same pollinator, but remain separate because of geographical exclusion. Only in the 'contact zone' in Albania is there a mixed population.

Cases of isolation in time, by having different flowering periods, are fairly common. In the species descriptions this information is given in the relevant cases ('flowers earlier/later than . . .'). One example is the pair of species *Orchis palustris/O. laxifolia* which are separated by about 3 weeks and thus produce hardly any hybrids. The separation by flowering time does not only apply between species: in *Ophrys*, for instance, the majority occur within a species. Morphologically similar variants are found growing in the same place with different flowering times. Such instances could be the early stages in the formation of a new taxon, since detailed examination of flowers will often show some slight, but constant, character difference.

Whether the infertility of orchid hybrids is a significant factor has scarcely been investigated. So far, only a few cases have proven that hybrids are fertile and back-cross with the parents under natural conditions. Probably the opposite is more common.

Fungal Symbiosis

Orchids feed with the help of fungi; they are mycotrophic. The relationship benefits both partners, so can loosely be described as a symbiosis. The fungi provide the orchid with water, salts and probably also with organic compounds, and for their part receive carbohydrates and other organic compounds. The fungi penetrate the cells of the orchid (endotrophic symbiosis) and are finally digested.

The extent of the dependence of orchids on the fungi changes during the life cycle. Since the tiny seeds have no endosperm and little if any food reserves, they are completely dependent on the fungus. Growth procedes slowly; a tiny spindle-shaped, pale structure (the protocorm) develops. Only when it becomes stronger – which may take several years under natural conditions – are roots and leafy shoots produced. Experiments in cultivation have shown that, under suitable conditions, some species can produce a first green leaf in a matter of months, rather than years. The fully grown green plant can feed itself independently, but still retains the fungus in nearly every case. The fungus then lives as a mycorrhyza in the root cortex.

A few species remain dependent on the fungus throughout their lives, as the plants have lost, in part or totally, the ability to produce chlorophyll and so cannot feed themselves. These orchids are parasitic on the fungi. They include a few European species – *Epipogium aphyllum*, *Neottia nidus-avis*, recognizable by their pale parts and absence of leaves – at most reduced to scales. They are also able to survive in deep shade, since they are not dependent on sunlight for assimmilation. The *Limodorum* species and *Corallorrhiza trifida* are in a transition stage towards parasitism. Their leaves are also reduced, but small amounts of chlorophyll are present, as can be recognized by the green colouration. Little is known about the symbiotic fungi. Orchids appear to live together with specific fungi. Few genera of fungi are involved and their taxonomy is as fraught with difficulty as that of orchids. It could be that a

fungus has its chemistry subtly changed by association with a particular orchid after invasion of the seed.

Distribution

The distribution of the species is described under three different headings in the species descriptions. If you want to know quickly where a plant lives, you can get this information from the section 'Distribution'. More exact information can be found under the sections 'Floristic Element' and 'Countries'. The floristic element will help anyone interested in learning about the climatic and ecological demands of a plant. The information about countries can be helpful when planning a journey, or for testing the accuracy of an exercise in identification, to see whether the species ascertained is likely to be correct.

Many of the species and subspecies dealt with will also occur wild, outside the regions covered by this identification guide. This wider presence is indicated in the section headed 'distribution'. On the other hand 'Floristic Element' and 'Countries' only apply within the geographical boundaries of the book. These are Europe, the Near East and north Africa.

The distribution of most plants is basically well known today. Some exceptions are, for example, those species which have only recently been discovered, or recognized as independent. Such cases are referred to when they occur. In general, it must be noted that floristic investigations in Europe and the surrounding areas are very uneven from one region to another and are largely dependent on historical interest in local botany. In general,

Orchis mascula x pallens: the hybrid is male-sterile; since pollinial stalks and viscidia are absent the pollen cannot be transferred (above). *Ophrys bombyliflora x tenthred-inifera* with functional pollinia but sterile, probably for some other reason (below).

there is a north-south gradient. Knowledge of many parts of the Mediterranean region is very poor compared with that of northern and central Europe. Realizing these shortcomings, intensive efforts have been made in recent years to fill the gaps. Various mapping programmes have contributed to this (*see* p275).

There will inevitably be discoveries which will enlarge the known areas of distribution. Many new records may still appear for a country, but fewer changes are to be expected regarding the floristic elements since these do not have arbitrary political frontiers, but are based on factual, biological knowledge. Recent first reports, for example, include *Epipactis phyllanthes* for Spain and *Ophrys levantina* and *O. reinholdii subsp. straussii* for Rhodes, and have increased the list of countries, without making any change in the floristic element necessary.

Area and Climate

That part of botanical science which investigates the distribution of species is entitled 'comparative distribution information' or chorology. Sometimes the term 'plant geography' is used, but the two concepts do not always cover the same ground.

An important result of such investigations is that species are not distributed at random over the earth. If you compare the distribution areas (areals) by projecting the occurrences of many species on a map, you will find a surprising result: the boundaries of the areas follow definite lines which recur for the different species with varying frequency and changing combinations. The areas included within such common boundary lines are called 'floristic regions'. The repeated occurrence of similar areals leads to the conclusion that the distribution of plants is determined by factors based on universally applicable natural laws.

Without doubt, an important factor in this is the climate. You will meet certain species only in particular climatic areas. Think, perhaps, of the evergreen trees of the rainforests in the tropics, or of the deciduous species in the woods of our temperate latitudes. Of the climatic factors affecting plants, temperature and rainfall play leading roles.

The earth is divided into climatic zones along the temperature gradient, from the equator to the poles. Zones run in belts parallel to the lines of latitude. In similar ways, floristic zones can be distinguished based on the plants. These only approximate to the climatic zones, since their frontiers are not schematically orientated along the climatic lines, but along the plant distribution boundaries. The boundaries do not coincide because plants reacts not only to climate, but also to other environmental factors such as soil and topography. The areals are also determined by historical (geological) developments. In the northern hemisphere, from the equator to the pole, the following regions are distinguished:

tropical, subtropical, meridional, sub-meridional, temperate, boreal, arctic.

This book covers the geographical limits from the meridional to the arctic zones. Each of the floristic zones is sub-divided into a number of floristic regions.

A division of the continent can also take into account the gradient from an oceanic to a continental climate. The two concepts are complementary and can each be used according to your own viewpoint. The following are distinguished:

oceanic, suboceanic, subcontinental, continental.

Further intermediate grades are also distinguished, as required. Regions affected by the sea are described as oceanic (even temperature, high rainfall), those with a land climate are described as continental (large temperature variation, low rainfall). Along the gradient, the plant-cover changes markedly.

The European orchid species are, almost without exception, confined to a more or less oceanic climate. Through a combination of demands for a particular degree of oceanic influence and the dependence on certain floristic zones, characteristic distribution patterns arise which are repeated by different plants. Even widely distributed species show astonishing conformity. For example, many of the Eurasian orchids in the continental area (eastern Europe and Siberia) are confined to the temperate zone, while in the oceanic region (western Europe) they are able to thrive from the meridional to the boreal zones. Some examples are: *Cephalanthera rubra*, *Orchis ustulata* or *Epipogium aphyllum*.

Floristic Regions
Floristic regions are the units used for the plant geographical classification of the earth. The science of distribution groups them according to their similarity — that is, according to their common species — and then arranges them in relationship to one another. The system often used, worked out mainly by the plant geographers at Halle under H. Meusel, distinguishes different size units in a range from floristic district (the smallest) to floristic kingdom, the largest unit.

System of Floristic Regions
Example:
Floristic-
     district (not distinguished in the book)
  sub-province s-subatlantic
   province subatlantic
  sub-region centraleuropean S.:
        m + s-atlantic, subatlantic,
        central european, sarmatic
      region central european R:
        areas of the sub-region, also
        alpine, carpatic
      kingdom holarctic
Floristic region is the universal expression used when no particular unit is meant.

The floristic regions used in this book are set out on the map on pp272–273. The regions follow the system described, but use different units. They are often floristic provinces, sometimes sub-provinces or sub-regions. This selection seems to be suitable for describing the distribution of orchids. It is an attempt to effect a compromise between a sufficient exactitude and a useful generalization.

List of Floristic Regions (West–East) by Floristic Zones (South–North)
Meridional zone: canarian, madeiran, w-mediterranean, c-mediterranean, e-mediterranean, oriental

Submeridional zone: azorean, w-submediterranean, c-submediterranean e-submediterranean, (caucasian*);
pannonic, dunubian, pontic (s-siberian*)

Temperate zone: s-atlantic, m-atlantic, s-subatlantic, n-subatlantic, s-centraleuropean, n-central european, (=baltic), sarmatic, (c-siberian*)

Boreal zone: n-atlantic, scandinavian, n-russian, (n-siberian*)

Arctic zone: lapponic, samojedic

Overlapping zones in high mountains: alpine, carpathian

*Floristic regions outside the geographical limits of the book.

Floristic element

The floristic element describes the distribution of a species (or a taxon in general) according to the plant geographical classification of the earth in floristic regions; it is the sum-total of the floristic regions occupied by a species.

The floristic element is given for each of the species and subspecies dealt with. It applies only within the geographical boundaries of the book; outside this, the floristic regions of those species which go as far as Asia or North America have been omitted.

The floristic regions are in each case arranged according to floristic zones from south to north. To simplify things, those with different prefixes have been put together (for example: c + e-mediterranean). Where all the related areas are occupied, the prefixes are omitted (for example: mediterranean means w + c + e-mediterranean; subatlantic means s + n-subatlantic). If the area of distribution stretches over (almost) the whole floristic zone, this is given instead of the individual floristic regions, (for example: boreal means n-atlantic, scandinavian, n-russian). Floristic regions or zones where a taxon is present only in small numbers near the boundary are put in brackets.

You can obtain a visual impression of the area of distribution if the floristic areas of a taxon are put together on the map on pp272 – 273. However, it must be noted that a taxon does not always occupy the whole area of a floristic region. In such cases, further information can be obtained from the list of countries given.

Orchis laxiflora can serve as an example to illustrate this point. Its floristic element is given as: mediterranean submediterranean s-atlantic s-subatlantic (*see* p112). From the map, it can be easily ascertained that the species is widespread throughout the whole of the Mediterranean region. However, North Africa is missing (no countries). It is nevertheless suited to a thoroughgoing

Gymnadenia conopsea.

Mediterranean climate so its absence from North Africa is more likely to be for historical (areal historical) reasons rather than for climatic ones. In the atlantic-subatlantic western Europe where, because of the oceanic influence of the Atlantic, a mild winter climate prevails, the species has been able to penetrate further north. If you now take into account the countries where it occurs, then you can see that the species reaches as far as France (actually to the Channel Islands, which are included in Ga) and in the subatlantic region as far as Switzerland (He), but not into Belgium (Be) or Germany (Ge).

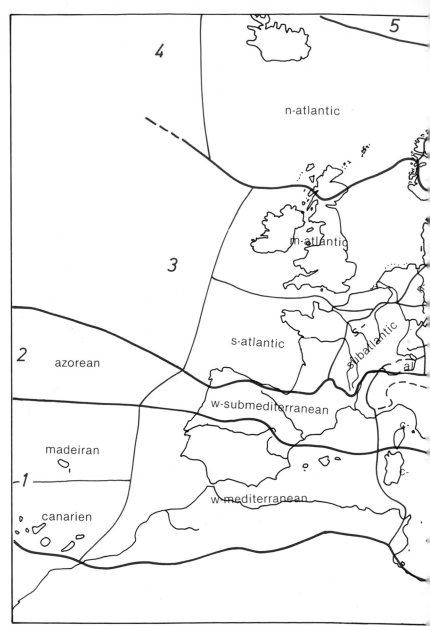

The *floristic regions* in Europe, the Near East and North Africa (turn to text, p270). The *floristic zones* are bounded by thick lines, the floristic regions within them by thin lines. The regions which overlap the zones in the Alps and Carpathians are in dotted lines. The zones are marked on the left and right of the map by figures: 1 meridional, 2 submeridional, 3 temperate,

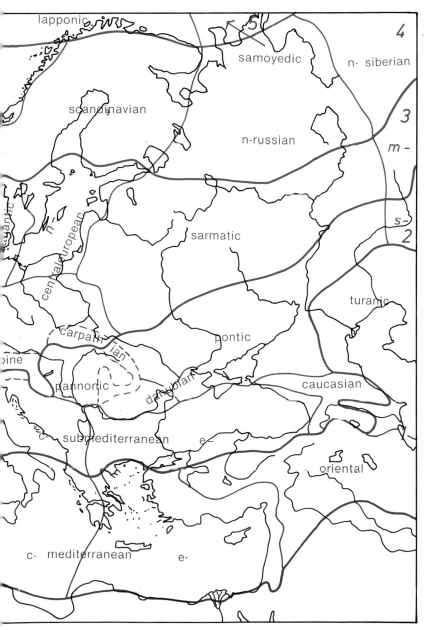

4 boreal, 5 arctic. The subtropical zone adjoins the meridional to the south. After H. Meusel, E. Jager, and E. Weinert, *Comparative Chorology of the Central European Flora*, Jena 1965, map 258 modified.

Countries

The countries in which a species has been found are shown in the distribution information by means of abbreviations. These consist of two letters, which correspond to the ones used by the various international botanical research centres, including Flora Europea (the 5 volumes of which appeared between 1964 and 1980), also by the Med-Checklist – a catalogue of species for the countries surrounding the Mediterranean which was started in 1981. In the majority of cases, the abbreviations refer to the present political frontiers, but there are deviations on geographical grounds.

In the distribution information, the countries are arranged according to a uniform system: first the European, then the Asian and finally the African. Europe starts with the group of countries in the south-east then the remainder in a clockwise direction.

List of abbreviations for the countries:

Eur: **SE** Cr Gr Tu Al Ju Bu Rm RK
    S Me Si It Sa Co
    SW Bl Hs Lu Az
    W Ga Be Ho Br Hb Fa
    C He Au Hu Ge Da Cz Po RB
    N Su No Fe RN Is
    E RW RE RC
Asi: Sn IJ LS Cy An AE
Afr: Li Tn Ag Ma Ml Cl

† The species or subspecies has become extinct.
* The species or subspecies is only a casual and not a native.
? Presence is doubtful and requires confirmation.

The meaning of the country abbreviations:

AE	eastern Aegean islands from Lesbos southwards (**A**rchipelagus, **E**ast)
Ag	**Ag**eria
Al	**Al**bania
An	Asiatic Turkey (**An**atolia)
Au	**Au**stria & Lichtenstein
Az	**Az**ores
Be	**Be**lgium & Luxemburg
Bl	**B**alearic **I**slands
Br	**Br**itain except Channel Islands
Bu	**Bu**lgaria
Cl	**C**anary **I**slands
Co	**Co**rsica
Cr	**Cr**ete, Karpathos, Kasos and Gavdhos
Cy	**Cy**prus
Cz	**Cz**echoslovakia
Da	**D**enmark (**Da**nia)
Fa	**Fa**eroes
Fe	**F**inland (**Fe**nnia)
Ga	France (**Ga**llia) and the Channel Islands
Ge	**Ge**rmany
Gr	**Gr**eece (without AE & Cr)
Hb	Ireland (**H**i**b**ernia) N & S
He	Switzerland (**He**lvetia)
Ho	**Ho**lland
Hs	Spain (**H**i**s**pania) and Andorra (not Bl & Cl)
Hu	**Hu**ngary
IJ	**I**srael and **J**ordan
Is	Iceland (**Is**land)
It	**It**aly (without Sa & Si)
Ju	Yugoslavia (**Ju**goslavia)
Li	**Li**bya
LS	**L**ebanon and **S**yria
Lu	Portugal (**Lu**sitania) (without Az & Ml)
Ma	Morroco (**Ma**rocco)
Me	Malta (**Me**lita)
Ml	Madeira (**M**adereses **I**nsulae)
No	**No**rway
Po	**Po**land
R.	European USSR (**R**ussia)
RB	**R**ussia, **B**altic: Estonia, Latvia, Lithuania, Königsberg region
RC	**R**ussia, **C**entral: Ladoga-Ilmen, Upper Volga, Volga-Kama, Upper Dnieper, Volga-Don, Urals
RE	**R**ussia, south-**e**ast part: Lower Don, Lower Volga, Transvolga
RK	Crimea (**R**ussia, **K**rimea)
Rm	**Rm**umania
RN	**R**ussia, **n**orthern part: arctic Russia, Karelia-Lappland, Dwina-Petschora

RW Russia, western part: Moldavia, Middle
    Dnieper, Black Sea, Upper Dniester
Sa Sardinia
Si Sicily
Sn Sinai peninsula
Su Sweden (Suecia)
Tn Tunisia
Tu European Turkey and Imroz

Altitude Distribution

Whenever distribution has been discussed, so far it has always meant the horizontal extent of the areal. This, however, is only one component of the complete distribution picture. The second is the vertical extent, or altitude distribution.

Each species has its own altitude distribution, depending on its requirements regarding climate and other environmental factors. Since groups of species growing together in different plant communities show that they have common requirements, the vegetation arranges itself depending on the altitude. The phenomenon is especially well observed in the high mountains where the vegetation types succeed one another over small distances according to the 'rules', and there is often a sharp demarcation between them. In Europe, the following altitude levels can be distinguished:

planar (plains)	oreal (high mountains)
colline (hills)	subalpine
submontane (lower mountain)	alpine
montane (mountains)	nivale (snow line)

The altitudes at the level boundaries depend on latitude and local climatic conditions.

Consistent with their evolutionary descent from an original tropical type, orchids have occupied Europe mainly in the lower, warmer altitude levels. Higher up the number of species fall off. Only a few thrive above the tree line in the alpine level – some examples are *Chamorchis alpina* and members of the genus *Nigritella*. A similar situation can be observed as you move towards the pole. Here too, the number of species fall off steadily. Finally, the arctic zone has no orchids of its own and only a few species venture into it.

The vertical distribution is briefly alluded to under the sections labelled 'Habitat' in the species descriptions. The altitude limits are given to the nearest 100m. The upper limit is shown when species are climbing from the lower levels, and conversely, the lower limit in the case of those types whose main concentration is on higher ground. The known extreme values are given; these apply to the southern part of the distribution area. Species which can be found at altitudes up to 2,000m in North Africa or Asia Minor reach their upper limit several hundreds of metres lower in the mountains further north.

As a general rule (not just applying to orchids) species are able to grow at a greater altitude the further south the mountains lie. Presence in the colline and submontane levels in central Europe (temperate zone) can be compared with the montane level in the Mediterranean region in the meridional and submeridional zones. In these cases, the altitude level is added to the floristic region in the section 'Floristic Element'.

Orchid Mapping

Since the 1970s, several map-making undertakings have been started to try and make a comprehensive survey of the distribution of the European orchid species. These special orchid-orientated projects run parallel with wider undertakings which involve the distribution of all seed-bearing and other plant groups.

In Germany, the map-making is entrusted to the working party on native orchids, A.H.O. (Arbeitskreisen Heimische Orchideen). In Switzerland and Austria, orchid societies are undertaking the work. Their secretaries will send information concerning the procedure whereby all known sites can be catalogued and described.

Addresses can be obtained direct from the societies. An orchid mapping scheme including the whole of the Mediterranean area is being undertaken by the Organization for the Phytotaxonomic Investigation of the Mediterranean area (OPTIMA); address: Blumenstr. 6, D—7016 Gerlingen, Germany (c/o S. Künkele).

Since there are so many unfilled gaps in our knowledge about the distribution of orchids, accurate information is always welcome, no matter the region concerned, and should be sent to the secretaries. The mapping is supported by many interested parties as a joint project. The larger the circle of enthusiastic helpers, the sooner they will come close to their goal of producing the fullest possible orchid distribution record. The effective protection and conservation of the many endangered groups of plants explicitly depends on its success.

Orchid Protection

Orchids are one of the world's most threatened groups of plants. This applies to many species growing in many lands. It is true that in Europe there is probably still no species which has been completely exterminated, but there have already been losses in some countries. In Britain, for example, *Spiranthes aestivalis* has disappeared from the New Forest. Check the Red Data Book for such information.

The real danger in the first place is the rapid reduction in suitable habitats or biotopes. It is not only the loss of such areas, but also the continual changes in the natural environment that play their part. Nearly all orchid species react sensitively to the introduction of new methods of husbandry: they will not tolerate any intensification — manuring, draining or over-use — as carried out in so many places today. In fact, orchids act as an effective 'barometer' as far as the pressures on a habitat are concerned. A few species only can withstand the continual pressure of people on the countryside — those such as *Epipactis helleborine* and *Listera ovata*, for instance, which can also invade disturbed woodland and plantations. The ecological flexibility of both is shown in the fact that these are the only European species which have also managed to make a home in North America.

Earlier methods of land utilization were, in fact, advantageous to the spread of orchids. Seen in this light, the orchids are not a special case, although often very sensitive to changes, but have succumbed to the same pressure as many other groups of plants and animals.

Compared with this generally dangerous situation, those special problems relating to orchids tend to take a back seat. They do, however, intensify the situation. In Turkey, for example, whole populations are decimated by people digging up the tubers for 'sale'. Sometimes, dealers plunder sites and illegally sell the tubers to 'amateurs' in the bulb-growing fraternity, well aware of the quick profit to be made.

Aware of the dangers, many countries have passed laws for the protection of orchids. However, the regulations are not uniform. In Germany, for example, protection is afforded to all species, whereas some of the more common species in the Swiss Cantons and Austria are only partially protected or not at all. In the UK, five orchids were on the original list of twenty specially protected plants, with the threat of legal action for any disturbance. Fortunately, the list has been substantially increased and an effective, though inevitably underfunded, system of orchid wardening helps protect against the unscrupulous in the flowering season. Orchids are included in the Washington 'Species Protection Agreement' which regulates trade in plants and animals. The whole orchid family belongs to the group of ' . . . species which are directly threatened with extermination' – which means that trading in orchids is prohibited, except for exceptional cases which require an export permit from the country of origin and an import permit from the destination country.

Laws are necessary, and in the case of tropical orchids, which are traded more than any other and provide considerable profits worldwide, they are an unconditional necessity. But laws concerning trade are not needed in the same way for European orchids. Legal protection for species cannot be effective unless safety of the biotope is assured at the same time. Therefore, additional strategies are needed for the protection of nature. Traditional nature reserves are necessary only as a first step. Further progress can only be made and the future of Europe's orchids assured if concerted action is taken and a strategy adopted by countries as part of a far-reaching policy for the future. How to achieve that is an urgent question, and it needs an answer sooner rather than later.

If you really enjoy orchids, then it is up to you to put something back, whether at local or national level, according to your own ability.

Bibliography

Guides – General

Baumann, H., Künkele, S. *Die Wildwachsenden Orchideen Europas*, Kosmos-Naturfuhrer, Stuttgart 1982.

Baumamm, H., & Künkele, S. *Die Orchideen Europas*, Kosmos-Naturfuhrer, Stuttgart 1988.

Danesch, O. & E. *Orchideen Europas. Mitteleuropa*, Hallwag, Bern and Stuttgart 1975.

Danesch, O. & E.*Orchideen Europas. Südeuropa*, Hallwag, Bern and Stuttgart 1969.

Danesch, O. & E. *Orchideen Europas. Ophrys-Hybriden*, Hallwag, Bern and Stuttgart 1972.

Danesch, O. & E. *Die Orchideen der Schweiz,* Silva, Zurich. 1984

Davies, P. & J., and Huxley, A., *Wild Orchids of Britain and Europe*, Chatto & Windus, London 1983.

Delforge, P., & Tyteca, D., *Europäische Wildorchideen*, Benziger, Zurich and Cologne.

Ettlinger, D.M.T. *British and Irish Orchids*, Macmillan, London 1977.

Kohlhaupt, P. *Mittel und Südeuropäische Orchideen*, Athesia, Bozen 1981.

Lang, D.*Orchids of Britain*, Oxford University Press, Oxford 1980, 1989.

Summerhayes, V.S. *Wild Orchids of Britain*, Collins, London 1951, 1968.

Sundermann, H. *Europäische und Mediterrane Orchideen*, Brucke-Verlag, Hildesheim 1980.

William, J.G. & A.E. and Arlot, N. *A Field Guide to the Orchids of Britain and Europe*, Collins, London 1981.

Folio and Lavishly Illustrated Works

Hermjakob, G. *Orchids of Greece and Cyprus*, Goulandris Museum, Kifissia, 1974.

Landwehr, J. *Wilde Orchideeën van Europa*, Amsterdam 1977.

Nelson, E. *Monographie und Iconographie der Orchidaceen*, Folios published with accompanying text:
Ophrys, 1962. Serapias, Aceras, Loroglossum und Barlia, 1968. Dactylorhiza, 1976.

Floras
Davis, P.H. *Flora of Turkey*, University Press, Edinburgh 1984. Orchids by J. Renz and G. Taubenehim.

Meikle, R.D. *Flora of Cyprus Volume 2*, The Bentham-Moxham Trust, Kew 1985. Orchids by J.J. Wood.

Tutin, G., et alia *Flora Europaea Volume 5*, Cambridge University Press, Cambridge 1980. Orchids by D.M. Moore, D.A. Webb and R. De Soó.

Journals and Other Works

Several publications have appeared from the OPTIMA project under the title *Projeckt Kartierung der Mediterrane Orchideen:*
1. *Index der verbreitungskarten für die Orchideen Europas und der Mittelmeerländer*, Willing, E. & B., Karlsruhe 1979.

2. *Orchideenforschung und Naturschutz im Mittelmeergebiet*, various authors, Karlsruhe 1981. (Dealing with the Greek Islands of Chios, Kos, Lesbos and Samos.)

3. *Die Orchideenflora von Euboea (Greichenland)*, Künkele, S., and Paysan, K., Karlsruhe 1981.

A.H.O. (Arbeitskreis Heimische Orchideen), Baden Wurtemburg Mitteilungsblatt. The quarterly bulletins of the *A.H.O* contain numerous authoritative papers. These range from complete orchid floras (Crete, Cyprus, Gargano, Sardinia etc.) through to taxonomic revision and descriptions of new species.

Details of publications and membership from: Otto Feldweg, Sconbergstr., 1, 7400 Tubingen, Germany.

Die Orchidee — Worldwide coverage with regular papers on European orchids.

Details from: Deutsche Orchideen-Gesellschaft, Arndstr. 8, D-2724 Sottrum, c/o L. Thiemann, Germany.

Orchid Review (from 1983). Occasional articles on Britain and Europe.

Details from: *The Orchid Review*, 5, Orchid Ave., Kingsteinton, Newton Abbot, Devon, TQ12 3HG, UK.

American Orchid Society Bulletin. Illustrated articles on European genera from 1985 — 1988, authors P. & J. Davies.

Details from *American Orchid Society*, 6000 South Olive Ave., West Palm Beach, Florida 33405, USA.

Alpine Garden Society Bulletin (quarterly from 1929 —). Various articles on plant-hunting relevant to European and Middle-Eastern orchids.

Details from: The Secretary (*AGS*), Lye End Link, St Johns, Woking, Surrey GU21 1SW, UK.

Index to the English Names

Index to the Scientific Names

Names set in *italic* indicate synonyms

Photographic Acknowledgements

a = above, b = below, r = right, l = left, m = middle.

H. Baumann: 23 bl, 23 br, 83 br, 123 bl, 215 ar; K. Baumann: 35 al, 41 bl, 45 br, 55 al, 55bl, 103mr, 149 al, 153 am, 211 bl, 231 bl; H. Blatt: 115 ar, 131 al, 195 al; H.W.E. van Bruggen: 20al, 20ar, 47 al, 47 ar, 89 br; B. Castelein: 13 bl, 13 br; R. Cramm: 13 al, 101 ar; B Corrias: 116 al, 133 ar, 165 bl, 165 br, 213 mr; D.D. Chesterman (Sammlung Kew): 73 al, 116 ar, 203 br; P.H. Davies: 53 ar, 53 bl, 99 bl; P. Delforge: 181 bl, 181 br, 225 ml, 225 mr; J. Devillers-Terschuren: 83 ar; H. Eisenbeiss: 69 bl, 143 br, 149 br, 213 al; J. u. L. Essink: 39 bl, 39 br, 81 bl, 83 bl, 83 bm, 133 al; X. Finkenzeller: 45 al, 67 al, 67 ar, 67 ml, 71 ar, 73 al, 75 al, 75 ar, 91 am, 91 br, 93 bl, 101 bl, 167 ar, 171, 199 ml, 233 al, 233 ar, 233 bl, 233 br, 235 ar; E. Garnweidner: 21 bl, 21 br, 23 al, 39 al, 41 al, 43 ar, 49 bl, 55 ar, 59 br, 61 al, 71 al, 87 al, 89 al, 95 ar, 113 ar, 113 br, 117 al, 121 ar, 121 bl, 129 al, 133 bl, 135 ar, 138 al, 175 mr, 197 al, 201 bl, 203 mr, 235 al; P Gölz: 171 ar, 181 ar, 209 mr, 211 al, 219 br, 223 al, 223 ar, 227 bl; R. Hasiberger: 115 br; G. Kalden: 65 mr, 179 al; M. Kalteisen: 209 al; E. Klein: 39 ar, 85 bl, 85 br, 87 bl, 87 br, 96 al, 96 ar, 159 al; H. Kümpel: 29 mr, 61 bl, 61 bl, 61 br, 97 ar, 101 br, 151 bm, 205 bl, 205 br; S. Künkele: 97 bl, 97 br; W. Layer: 43 al, 115 al; W. Loos: 107 ar, 145 al; G. Lopez: 65 ar, 153 ar, 155 al, 155 ar, 193 ml; J. Mehl[2]: 258, 259 al drawing; D. Mitchell: 13 ar, 23 ar, 26 al, 26 bl, 26 br, 29 bl, 29 br, 33 ar, 85 ar, 87 ar, 91 ar, 91 bm, 95 bl, 95 br, 107 bl; A. u. C. Nieschalk: 19 ar, 25 al, 29 al, 71 bl, 73 ar, 73 br, 77 br, 259 ar; R. Peter: 19 al, 29 ar, 37 ar, 37 br, 69 br, 91 al, 105 ar, 107 al, 119 br, 123 al, 127 al, 127 ar, 139 al, 159 ar, 159 bl, 169 al, 173 al, 173 br, 175 ml, 185 br, 187 al, 191 bl, 193 br, 195 bl, 197 mr, 199 mr, 207 ml, 217 br, 221 ml; W. Pilz: 41 ml, 55 ml, 121 al, 179 ml; H. R. Reinhard: 35 mr, 45 ar, 49 br, 55 br, 63 al, 67 mr, 69 al, 91 bl, 93 al, 93 br, 95 al, 97 al, 99 al, 99 ar, 101 al, 103 br, 113 bl, 115 bl, 123 ar, 131 ar, 131 ml, 137 ml, 137 bl, 137 br, 159 br, 161 bl, 163 ar, 167 al, 169 ar, 169 mr, 171 bl, 171 br, 173 ml, 173 mr, 175 bl, 179 mr, 179bl 183 ar, 187 bl, 187 br, 193 mr, 201 al, 203 bl, 205 al, 205 ar, 205 ml, 207 bl, 207 br, 209 al, 209 ml, 209 br, 211 ar, 213 ar, 213 ml, 213 bl, 213 br, 214 al, 214 ar, 215 al, 215 mr, 215 bl, 215 br, 219 al, 219 bl, 223 bl, 223 br, 225 al, 225 ar, 225 bl, 227 ar, 227 br, 228 al, 228 ar, 228 ml, 228 bl, 228 br, 229 al, 229 bl, 229 br, 253, 256 l, 259b, 260 l, 261 al, 261 ar, 262, 264 a, 266, 268 a, 268 b; J. Renz: 37 al, 81 al, 173 bl, 177 mr, 189 al, 189 ml, 189 mr, 189 bl, 195 br, 199 ar, 199 br, 219 ar; K. Robatsch: 21 al, 21 ar, 31 bl, 31 br, 53 al, 57 bl, 57 br; D. u. U. Rückbrodt: 15 al, 15 mr, 26 ar, 31 al, 31 ar, 33 bl, 33 br, 35 br, 39 ml, 41 ar, 41 br, 47 bl, 47 br, 49 al, 51 al, 51 ar, 51 bl, 51 br, 59 al, 59 ar, 59 bl, 61 ar, 63 ar, 63 bl, 63 br, 65 al, 65 bl, 65 br, 69 ar, 75 br, 75 bl, 77 al, 77 am, 77 ar, 79 ar, 79 bl, 79 br, 81 ar, 81 bm, 81 br, 83 al, 93 ar, 93 bm, 99 br, 102 al, 102 ar, 102 bl, 102 br, 103 al, 103 ar, 105 al, 109 al, 109 ar, 109 bl, 109 br, 111 al, 111 ar, 111 bl, 111 br, 113 al, 113 mr, 117 al, 117 ml, 119 bl, 121 br, 125 al, 125 am, 125 ar, 125 br, 127 bl, 127 br, 129 ar, 131 mr, 131 bl, 131 br, 135 bl, 135 br, 137 ar, 138 ar, 139 bl, 139 br, 141 al, 141 ar, 141 bl, 141 br, 143 al, 143 ar, 143 bl, 145 bl, 145 mr, 145 br, 147 al, 149 ar, 149 bl, 149 mr, 151 ar, 151 br, 153 al, 157 al, 157 ar, 157 br, 161 al, 161 br, 163 bl, 165 ar, 167 br, 175 al, 175 ar, 175 br, 179 br, 183 ml, 183 mr, 183 bl, 183 br, 185 ar, 185 bl, 187 ar, 189 al, 189 br, 191 ar, 193 al, 195 ar, 197 ml, 203 al, 219 ml, 221 al, 221 bl, 228 mr, 231 al, 231 ar, 231 br, 260, 261b, 263r; J. Rydlo: 25 bl, 25 br; J. Schimmitat: 17 al, 17 ar; W. Schmid-Fisler: 103 bl; H. Schrempp: 35 ar, 163 al, 231 bm, 235 am, 256r; W. J. Schrenk: 57 al, 57 ar; W. Schubert: 15 al, 35 bl, 147 ar, 151 al; Silvestris Fotoservice: Bellmann: 25 ar, 45 bl, 49 ar, 111 am, 169 ml, 177 ar, 181 al, 185 al, 203 ar, 215 ml; H. Sundermann: 19 bl, 53 br, 117 bl, 117 br, 123 br; G. Synatzschke: 151 bl; G. Taubenheim: 15 bl, 15 br, 17 bl, 17 br, 27 al, 27 ar, 43 bl, 43 br, 45 mr, 71 br, 77 bl, 79 al, 105 bl, 105 br, 147 bl, 147 br, 157 bl, 163 br, 169 br, 173 ar, 177 bl, 177 br, 191 ml, 195 ml, 195 mr, 199 bl, 207 al, 207 mr, 209 bl, 221 ar, 221 mr; H. Teppner: 67 bl, 67 br, 235 bl, 235 mr, 235 br; W. Teschner: 27 bl, 27 br, 37 bl, 129 bl, 129 br, 145 ar, 153 bl, 153 br, 155 bl, 155 br, 171 al; D. Tyteca: 19 br, 85 al, 89 ar, 119 al, 119 ar, 177 al; E. Vimba: 89 bl; W. Vöth: 263l; K. Wagner: 107 br, 125 bl, 133 br, 135 al, 137 al, 139 ar, 165 al, 169 bl, 179 al, 183 al, 191 al, 191 mr, 191 br, 193 al, 193 bl, 197 ar, 197 bl, 197 br, 199 al, 201 ar, 201 br, 205 mr, 207 ar, 211 br, 217 al, 217 ar, 217 bl, 219 mr, 221 br, 225 br, 227 al, 229 ar; K. Weihs: 33 al; W. Zepf: 161 ar, 167 bl.